How
to Conduct
Training
Seminars

How to Conduct Training Seminars

A Complete Reference Guide for Training Managers and Professionals

Lawrence S. Munson

Second Edition

McGraw-Hill, Inc.

New York   St. Louis   San Francisco   Auckland   Bogotá
Caracas   Lisbon   London   Madrid   Mexico   Milan
Montreal   New Delhi   Paris   San Juan   São Paulo
Singapore   Sydney   Tokyo   Toronto

Library of Congress Cataloging-in-Publication Data

Munson, Lawrence S.
   How to conduct training seminars : a complete reference guide for
training managers and professionals / Lawrence S. Munson.
     p.   cm.
   Includes index.
   ISBN 0-07-044201-0
   1. Executives—Training of. 2. Seminars. I. Title.
HF5549.5.T7M86 1992
658.4'0712404—dc20   92-7564
                                            CIP

   3 4 5 6 7 8 9 0   DOC/DOC   9 8 7 6 5

ISBN   0-07-044201-0

*The sponsoring editor for this book was Betsy N. Brown, the editing supervisor was
Caroline Levine, and the production supervisor was Donald F. Schmidt. It was
set in Baskerville by McGraw-Hill's Professional Book Group composition unit.*

Printed and bound by R. R. Donnelley & Sons Company.

This book is printed on recycled, acid-free paper containing a minimum of 50% recycled de-
inked fiber.

Contents

5. How to Plan for Maximum Impact   79

Preface

A lot has happened in the field of corporate human resource development in the past 8 years, and more particularly in the use of training seminars. But at the same time, a lot has remained the same.

At the time of the first edition of this book, 1984, training seminars had already seemed to have come of age. The early classroom lecture format had given way to a U-shaped table so that every participant could see and react with every other participant. Seminar leaders had learned to hold the interest of their classes through the use of cases, small group assignments, and experiential exercises. Lecturing had been largely reduced to making subject matter transitions and summaries. Animated group discussions had become the rule rather than the exception. Visual aids had progressed from flannel boards and the 16mm. motion picture to the more versatile overhead projector. More and more organizations were recognizing the need for a training and development function, although this was by no means universal.

In the intervening years, the role and characteristics of the training seminar have changed in many ways. Perhaps most importantly, the managements of a substantial number of leading corporate enterprises have learned to use the training seminar as a means of furthering their own broad initiatives. We had already begun to see some of this by 1984, but it has spread much more broadly.

At that time we had seen some interest in using the training department to implement various kinds of planning and control systems, most notably management by objectives and performance appraisal. The im-

portance of developing a common vocabulary also had come to be recognized in some quarters.

But in recent years, as America has had to struggle against toughening global competition, a large segment of corporate America has become almost obsessed with total quality management. In order to introduce and maintain these programs, huge populations of employees
have had to be trained in strategic quality-control concepts and taught
the skills necessary to make them work. The training had to start at the
top and proceed throughout all levels of the enterprise. The training
and development function in these organizations has become a true
partner of top management.

In my own case, I've seen the clients of Louis Allen Associates looking
at management training more and more as the means to an end. It
helps establish some area of common understanding preliminary to establishing new or revised management leadership systems. Training becomes an essential first step in order to embark successfully on improved strategic planning methods, to prime a task force to analyze and
streamline organization structure, or to understand and implement a
system of planning that links corporate strategies to down-the-line operational planning. Once these systems are established, people have to
be helped to develop skills in using them.

The accelerating use of the computer, especially desktop, personal
computers, has brought with it a whole new demand for training: developing computer literacy. Then, as new and improved on-line systems
and new software became available, computer training and retraining
became a major workload for training departments. The sheer size of
the task makes it a matter of top-management importance.

These forces have resulted in greater management recognition of the
need for a high order of seminar development and delivery capability.
We see the spread of highly professional training and development
staffs, now increasingly referring to themselves as human resource development professionals. More companies are establishing well-
equipped training centers and using them to further corporate strategic
initiatives.

The changing role of the training function has been accompanied by
major changes in the form of the seminar itself. The age of electronics
has swept through on a wide front to substitute the videotape for earlier
forms of visual reinforcement. Video can now be hooked up with computers to offer a wide variety of controllable audio-visual messages.
These can be cast on huge screens with the result that we can combine
the broad impact of the cinema with the versatility of the videotape. A
new generation of computer-expert trainers is arriving on the Ameri-

can and, indeed, on the international scene and will continue to grow in numbers and importance.

And yet some things haven't changed much since 1984. The training seminar continues as the workhorse of the training and development function. The overhead projector and flip charts continue to play their useful part in the conduction of seminars. The U-shaped table is still with us, except in some cases where participants have to use computer terminals set up in a different configuration. And none of us foresees the decline of seminar leaders. There is no substitute for the sensitive discussion leader who can "read" and respond to the reactions of participants and who can relate seminar subject matter to the business realities faced by seminar participants.

The extent of the changes, however, is what has led me to bring the 1984 edition of *How to Conduct Training Seminars* in line with the new times. At the same time, I have to recognize that not all companies have moved ahead at the same speed. Many readers, I suspect, will be envious of those trainers in companies which accept the training function into top-management circles. And even today, I am aware of important companies which have no training function at all.

The material in the book follows a natural sequence. After an introductory chapter, the next nine chapters are concerned with how to do all the things that have to be done in advance of the actual seminar presentation. Chapters 10, 11, and 12 tell you how to deliver the seminar. Chapter 13 explores the methods available for evaluating the seminar and for evaluating the training function itself. Chapter 14 summarizes the whole work.

Where appropriate, checklists, diagrams, and extended examples from actual experience are included in the book to make the work as useful as possible to fellow professionals. It provides information more by way of anecdote than statistical tables. It attempts to keep the enduring parts of the original work while building in 8 years of change and new experiences.

This book came about through the contributions of a large number of experienced professionals, who are listed below, and to whom I am deeply indebted. It is based on their inputs and on my 20 years of personal experience.

> Bernie Abramowitz
> Louis A. Allen
> Mike Allen
> Mim Anzolut
> Steven J. Azzaro
> Philip Cooper
> Lee Dailey

Scott Gassman
Dennis Harr
Deb Jarvis-Valentine
Nick Kourkoumelis
Robert LaMontagne
Mary K. Lindberg
Mary Meanwell
Tom Quick
Doug Raynor
Geraldine Ruthchild
Gary L. Schulze
Karen Stein-Townsend
Mary Sullivan
Al Versacci
Ron White

Lawrence S. Munson

How
to Conduct
Training
Seminars

1

The Escalating Demand for High-Impact Training Seminars

You'd better be prepared to face it. If you are a manager or professional concerned with training in the workplace, you're on the spot. You're going to face enormously increasing demands for providing high-impact seminars in the decade ahead.

A great deal of your success in putting on effective training seminars will depend importantly on how well you can apply a wealth of ideas that represents the accumulated experience of seasoned professional trainers. To some extent, it will also depend on your shrewd management of the opportunities being made available through rapidly advancing technological change.

The Huge and Accelerating Need

The pressures for greatly expanded training programs come from several sources. One of them is the continuing increase in the knowledge and skill requirements of new workers, as our economy shifts toward high-technology products and services. At the same time, the demand for unskilled labor has been steadily declining.

Then there is the growing need to provide additional training for workers already on the job, estimated today to be $15 billion annually, or half again as much as the $30 billion employers are currently spending each year.* Much of this stems from the acceleration of technology changes and toughening global competition.

Another underlying force is the increased concern with cost-effectiveness coming out of the widespread adoption of strategic quality management with its heavy emphasis on performance standards and continuous improvement. The day of accepting training as a matter of faith — something that all good companies ought to do — is gone, and so is the heavy reliance on participant evaluations, not inappropriately termed "smile sheets," as the main avenue for evaluating training results.

The Critical Role of Seminars in Meeting This Need

Right in the middle of this powerful trend is the training seminar which will continue to be the primary vehicle for meeting training needs in the decade ahead. I'm using the term "seminar" here to mean a structured, group learning experience involving small groups of people (usually 9 to 25) and providing a high degree of interaction and participation. This definition will include "workshops," a term often used to describe seminars with a very high degree of individual application exercises.

The seminar has a much broader and more effective reach, by and large, than the other forms of training delivery. There is a proper place for lectures, on-the-job coaching, self-development, informal discussion groups, and planned work experiences. But the seminar, which incorporates many of the other techniques within its design, offers persuasive advantages that will continue its future dominance.

"No matter what advances we will continue to make in computer driven, inter-active video, computer based training, and other technological developments in the field of training, there will always be a primary need for group interaction under the guidance of a skilled program leader." This is the kind of comment I received from innumerable training directors with whom I talked in preparation for this new edition of my book.

---

*The American Society for Training and Development, "National Report on Human Resources," Jan/Feb 1991, p. 1.

The Rationale for the Dominance of the Training Seminar

There are many practical reasons for the dominance of the seminar as a training vehicle. Other training conduits have their special niches, but the seminar offers the greatest overall advantage.

Motivational Learning Environment

There is nothing that compares to the excitement and stimulation that can be provided by a fast-moving seminar with a high degree of stimulating interplay among alert, informed participants. It has the same potential for holding your intense interest as a good adventure novel or top-quality television drama. But in addition, you can perceive how it will help you become a more effective person in the pursuit of your career and in your life. There's something in it for you beyond the pleasure of the experience itself.

Even in the hands of inspirational spellbinders, like Tom Peters or Morris Massey, the lecture form can't come close to the seminar from a motivational point of view.

Neither can individual self-development. It takes more discipline than most people have to go through a self-instructional program in the first place. And without someone to share your experiences with, it's like going to the movies alone. Your experience is incomplete. It can even be frustrating.

In special situations, being thrust into a work situation that provides a challenge beyond your present capabilities can produce a high level of determination. I have a good friend who operates a one-person office for a company that adopted an incentive compensation system based upon profit contribution. He immediately took a closer look at the $1000 he was paying monthly to sublet office space and the $350 he spent on the average each month for word processing services.

It took very little analysis for him to persuade himself to move his office into an extra room in his apartment and to equip himself with a computer and word processing equipment. He didn't want to spend the time and money to go to a computer literacy course. Nor did he find the manuals that came with his equipment very helpful. They were written in a language he didn't understand and were incredibly complex and difficult to read.

Instead, with enough help from a friend to get started, he found his way by trial and error. Within about a week he was able to create a few simple files, store them, retrieve them as needed, and print out quite acceptable memoranda and letters. He probably only uses 10 percent or less of the total capabilities of the system, but he found out how to do what he wanted to do, which was enough for him. And it had a major impact on his incentive compensation!

This kind of motivation, however, is rare. For massive populations to be reached in the next decade, the seminar seems to provide the best answer all around.

Sometimes as part of a formal seminar, informal discussion groups are used effectively. A class is subdivided into small teams which are asked to analyze some assigned question and report back to the rest of the participants. As we'll see, this is a very good way to maintain a high interest level. It's essential to the extent that we want people to learn through self-discovery.

Efficiency

Training seminars are clearly far more efficient in reaching large populations than all but one of the other training vehicles. The reason is that you can train groups of 9 to 25 people at one time with one instructor. One-on-one coaching on the job, when performed by a truly professional management leader, can be extraordinarily effective. But it takes one teacher for each learner, a ratio that is unacceptable in view of the huge demands. Furthermore, most managers are not good coaches. They either cannot find the time or they lack the skills to do the job right.

Seminars can reach large populations with common needs at a low per capita cost. If so desired, they can be tightly structured around standard audio-visuals and participant workbooks so that a number of different trainers can deliver essentially the same program. This is a special advantage for global companies who can then use local people to train their company employees who are spread out all over the world. It also permits the use of line managers as trainers, part-time, with the extra credibility they can sometimes provide.

Union Carbide Corporation, for example, puts on essentially the same modular management training program in dozens of different countries of the world in dozens of different languages. The result is that all managers come to understand and apply the same management leadership philosophy and common approaches to such fundamentals as forecasting the external environment, setting objectives, establishing standards of performance, and conducting performance appraisals and performance counseling.

The one method that appears at first glance to be more efficient than seminars is lecturing. You can have instructor/learner ratios as high as 200 to 1 or perhaps even higher, as in some survey courses in our universities. You can certainly cover large populations more efficiently with this kind of ratio. The big problem, though, is the degree of real learning that occurs.

Although lectures reach large numbers of people efficiently, the lack of listener participation encourages mind wandering and impedes learning. Such a result would be of particular concern in the case of employer-initiated training where the participants' attendance is a requirement imposed by the employer and not due to a self-generated interest in the subject matter.

Some teachers have found ways to overcome, at least in part, the limitations of lecturing to huge classes. Professor A. James Casner at Harvard Law School would assign one side of a hypothetical case to one half of the room and the other side to the rest of the class. He would then pit one side against the other in such a skillful way that he generated a very heated competition between the two sides. The result was very high involvement by all members of the class and a great deal of real learning.

Another approach is to break a large group into smaller subgroups for discussion and feedback. If the group isn't too large and the seating arrangements not too restrictive, it can be an effective way to avoid the limitations of large classes. If they are discussing something in a team of five to seven people, the participants are literally forced to get personally involved.

If the circumstances are such that there is a very high level of desire to learn, a lecture can get a lot of information across in a short time. An example is at Texaco Corporation where a 3-day course in strategic decision making is given. The first day includes 5 hours of lecture. The rest of the program is conducted in teams of two, making and entering strategic decisions into personal computers in a highly competitive environment. If they want to prevail over the other teams, the participants have to know how to play the game.

As we'll see, a certain amount of lecturing may be necessary in conducting seminars, but straight presentation (as we prefer to call it) should be carefully controlled as to time and delivered with polished platform skills to avoid loss of attention and interest. These skills include keen awareness of the interest level of the class and an ability to respond quickly to symptoms of listening fatigue.

Adaptability

Almost any subject can be taught in a group learning setting. The subject can be very broad, such as a comprehensive course in the fundamentals of management leadership, or it can be very narrow, such as how to operate a specific machine tool.

Furthermore, a skilled discussion leader can adapt essentially the same subject matter to the needs and interests of different groups. In fact, it is almost inevitably so. The questions raised by the participants and the experiences they share provide for different and more relevant group discussions from class to class. This can occur without conscious effort by the program leader.

By way of contrast, the materials used in self-development, whether by way of reading relevant texts or computer-based instruction, are structured in advance. The texts can be skimmed or studied in depth, which provides for some flexibility, and computer-based training can provide for many alternate tracks to follow. But they nevertheless fall far short of the adaptability of the seminar in the hands of a skilled discussion leader.

High Impact

The seminar also has the potential for securing a very high level of participant commitment and learning. As the participants interact with each other during the learning process, a mutual reinforcement occurs that produces deep commitment and facilitates understanding on the part of all.

The group experience is the seminar's big advantage over self-instruction and lectures. Much less self-discipline is involved. The setting itself provides a serious forum for learning and stakes out a period of uninterrupted time for learning to take place. Furthermore, the exchange of views and greater opportunity to pose questions permits deeper understanding to be gained.

In terms of impact on the individual, the seminar would have to yield to work experience. Since our focus is off-the-job learning, the comparison here has to be to special, one-time projects. These offer excellent learning experiences but can be offered only infrequently and usually to a very few people, which means they can only have a limited role as we face the huge demand for training in the years ahead.

For example, general line management consulting firms such as McKinsey & Company, Booz Allen & Hamilton, and Arthur D. Little provide services to clients through teams that are organized especially for each assignment. Team members are chosen so that they represent in total the combination of skills and experience deemed to be most appropriate for the particular assignment. At the same time, they are trained to reach conclusions in teams and to challenge each other's ideas. Usually, the team effort is accompanied by performance appraisal and skilled coaching. Sometimes at the end of a client project, the team members reassemble and ask themselves how they would carry out the assignment more effectively if they were to start it all over again.

The end result is a powerful learning experience. The professional staff people in these firms are said to get 5 year's worth of experience in their first 2 years. I know that was my own experience in my early years with McKinsey & Company.

This technique is also widely used in corporations generally, sometimes being referred to as "task forces." On occasion, project teams are organized to work with an outside consultant. Other times they are completely internal. Typically these task forces are made up of representatives from different functional groups within the company. In some strategic quality-management programs, suppliers and/or customers are included on the task forces.

United Technologies in Farmington, Connecticut, uses this team technique in conjunction with a formalized group learning process as part of its executive development program. An outside professional is engaged as facilitator, and the "task force" develops a detailed plan of action in a seminar-type setting. The company reports that in one such experience, involving Carrier Corporation, a subsidiary, a follow-up survey 18 months later was able to document a 276% return on the cost of the seminar!

Availability

Training directors know only too well that there is a thriving industry that develops and sells them educational materials for use in seminars that have been tested and proven. The problem, if any, is an overabundance of easily available programs or program components.

In recent years, there has been a significant decrease in the use of "off-the-shelf" programs that can be purchased and presented as is. The trend has been very strongly toward adapting and customizing these generic programs to make them more company-specific and more relevant to the participants' own working environments.

Perhaps for the same reason, we have seen in recent years—at least among the more prominent and larger corporations—a strong move toward building an internal training capability complete with modern "training centers." This trend is undoubtedly a reflection of the increasing investment corporate America is making in employee training and development.

Nevertheless, even these larger and more self-sufficient training organizations make effective use of outside educational materials. Sometimes they bring in complete programs. Other times they adapt individual program elements and build them into their own programs. A case in point is the use of video. Many leading companies, among them the prominent insurance brokerage firm of Johnson & Higgins, will pick and choose individual video sequences to fit their particular needs.

At the same time, for companies that have elected not to develop ma-

jor internal capabilities, the availability of complete programs from outside vendors is still an advantage. It's a lot less expensive and less risky
than building training programs from ground zero. Also, the vendor's
programs can be easily adapted and customized to give them greater
relevance. So long as the changes are represented in hard-copy material
(as opposed to videotapes and courseware), they are not very costly.
Most workbook text material is stored on compact discs and is easily
changed.

Most professionals in the field would say that people learn best by doing. While this may be true in a general sense, it won't work well in
meeting the massive training needs that we foresee in the next decade.
It won't work unless the work experience provided comes *after* some
initial training by other means, usually seminars. Putting people to work
at something without some preliminary training may not work at all or,
if it does, will take too long a period of time.

Adding Impact Through Emerging Technology

Important technological advances promise to make training seminars
an even more powerful means for training our work forces in the years
ahead. Let me share a personal experience on this count with you.

I'm not a very sociable airplane traveler. To use my travel time to best
advantage I'm usually busy working on something I brought with me.
But a few months ago I happened to fall into a short interchange with
the passenger sitting next to me that somehow captures the anomaly of
marching technology.

How the conversation started I don't remember, but I learned that he
was a professor of physics at Stanford University in Palo Alto, California. "That's interesting," I commented. "I'm in the education business
myself—conducting management leadership seminars for employees of
business and other organizations.

"Tell me," I continued, "just out of curiosity, do college professors
still use blackboards?"

"I couldn't get along without them. I use them all the time." He paused
for a moment, and then continued: "But sometimes I use a small pad or
chart for the TV students who get my lectures via satellite!"

He explained to me that companies paid Stanford a respectable fee
for this service. Although it was only a one-way telecast—the remote audience could not be seen or heard by the professor—the TV students
could telephone in any questions or comments. Videotapes of the pre-

sentation were made available for reference in the university library for several weeks after the lecture.

The anomaly I saw was this. In all my experience with training in the workplace, I haven't seen blackboards used for the last 15 years! They're messy. Chalk dust flies all over, and the instructor has to spend an appreciable amount of time with his or her back to the class, erasing the blackboard.

When I reflected on this conversation, I realized once again that people tend to cling to familiar ways, just as college professors stay with blackboards. But as the economics of advancing technology finds cost-effective niches, new ways become accepted.

I never really researched the subject afterward, but I presumed that a number of universities — which one could view as being in the "business" of selling education — were expanding their markets by televising courses to a geographically dispersed population much in the same way that correspondence courses have been doing for many generations.

There is an underlying dilemma attached to the rapidly expanding application of technology in the training and development field (of which my example is only one piece): when and how to make the plunge. It reminds me of the first romance on the part of industry with mainframe computers.

When I moved from McKinsey & Company to become president of Loral Corporation, I found myself in the middle of this dilemma. Like so many other companies, Loral had invested in a huge computer in large part to establish an image of "being with it." But then after the computer was in place, there was a mad scramble to find productive things for it to do.

I hope we don't make the same mistake with some of the computer-driven, interactive techniques becoming made available with access to huge banks of information stored on magnetic discs. Training directors will have to establish their own strategies on this. My own thought is to keep yourself apprised of what's going on but relate it always to your own forecast of training and development needs. As you begin to get some technology experts in your organization, make sure your focus is always squarely on the objective and not the means.

Getting the Most for Your Money

So let's accept the idea that training seminars will continue to be the workhorse of workplace training and will play the largest role in meeting the huge demands foreseeable in the future. We probably have to agree as well that we will be caught up, to some degree, in the new technology.

In any event, as we look into the future, the key question is, What must you do to ensure that you get the best return on your large investment in training seminars? And that's what this book is about.

Here are some fundamentals that will be elaborated on in succeeding chapters:

1. Build a positive climate for training in your organization, at all management levels.

2. Make sure you are operating from a sound organization structure that is properly staffed.

3. Use outside resources wisely to supplement your internal capabilities.

4. Operate from a comprehensive annual plan that has the backing of top management.

5. Insist on the use of sound seminar design and top-quality educational materials.

6. Develop an acceptable strategy for participating in the technological advances in the training field.

7. Use truly gifted, properly prepared program leaders.

8. Plan to use a setting and seminar room setup that will add to the seminar's success.

9. Take advantage of the accumulated experience of successful practitioners in presenting your seminars.

10. Watch your costs and measure results.

2

How to Build a Favorable Corporate Environment

An essential starting point for a successful corporate training function is the right organizational culture or climate. If this already exists for your company, you have a good start. If it doesn't, you have to try to do something about it, difficult though that may be.

For an increasing number of companies in recent years, the bond between corporate management and the training function has become a close one. In order to launch the kind of fundamental change involved in, for example, strategic quality management, top management is literally forced to use its human resource development staff. There's no way they can introduce a change of such magnitude successfully without bringing these professionals into their planning and giving them a major role in the implementation of these changes. This top-level involvement almost by necessity creates the favorable climate you need.

Introduction of the Malcolm Baldrige National Quality Award has added impetus to this trend. A major criterion established to qualify for this award is human resource utilization and, more specifically, quality education and training.

If you are a training director of a company with a good climate, your challenge is to *maintain* and not to *develop* a favorable environment. We can envy you. You are in a position to maximize the impact of your function on improving the effectiveness of your corporation. This chapter is not for you. You will keep your position of importance by doing well all the things we will be talking about in succeeding chapters.

Nature of the Problem

Some years ago, a thoroughly frustrated training director* shared his feelings with me. He found himself in a company that provided funds for essential technical training and for some management training as well. His problem was that top management clearly didn't believe in the concepts of management leadership being taught in the management course. They behaved in an autocratic way, keeping virtually all the operating decisions in their own hands. They cared little for communicating with their people. They controlled through personal inspection and tight financial controls. More importantly, they wouldn't listen to the training director when he tried to do something about it.

"I sometimes think of myself as the minister in a small village," he confided in me. "Corporate management is the wealthy element in the village that supports the church financially but doesn't go to church. They think of religion as a good thing for the people, but don't really believe in it themselves. That's why they support it with money.

"That's how management thinks about management training courses. It's a 'good thing,' so they fund it. But everything they do on the job negates what we are trying to preach. Even in the management meetings I attend, they belittle the ideas I try to advance about how to improve human productivity. It's humiliating. But I'm only 8 years from retirement. I have to stick it out."

Fortunately for him, soon after this conversation he was given early retirement. He didn't have the courage himself to make a move, but when it was literally forced on him, it turned out to be the best thing that could have happened to him. He found a job with a travel agency and started a happy new life.

At one time, the situation just described was fairly typical. Although times are changing, there are still large numbers of organizations in which the training function exists but has to function without real backing from top management, without the kind of environment that the training function needs to be fully effective. Although it's difficult to generalize, I suspect that these companies are not major defense contractors (who are required to institute quality-improvement programs).

---

*"Training director" is a term I'll use to refer to the individual responsible for the training function.

They are probably not struggling for survival against tough competition. Many of them, unfortunately, have managements which, for whatever reason, fail to see the crucial importance of improved human productivity in their particular situations.

The need to improve the organizational environment is probably most apparent when it comes to management training. Climate is less important in technical training where the end results are more directly translated into more sales, lower costs, increased output, or shorter turnaround times.

In the short term, training directors themselves probably have little influence over the readiness of their companies to embrace management training and put it to work on the job. Over a period of time, however, there are some things they can do, which we'll review in this chapter. But first, let's examine the various influences on corporate climate.

Importance of the Climate

To illustrate the significance of organizational environment, assume that Harry and Joan come back from a 4-day management training seminar full of ideas and enthusiasm. They've taken essentially the same course but at different times and under different circumstances.

Let's take Harry first. Harry goes to a seminar conducted by an accomplished outside consultant and is very impressed. When he returns, he calls a meeting of his staff. He tries to teach them in 20 minutes what he learned over the entire 4 days of the seminar. His people listen politely. Some even show enthusiasm. But below the surface, Harry's announced intention to "start doing things differently around here" meets a wall of quiet but determined opposition. Two weeks later, Harry is back in his old routine. His seminar workbook is displayed proudly on his bookshelf—gathering dust.

Now let's see what happens to Joan. Her seminar had the same basic subject matter, same educational design, and an equally able discussion leader. But it was set in quite a different organizational environment. A group of 20 managers with roughly equivalent management experience were gathered together in the seminar room filled with positive expectations. They had heard good things about the program from their managers and peers who had already been through it. As they settle down in their places, the president of the company comes in and says to them:

> "Welcome to our seminar on management leadership. I think you'll get a lot out of it. I know I did when I went through it with the first group, which consisted of all the senior officers in the company. The program has

been adapted from a proven training program that has been used with hundreds of other companies and many thousands of other managers. It has been customized to our specific needs, including the incorporation of our strategic planning processes and established management terminology.

"Some of the most important parts of the program are being built into our own performance planning and appraisal practices. You'll learn about 'mission statements' and 'measurable standards of performance.' You'll be expected to develop a mission statement backed up by standards of performance for the function or area you manage.

"You'll also hear about something called 'action planning,' which is a powerful way for a manager to visualize some result that he or she wants to make happen, to think through the best way to make it happen, and then to make sure it really does happen. You'll be able to apply this technique and many others included in the course back on your job.

"But don't misunderstand me. We don't want you to fit tightly into a carefully defined mold. We value individual creativity and recognize that individual styles may, and perhaps should, differ. But if we all use the same common vocabulary and certain common management processes, we can work much more effectively together as a team."

Needless to say, Joan and the other participants in the second group showed significantly greater commitment during the seminar and now demonstrate a clearly identifiable behavior change on the job. It needs to be footnoted that this particular president set a living example of a true management leader. He means what he said, and he practices what he preached.

The example makes the point. Harry probably gained some useful knowledge, but he showed little if any improved management performance on the job. Even the knowledge he gained will be gradually lost through lack of use.

Joan probably absorbed the same amount of knowledge as Harry, but, unlike Harry, she did change her behavior patterns on the job. She put this knowledge to work and kept it as part of her ongoing knowledge inventory. A good part of the reason was that the president of the company established the importance of the training seminar and made her understand that she was expected to use what she learned in her job. He also demonstrated a personal understanding of the subject matter.

Another part of the reason was that a large number of managers had already gone through the program and it was known that more would follow. The growing population of past participants were themselves creating a working climate featuring the use of the management concepts and methods taught in the course. They were reinforcing each other, unlike Harry's experience.

The organizational influences on the training function can usefully be considered in terms of three groups: (1) top management, (2) the immediate managers of seminar participants, and (3) their peers. Top management doesn't necessarily mean the chief executive officer of a corporation and his or her immediate staff. It's a convenient term to describe any team of managers heading up a reasonably autonomous organizational component.

The immediate managers of the participants in any seminar is a population that changes with every seminar, but it is helpful to identify this group separately because of its importance to the immediate post-seminar environment.

The peer group is made up of fellow employees, other than top management or immediate managers, regardless of organizational rank. The most important peer group is made up of those with whom the participants associate in a working relationship on the job. The other participants in any seminar group are also important peer influences.

How Top Management Influences the Climate

Of all three groups, top management clearly has the greatest impact on organizational environment. It's the power center that decides whether there should be any training function at all. It determines what resources should be made available to training. How it relates to the training function can enhance or lower the prestige of the function and hence affect its overall acceptance. How the individuals that constitute top management behave and what they say are also important influences. At the same time, this influence may be the most difficult for the training function to harness.

Budgetary Support

The resources made available to the training function by top management are a direct determinant of its potential effectiveness. At one extreme are companies like Digital Equipment, General Electric, Western Electric, and Waste Management (among undoubtedly many others) that have established large, well-equipped training centers whose very existence establishes the importance of the function. Merrill Lynch & Company dedicated a whole floor of its corporate headquarters on Liberty Plaza in New York City to the training function. Swiss Bank's New York branch has taken two floors at 222 Broadway for a training center.

At the other extreme are companies, sometimes of substantial size, who don't recognize the function at all. Just for example, a prominent

$2-billion electric utility holding company system relies wholly upon on-the-job training. For key positions it will appoint understudies some months in advance of an incumbent's retirement or reassignment. The practice provides assurance of continuity and recognizes the superior value of learning by doing.

But it may entail paying the penalty of less innovation. By the time the understudy takes over, he or she is brainwashed to do everything exactly the way it has always been done.

One large manufacturer in the paper industry simply doesn't recognize the value of a training function. They've never had one, and they can't see undertaking the expense to set one up. They are fighting every quarter to report an acceptable earnings per share performance.

Most companies will fall somewhere between these extremes. They are most likely to provide needed resources in good times and cut training budgets in bad times. Training professionals, certainly those at lower organizational levels, seem to have unusually high turnover compared to other specialized fields.

Sometimes in an effort to maximize return on an investment, companies will try to operate the training function on a starvation diet. In such cases, training directors may have to conduct programs for which they are not fully qualified, or they may shop around for bargains in outside program leaders. Another cost saver is to use inexpensive facilities that may seriously detract from learning.

One aluminum rolling mill used as a seminar setting a portion of a public restaurant with very inadequate dividers. The result was that seminar proceedings came to a halt during a busy 2-hour lunch period. Later in the day there were some company parties, with the same result.

A more usual mistake is to hold the training session in a company's own conference room without providing the discipline necessary to prevent interruptions and discourage participants from dividing their allegiance between the seminar and their regular jobs.

Naturally, budgetary support in itself does not alone provide for the right organizational environment, but it is an essential starting point. Without funding there can be no training function. With inadequate funding, it cannot have a significant effect.

Training professionals may have difficulty exerting a direct influence on increasing their budgetary authorizations. Budgetary decisions come out of the availability of funds and management's perception of the function's relevance to the success of the company, which comes about through the totality of their activities. They can protect themselves to some degree against uniformed reductions by making the clearest possible presentation of their cases.

Active Involvement

Of increasing importance in recent years is the visible, active involvement of higher-level executives with the training function. They are increasingly likely to participate in the identification of training needs, with specific reference to the company's own strategic directions. Then again, they are understanding more and more that significant change must be introduced through the training function. You can't simply send out a directive and expect the right things to happen.

It would seem fairly obvious that improving human productivity is becoming increasingly critical as the demand in the United States is moving away from unskilled jobs to those of an increasingly high technical content. Enlightened executive teams have come to recognize that they have to play a more important role in planning and guiding human resource development activities of all kinds.

For example, at United Technology the heads of the many operating units constitute an advisory body that meets several times a year to generate guidelines for the corporate executive development function — guidelines that are rooted in the strategic planning of the various units. The major concern of this company and many other companies these days is quality improvement as measured by the determination and meeting of customer needs. Improvements in such things as product performance, cycle time, and waste have to have a real, bottom-line importance to companies, and companies must recognize the role of training in getting people to function effectively as individuals and teams in securing these continuous improvements.

Some years ago, the corporate training center for Western Electric in Hopewell, New Jersey, organized a training committee composed of a number of high-ranking executives to do essentially the same thing. The staff of the training center would propose a curriculum, and the training committee would discuss, revise, and improve it. The arrangement has the incidental advantage that these senior executives encouraged their own people to sign up for the seminars that are offered.

Recently, Bristol-Myers Squibb decided to introduce flextime in its research facility in Wallingford, Connecticut. The company realized how critical it was to get all employees to understand the program and buy into it. How did they do it? Through a series of workshops conducted by the training function.

But surely the outstanding example is the way top managements of so many major corporations are using their training functions to make a major shift in their total culture with regard to continuous quality improvement. Lockheed, Philips, and Rockwell (and countless others) are ready examples.

Perhaps the lesson to be learned here is for the training function to get and keep close enough to top management to be able to anticipate ways in which it can assist in the sound introduction of new programs. A corollary is that the head of the training function cannot get too involved in the delivery of training. It's an easy mistake to make. But the penalty is the lack of sufficient time to work with and anticipate top management needs.

Management Practices

The kind of management practices established by top management constitutes the third way that top management influences the environment within which training takes place. Sometimes there is a very direct relationship.

For example, if top management introduces a new companywide system of operational planning and control, managers have to be taught how to use the system. They have to learn how to develop and write up objectives and standards of performance in a way that will link different levels of management, a way that makes each other's operating plans easy to understand.

Similarly, if a new performance appraisal and performance counseling system is adopted, it almost necessarily has to be implemented through training. In this case, there is a continuing need to overcome the natural reluctance of human beings to sit down and pass judgment on each other. There is always some uncertainty about the quality of performance itself, but more importantly, if the counseling interview promises to be difficult, it's only human to try to avoid the unpleasant.

In these examples and other instances in which a change in management practices is to be made, the participants in the training sessions know they will be expected to put their new knowledge to work on the job. Even more importantly, they themselves will be evaluated on how well they do so. Therefore, they come to training seminars with positive attitudes.

At other times the influence of top management may be somewhat less direct. For example, if a company adopts a new performance appraisal form that includes an item that evaluates managers on their performance in training and developing people, managers will be encouraged to give the training function a higher priority. They will be more inclined to send their people to training seminars. If need be, they can provide a head-count measurement on this item when they are being evaluated.

Then again, if corporate management adopts career planning and management development programs that require the successful completion of certain prescribed training courses, it necessarily creates a demand for these courses.

Training directors can play an important part in getting their companies to see the need for changes in management practices that will enhance human productivity. As professionals in the field, they are the most competent to anticipate the need for them, to help define the content and scope of the changes, to plan the communications and training programs necessary to implement them, and to carry out those programs effectively.

Public Manifestations

A fourth way top management helps is through public manifestations of support. These may be in the company's annual report, in company publications of various kinds, or at meetings.

For example, Paul Sticht, then chairman of R.J. Reynolds, Inc., attended a dinner held before the start of a series of top-down management training seminars for a subsidiary, Sea-Land Service, Inc. Although he only made brief remarks, his presence said a great deal and added significantly to the importance of the occasion.

Joseph Dionne, then president of McGraw-Hill [later chairman and chief executive officer (CEO)] and James Corcoran, chairman of General Accident and Indemnity, used this approach too, with similar effectiveness.

Serving as a Behavior Model

The fifth means, top management as a behavior model, applies most appropriately to management training seminars and, perhaps, to broadly aimed programs such as computer literacy. The model, unfortunately, can work both ways. It can be supportive, or it can be nonsupportive.

If, as in the illustration provided at the start of this chapter, top management conducts itself in accordance with generally accepted concepts of management leadership, it can be a real plus. If the chief executive is a good delegator, provides sufficient authority and freedom to act, but insists on completed work, his immediate staff members are more likely to do the same, and similarly throughout the organization.

If the CEO is observed to be a wise user of his or her personal computer and evidences full understanding of computer usage in day-to-day conversations, it tends to encourage others to become computer literate. There is a danger in this example, however; computers have a fascination that can cause executives to spend too much time at the keyboard. It also opens the risk that they may seek and use detailed operating information that undermines the authority of their subordinates.

The president of a major division of a food service company is a case in point. He was observed for hours at a time at the computer terminal in his office. It was generally believed he was "soaking up" operational information that he could use later to keep his regional vice presidents off balance. In any event, it took up valuable time that he could have used better in strategic planning or getting closer to his key people.

It is strange, in a way, to reflect upon the influence of the top team, especially the chief executive. Some years ago, a new president came into a very conservative, old-line insurance company in Philadelphia from another company. Much to the astonishment of the management bureaucracy, conservatively clad day after day for many years in white shirts and dark suits, the new president was observed wearing a *yellow* shirt on two separate occasions within the first 2 weeks of his arrival! Within 3 weeks, I am told on reliable authority, all the men's clothing stores in downtown Philadelphia were sold out of yellow shirts!

Here's another one. For many years it had been an unwritten rule at McKinsey & Company that members of the professional staff had to wear hats. It was a practice originally started by Marvin Bower who felt it important for the firm to project a professional appearance. This practice continued until long after President Kennedy introduced the wind-blown, hatless look. But one day, Marvin Bower was seen going out to lunch without a hat. In an incredibly short time, the word was flashed all over the firm. It proved to be a great relief to the McKinsey associates in Los Angeles. They had been uncomfortably conspicuous for many years: the only people walking along the streets in downtown Los Angeles who wore hats!

The influence of the top-management behavior model can often be a negative one. The president of a large, east coast utility company was the type that had to be deeply involved in every aspect of the company's operations. He was the first to arrive in the morning and used this opportunity to scan and sort the incoming mail. He would also telephone the superintendents of all the company's electric generating plants to get a first-hand, current report on all operating conditions. In doing so, he effectively bypassed two levels of intermediate management, undermining their effectiveness and motivation. It is no wonder that he had little time left for strategic planning and upgrading the effectiveness of human resources at all levels. Quite understandably, his management style was emulated by everyone else throughout the system, creating an environment that discouraged any efforts to introduce more enlightened management leadership concepts and methods.

Seminar Introduction

The sixth vehicle for top-management influence is personally introducing training seminars. When Union Carbide went through a massive, comprehensive management training effort from top to bottom, the company's top management made it a point for one of them to be personally present at the start of every session. They drew up a duty roster to ensure that one of the four top corporate executives from corporate headquarters (then on Park Avenue in New York City) would be present at the start of each seminar held in their conference facility in Tarrytown, New York. The corporate executive who was present would welcome the group, explain the background leading up to the program, and stress its critical importance to the company and to each individual.

In a series of programs conducted by the company's own trainers all around the world, the then chairman and chief executive, William Sneath, appeared at the outset in a short sound-movie segment doing the same thing. Most importantly, he made a point of using some of the same buzz words the participants would learn in the program. It had a great impact, many of the participants never having seen their chief before.

Kennametal, a fast-growing company in the high-technology cutting tool business, used a similar approach. With very few exceptions, Quentin McKenna, then president of the company (later, chairman of the board), appeared personally to start off each seminar session of a broadly based management development program. It had a very positive effect on each class.

How to Gain Top-Management Support

Given its importance, how can training directors get top-management support? Underscoring concern over this question is a constant topic of discussion by the American Society for Training and Development.

But it's not an easy question to answer. Perhaps the question has to be rephrased to ask, What practical steps can training directors initiate and carry out that will, over time, strengthen top-management support and thereby improve the organizational climate? Surely, training directors have some professional obligation to provide some leadership in effecting change in the overall climate. They should not sit idly by if they are not getting the support they need to do their jobs.

Know the Business

As more and more leading companies are turning to their human resource development professionals to help them implement major management initiatives, the latter must become contributing members of their respective top-management teams. They have to be in a position to anticipate the need for these major programs, perhaps even initiate them, to earn full top-management recognition and support.

At a recent work session held with experienced training directors from some of the most prominent corporations in metropolitan New York, there was unanimous agreement on their number one priority: getting to know as much as possible about the business their corporation is in. This would allow them to participate meaningfully in meetings at top corporate levels and earn credibility for their views.

Here is a typical viewpoint from a leading practitioner. William Yeomans, then manager of training and development for J.C. Penney, and president-elect of the American Society of Training and Development (ASTD), offered a list of recommendations for human resource development professionals.* First on the list was that training professionals should "learn and be part of the business they work in."

Do Good Work

Doing good work is essential in winning top support. Do the best possible job within whatever parameters have been set and do everything you can to make sure this is recognized by top management. Sales representatives know that their success is very dependent on the quality of the product or service they are offering, as perceived by their customers.

During the 40-odd years that he headed up McKinsey & Company, one of the world's most successful management consulting firms, Marvin Bower repeatedly said that by far the best way to sell the firm's services was to do outstanding work for present clients. The same advice applies here, except that you are selling your services to internal "clients."

Make sure your training seminars are so good that people will talk about them. I was visiting the west coast office of a client organization

---

*Presentation, February 2, 1987, to the New York Metro Chapter of the ASTD, as reported in the *Lamplighter,* April 1987, p. 13.

recently and happened to encounter the regional vice president in charge. I was in the company of a training specialist employed by the company. She conducted a number of programs in-house for this particular company, including a 1-day workshop on presentation skills.

The vice president's face broke into a broad smile when he saw us. He told me what an exciting experience it had been for his people to go through a session of the workshop she had only recently conducted. By the end of the day, he reported, even the most self-conscious participants were getting up, making first-rate presentations to the whole group, and getting a great kick out of it.

You can be sure this vice president made similar comments to other officers in the company. I know that I passed his comments around!

Know Your CEO

Another thought is to analyze your problem. Most successful sales representatives do a good deal of background research to assist in formulating a winning sales strategy with key prospects. Can you afford to do less in pursuing your own top target?

Perhaps you can pick up some clues from his or her early upbringing. Was your chief raised on a farm as a hard-working member of a large family? An only child of a wealthy east coast family? Brought up in a deeply religious environment? An army brat, hauled from station to station every few years? It can make quite a difference.

Did your chief work up through the ranks or come in from another company? Can you get any clues from associates or people who were former colleagues or subordinates as to underlying motivations? From the texts of letters to stockholders, speeches to security analysts or other public utterances? Your observation and analysis should give you some clues.

Many chief executives these days are strongly motivated to win the Baldrige award. If yours is one of these, you may be able to align some program you believe important to one or more of the seven categories used in the National Quality Award Examination: (1) leadership, (2) information and analysis, (3) strategic quality planning, (4) human resource utilization, (5) quality assurance of products and services, (6) quality results, and (7) customer satisfaction.

Even more fundamental than the desire to win an award is the appeal of productivity. Most observers foresee toughening, global competition in the next decade. This forecast comes at a time when productivity has been generally decreasing in the country. It may seem obvious, but it is nevertheless a powerful appeal, particularly for companies who are fighting to maintain market share and profitability. Yet, unless training directors have trained themselves to think like chief executives, they may stress the features of some desired programs in their appeals for funds instead of linking the programs to competitive survival.

Another appeal that has worked in the past in gaining support for management training is for a chief executive to leave a "monument" behind. It is frequently frustrating for chief executives of larger companies to realize what a limited influence they have on day-to-day operations. In this case, you might be able to link management training to the installation of a total management system that will represent a long-term improvement in management effectiveness, a system that will last long after the executive has retired.

Sometimes we have found that the chief executive of a loose federation of subsidiaries, usually representing a number of past acquisitions strung out in time, wants a means to instill a greater sense of common purpose or direction. Again, the time may be ripe for a massive management development program hitched to a new system of planning and control.

For example, in the early 1970s, William S. Sneath, then head of Union Carbide Corporation, believed that the financial community was undervaluing the company's common stock (a frequent aggravation of chief executives). He felt further that the reason for this valuation was their view that the parent corporation was nothing more than a holding company. It didn't provide any leadership or unifying sense of direction. It simply meted out financial resources to meet the greatest opportunities presented by the subsidiaries and chose the top executives of the operating units as the need arose.

Sneath wanted to change this perception. He wanted to establish a comprehensive, integrated management system to provide for effective corporate leadership while maintaining the benefits of decentralized operations. Implementation of the system involved a massive management training effort, from the very top executive team down through managers at all levels of the organization throughout the world. In this instance, the initiative came from the chief executive, but training directors might be alert to the possibility of this motivation in their own companies.

Sometimes the need arises for an orderly management succession. If a chief executive and a number of other top executives are all, say, within 5 years of retirement, the time may be ripe for launching an executive development and career planning program.

These are appeals that have worked in my experience. There are undoubtedly others. But perhaps these examples can serve to illustrate a way of thinking that could reveal the appeals that could work in your company. We have focused on the chief executive, but the same line of thinking would work for higher-level executives with a good deal of autonomy over operating segments of the total organization.

Whatever appeals you use, use them carefully. You have to believe sincerely that they are valid and can be effectively addressed through training. By all means, avoid creating unrealistic expectations as to what training can really accomplish. If you do, and then fail to deliver, you may deal a death blow to your efforts to create the proper environment.

Demonstrate the Benefits

Providing proof, another means of securing top-management support, has two closely related aspects: proving the need and proving the benefits. In a sense, they are the before and after aspects of providing proof.

There are some instances in which proof is less important. For example, if you have successfully involved management in determining training needs, you may not need any proof. Then again, some needs, like sales training or technical training on specific jobs, are not difficult to sell. They are almost self-evident.

Success in getting other needs accepted will be influenced by the extent to which they are backed up by comprehensive, fact-founded analyses presented in a persuasive way. Methods of needs analysis are treated in greater detail in Chapter 5.

Here are two ideas for getting the proof you need to launch new programs. Try to get success stories from other companies, perhaps through your network of fellow training professionals. A second way is to set up a pilot program with special emphasis on practical methods for identifying and measuring operational improvements. Dedicated follow-up to a pilot program can often provide bottom-line benefits that are identifiable and measurable.

A case in point comes to mind from the experience of a training director in a manufacturer of paper products. He got sold on the idea of a management program that featured an action planning segment. Participants learned how to put any project into a simple action plan format which helped them plan the best way to carry the project out and gave them the means to make sure it was carried out properly. He set up a pilot session and had the participants bring in "real world" projects aimed at specific operational improvements. During the workshop they each developed an action plan around their project to take back to their place of work. The training director then followed up carefully and was able to measure operational improvements that exceeded the cost of the workshop by a factor of 5. His boss was so impressed that he approved a major program.

Overcome Common Objections

If you are having difficulty in gaining greater top-management support, try to find out what the objections are and why they exist. You can't deal with them unless you can define them clearly.

Budgetary.   One of the typical problems you are likely to meet is budgetary: "We can't afford it." This is an easy excuse. It may be just a way of getting rid of you. Consultants face this barrier all the time and have learned that it is usually, although not always, a convenient way to say "no." What they do, and what you have to do, is to probe more deeply to discover the real objection.

"I know it may seem too costly, in view of all the other demands you have to meet. It's difficult sometimes to sort out the necessary from the not so necessary. But let's look at what you'll get from the expenditure. That's the real test. Then compare the result against the return you'll get on the other alternatives you're facing. Fair enough?" This kind of response will often uncover the real reason. Once the true objection is known, you may be able to deal with it. If you don't know the true objection, you can't deal with it.

If the objection is made in a hostile or challenging way, you might want to respond with equal energy: "We can't afford not to! I believe I can show you that we'll produce measurable benefits far in excess of the initial outlay. Would you hear me out?"

In both these examples you have a good chance of getting the management representative to listen to you. From that point on, you have to present your case in the most persuasive way, being sensitive to the reactions you're getting so that you can deal with any further objections along the way.

If you find that the budgetary problem is a real one, then you may have to settle for something less than immediate approval. "Can we approve this 'in principle' and implement it during the third quarter if earnings hold up?"

In some non-profit or government organizations, you may be able to get approval contingent upon securing outside funding. Essex County, New Jersey, successfully used this technique. The new county executive had some personal friends on Wall Street who were able to get their companies to underwrite a major management development program.

Too Busy. Another objection frequently encountered is this one: "We're too busy with other pressing projects. You can only do so many things at one time." This response too may represent an easy way to get rid of you. You have to probe in much the same way to see if this is an excuse or a real reason.

If it is a real objection, perhaps your timing was poor, in which case you may have to gracefully retire until another time. If your company is always in a frenzy of work, you should have anticipated this objection and come prepared with something like this: "It *does* seem that we have a lot going on right now, but I think we have a way of avoiding that problem by getting started in a way that doesn't interfere with these other projects. Would you at least listen to how we might do this?"

Another response might be: "You are absolutely correct. That's why we are scheduling the first session for the second quarter when things should have quieted down a bit." If you use this one, you have to be able to back up your statement with some specifics.

If you do make a proposal and get a negative response from the chief executive, do everything in your power to get the real reason for the refusal. If you are separated by intervening management layers, it may be difficult to do so. You may have to rely on the opinions of others. But the point is, you have no way to cope with the problem unless you can identify the true objection.

Sales representatives learn this guideline in their initial training. The best of them always work to uncover objections. In fact they are happy to get them. Often these objections stem from a failure of communication, which can be quickly corrected, or from a lack of information, which can then be supplied. Training directors have to be skilled at selling too.

Build a Network of Allies

Another avenue of attack, which can go on together with other efforts, is to proceed to build a base of support below the chief executive level of the organization. You may be able to find some allies near the top of the organization that you can cultivate and use as advisors, perhaps even as sponsors.

In any event, as employees go through your programs, keep an eye out for the "movers." Keep in touch with them. Over a period of time you may be able to build a network that can serve as a valuable source of information and advice. Some of them will work themselves into higher positions and become even more important to you.

The step-by-step approach is the easiest to follow. But if it is relied upon exclusively, you need to accumulate and merchandise success stories and have them find their way upward to the chief and the top staff. The danger is that the training function continues to be viewed as something that exists for lower organizational levels. This viewpoint will make it quite difficult to penetrate into the executive suite.

Bring In Outside Consultants

Outside consultants can also be of value in gaining top-management attention, commitment, and support. If some outside firm captures the attention of a key executive for some program they are selling, look upon this as a possible opportunity and not as a competitive threat. You may be able to join forces with the executive and the outside consultant to find a way to top management that you didn't have before. You may even be in a position to put a key executive, perhaps the chief human resources executive, in touch with the outside consultant to achieve the same result.

If you choose carefully, you can usually find consultants who are highly skilled in dealing confidently and persuasively with top management. They may be able to help you open doors that you have not been able to open yourself. Possibly because they are outsiders and can draw from a wide variety of experience with other companies, consultants tend to have a greater credibility than inside professionals.

Sometimes you may be able to get the top team involved in the process of reviewing a proposal from an outside consultant. This is frequently the case in the area of management development. You can explain that you need reassurance from top management that the proposed approach is consistent with their own philosophy of management. You then counsel and coach the consultants to get the maximum benefit from their presentation.

Be Persistent

It's easy to get discouraged in this whole process. It often takes a long time. It may involve a lot of emotional wear and tear and a lot of disappointments and delays. You may have to develop a thick skin.

But remember that circumstances may change, and probably will. Changes in business conditions or new faces in the executive suite can improve the likelihood of strong top-management support. In view of the powerful influence of this support on the success of training seminars, especially management training programs, it can be well worth the watchful waiting.

How Managers Influence the Climate

A second important, though less powerful, influence on the success of training seminars is that of the immediate supervisors of seminar participants. Presumably, it is the group that is being the most directly benefited through the training of its team members. These managers send people to seminars, or at least acquiesce to their being sent; and they will receive the newly trained seminar participants back on the job. In both roles, and particularly in the latter, they can have a very significant influence on how much the participants learn and how much of the new learning gets put to work on the job.

Preseminar Conditioning

Their influence begins before the seminar starts. Potentially, these managers can condition their people so that they arrive at the seminar with a positive attitude. Ideally, the seminar attendance comes from a performance appraisal and counseling system and is part of a personal development plan that participant and manager have jointly developed.

Even if it doesn't, the participants' managers can be a positive influence by meeting with their people before the seminar, explaining what they should get out of it, and informing them that they will coach them after the session in using their new knowledge effectively. This type of meeting doesn't take a great deal of time and needn't be a formal session. It can happen naturally in the course of working together.

Unfortunately, in my experience, this kind of preseminar counseling rarely happens. Managers are just too busy, it seems, to find the time. They live a frantic life with never enough time to do all the things that should be done. Or they don't realize its importance. It's far more likely, if anything is said at all, that the future participants may receive a passing comment, intended humorously, about taking some "rest and recreation" at the managers' expense. Or else they're subjected only to a quick, worried consultation on what important items are likely to come up while they're gone and how they will be handled.

During the Seminar

After the training seminar starts and while it is being conducted, the influence of the participants' managers is rarely positive. It may be neutral and it can be negative.

There are several ways that these managers can adversely affect the success of the seminar. In the worst scenario, they may call participants out of the seminar to attend important meetings. They may interrupt by telephone to get information on some matter for which the participant is responsible. They may make it evident that they expect the participants to carry on their responsibilities by telephone, or before and after seminar hours, if geography permits. In all these instances, participants can be prevented from giving their undivided attention to the seminar, perhaps even being made to miss portions of the program.

After the Seminar

The most important impact of this manager group is by way of reinforcement after the seminar, or lack of it. Their influence may come from direct interpersonal relationships or less directly from their own roles as behavior models.

It's a truism that by far the best way for people to learn new skills is on the job with the guidance of a skilled coach. Some training directors have said that skill building is 20% classroom and 80% on the job. Regardless of the precise percentage, the influence of participants' own managers on the job is crucial.

Managers who played an active role in identifying specific improvement needs for their people and in sending them to seminars to meet those needs are far more likely to provide the necessary reinforcement after the seminar. In fact, to the observer, this kind of interplay would not be difficult nor time-consuming and could have a very powerful motivational plus. It shows the participants that their managers are really concerned about them and about helping improve their capabilities.

Sadly, the reverse can also be true and often is. Participants' managers can quickly undo the learning that took place in the seminar or make it seem unimportant. They can insist upon or encourage behavior that is contrary to what their people learned. For example, "I wouldn't waste my time writing up a mission statement with standards of performance for your function. I know they teach you that in the course, but we all know what needs to be done here. Let's not waste time writing about it. Let's get down to work and do it." Comments like this will reestablish the behaviors exhibited by the participants before the seminar. It will reinforce their natural reluctance to change.

The postseminar influence of the participants' managers can show up in a less direct way. The managers serve as role models for their people. Just as in the case of the chief executive, as we saw earlier, if these managers consistently demonstrate the desired behavior, their people will more surely adopt it—and vice versa. Actions surely speak louder than words.

Let's look at a few examples. If a time-management course offers a simple work planning form that participants see their own managers using effectively, they will more surely adopt it themselves. If they have learned a five-step technique for delegating which they see their managers applying, the same is true. If a course provides a problem-solving model that the participants' managers are observed to be following, they again will more likely use it themselves.

In my experience, most managers don't understand or else don't fully appreciate the important modeling role that they play for their people. Simply by setting a good example, managers can inspire their people to follow that example.

How to Win the Support of Managers

The powerful role played by participants' managers, particularly during the first 3 to 6 months after a seminar, is well recognized. But there is considerable frustration over what to do about it.

Part of the problem stems from the time pressures on both the manager group and on the training director. But part of it may be the lack of a clear, practical course to follow. We all probably have a lot to learn on this subject, but there are a number of approaches that are available. Getting the support of this manager group is difficult, but it can be done.

Mount a Communication Campaign

One approach is to borrow ideas from the professionals in advertising firms. They have developed some very effective techniques for molding the attitudes of selected populations of consumers. Although these techniques may sound "way out" to some, they are still worth considering.

In advertising, the modus operandi is (1) clearly define your target population and your objective, (2) develop attention-getting, high-impact messages to serve that objective, and (3) deliver these messages repeatedly through cost-effective media. Why not try this approach to influencing managers who will sooner or later be in this group of participants' managers?

The first thing you are likely to discover is that your target population has to be more clearly defined. You will have to think separately about plant managers, sales managers, and data processing managers, for example. Suppose we take plant managers as the target population, just to illustrate the approach.

Now you have to clarify your objective. What is it that you want them to do? It may be to send people to seminars or to coach people who have returned from seminars to apply their new knowledge effectively on the job. These are different objectives that will require different approaches.

Let's say your objective is to get plant managers to send people to a course on supervisory management. You then have to think about your message. You do this by asking yourself, in Madison Avenue's terms, What is the "unique selling proposition"? What key benefits will plant managers realize? Perhaps you will come up with the answer of improved productivity. If so, this benefit has to be translated into your message.

Now in developing copy for this message, you have to think of a "headline" right up front to capture attention. It should incorporate the key benefit in a high-impact way. Perhaps you could say, "Section heads at the Springfield plant reported a 20% improvement in productivity after their supervisors attended the company's 3-day supervisory training course." That message ought to interest the other plant managers!

After whatever elaboration is appropriate in your message, you should end with your objective — a call to action. "Sign up for places in the seminar now, while there are still openings at the times of your choice."

The use of media is also important. To get the message across you can send plant managers the year's seminar schedule with a prominent red circle drawn around the seminar to be promoted. Maybe you'd prefer a single-sheet flyer with specifics on the seminar attached to a short covering memorandum. At the very least, you could discuss seminar specifics when making personal appeals to these plant managers.

Note that this example assumed a specific target population, a clear objective, and an attention-getting message directly serving that objective. The same approach could be used for other target groups and other objectives. By necessary implication, the least effective communication is the one most commonly used: a brochure promoting all seminars sent to all target groups!

One final thought before leaving the advertising analogy: Why not develop a "tag line" to go along with all your communications to your clientele? It would not be a part of each message but a continuing reminder of the need for active line involvement before, during, and after the seminar. How about using the slogan "We need *your* help to help *you* best"?

If you stop to think about it, you are in continuing, regular contact with the managers using your services. You are making needs analyses, announcing seminar schedules, soliciting registrations, confirming registrations, or following up participants' performance after seminars. If you have organized a training committee, you are sending out reminders of meetings, agendas, background information for meetings, minutes or follow-up notes (as some prefer to call them), and progress reports. Just think of the stream of written communications from your office. Suppose each one of them contained your own tag line in an attention-getting, high-impact way. Over time, it could have an effect.

Get Them to Buy Into Your Plans

Getting participants' managers involved in determining the training needs of their people is another good approach. But make sure that you make acceptable demands on their time, that you meet the needs they identify, and that the managers understand that you have.

If you can get these managers actively involved in this way, they are more likely to use the services of the training function—and more likely to make sure ideas learned are applied on the job. A properly conducted needs analysis is one way to get them involved. Another is to get them membership on a training committee or advisory group. Sometimes informal discussions with individual managers will serve the purpose.

Even though you want to get this managerial group actively involved in determining needs, there are times when you may have to shape their perceptions. After all, the training director is the skilled professional. You can't sit back and accept *their* views. You have to provide some leadership. For one thing, they may have some misconceptions as to what training can accomplish. Some performance deficiencies or improvement needs may require other forms of corrective action, such as improved standards of performance, better feedback systems, or correction of individual motivation problems. You may have to sell these managers on some needs and unsell them on others.

A third approach is to get participants' managers to play an active role in scheduling seminars and selecting participants. In most companies they will almost necessarily be involved in deciding who goes to seminars from their teams and when they go. But usually they are presented with a seminar schedule and have to fit into it.

Scheduling. Getting these managers involved in the scheduling process sometimes occurs naturally. When line managers take the initiative in getting training sessions set up for their own people for some special reasons of importance to them, they will have a lively interest in determining when it should take place. They will be more concerned than usually with the problem of taking employees off the job. They have to schedule the training in a way that minimizes lost production.

Usually though, particularly in larger organizations, the scheduling of seminars takes place 6 to 18 months in advance of the actual seminar dates. Typically, an annual program with many different courses has to be finalized and funded as part of the budgeting process, which necessarily means a long lead time. But even in this case, you could circulate a "draft" or "coordination" copy of the proposed schedule for comments and suggestions.

Selecting Participants.   For some training directors, the real challenge comes after they have their funding and their catalog of courses has been published. Some of these professionals succeed in getting the cost of conducting the courses in their own budgets, which makes it easier to fill seminar seats. But in most cases they have to persuade line managers to send their people at their own cost.

It often seems at this point that training directors and line managers have adversary roles. The latter often want to postpone or even avoid off-the-job training. They are so intent on getting the work out, they find it difficult to spare their people.

On the other hand, training directors have a natural compulsion to fill their seminars. They know that if they don't get enough registrations, they may have to cancel a session. If so, they will be criticized for improperly forecasting training needs, and perhaps also for incurring some non-productive training expenses. Those who did register will be irritated because they will have had to change their plans, usually on short notice. No wonder that cancellations are viewed as calamities.

Ideally, the line managers should have identified individual development needs through the performance appraisal and counselling processes established by the company. They then match up these needs with what is offered. In this situation, they are literally forced to participate in the selection process because of the established management processes of their companies. Otherwise, they may be criticized by their own managers.

Curiously enough, in selecting employees to go to seminars, training and development specialists may be happy not to practice what they preach. In one fairly large company that I know, the training director agrees with the president on the list of attendees for a given seminar. And that's it! Even though training directors may profess the benefits of decentralized decision making, it's a lot easier simply to send out a memorandum in the president's name listing those who are expected to attend. You can't help wonder, though, about the attitudes of the managers whose people are being taken from them in this way.

Top-Down Training

Another way to win the support of participants' managers is to cascade the seminar from higher to lower organization levels. In this way, the managers of any seminar group will have been through the experience first. If they have had a favorable experience, they are more likely to provide positive reinforcement to their own people.

The top-down approach is used effectively in support of major management initiatives such as total quality management or installation of an integrated planning and control system. Another example would be creation of a common culture or management leadership system.

Pilot Testing

Sometimes it's possible to get a higher-level management team to pilot test a new seminar before lower-level employees are put through the program. Essentially a variation of the top-down approach, it has an additional advantage: It solicits the participation of the higher-level managers in the adaptation or redesign of the seminar. Even if the changes made are only in terminology, they provide an element of emotional ownership that adds greatly to the management support provided to future participants in the program.

Let me cite a pertinent example from my own experience. We use the term "Position Charter" in our management programs to describe a statement of the measurable results that a manager or management team is accountable for achieving through the ongoing, continuing operations for which the manager or team is accountable. The Position Charter plays a central role in planning, organizing, leading, and controlling ongoing responsibilities. It serves as a necessary counterbalance to any system of management by objectives, which tends to overly weight short-term changes to be made.

The term itself is unimportant. It's the substance that counts. But several client organizations preferred to call it something else. The top-management team of Sea-Land Service opted in favor of "Accountability Charter." The county executive's team in Essex County decided to call it a "Performance Charter." In both instances, by accepting these changes, we were able to get the top-management team to consider the whole program as something more clearly their own.

Priming the Participants

Getting the participants' managers to identify specific individual development needs before the seminar is another way to get their support. This effort will motivate the participants to pay particular attention to those needs during the course of the program. They will want to be able to show their managers that they have learned and will apply on the job specific knowledge relating to their identified needs.

But the approach has the secondary benefit of stimulating the managers' interest in the seminar as a means of specific performance improvement. These managers are far more likely to follow up on the job and do the kind of coaching that will ensure appropriate skill building.

Take as an illustration a hypothetical Barbara Green who learns from her manager that her interpersonal relationship skills need to be improved. Not only does she have a keener interest when this subject is covered in the seminar, but she is stimulated to demonstrate new and improved behavior. At the same time, her manager will feel a keener sense of commitment to follow up on the job to observe her behavior and provide essential feedback.

How Peer Pressures Influence the Climate

The aggregate impact of peer group values, attitudes, and behavior is the third major environmental influence on the success of training seminars. Peer pressures make themselves felt before, during, and after the seminar. Potentially they can be fully as important as pressures from the participants' managers, though perhaps less direct.

Attendance

For one thing, the overall opinions or attitudes of peers can affect attendance. If the feedback from past participants is favorable, the influence of the peer group is likely to be positive. Chances are that seminars will be well attended. Cancellations will be few. Seminar leaders start out with an advantage if individual attendees share with each other the previous favorable experience of specific named individuals. These can sometimes be induced if the leader gets the attendees to tell the rest of the group their expectations for the session.

If, on the other hand, the previous sessions have generated various degrees of negative responses, the reverse is true. Training directors will have to use every imaginable resource to fill up scheduled seminars. Partly filled seminars and even cancellations may result. In extreme cases, the whole series may have to be dropped.

In-Seminar Commitment

The participants in every seminar are themselves part of this overall aggregation of peer values, attitudes, and opinions. It is all brought with them into the seminar, although tempered by the particular mix of each seminar group. The result can range from a very high level of commitment to a fairly low level; from an eagerness that is willing to take a great deal on faith, to a cynicism that will question and weigh at every step.

There are times when a seminar group might view the experience as a bit of well-earned rest and recreation. Such a concern has been expressed to me on more than one occasion by training directors that have large, comfortable corporate education centers on large tracts of landscaped properties that resemble some of our finest country clubs.

This kind of group will respond enthusiastically to the program leader's humorous stories. More often than not, they will contribute their own favorite jokes. One laugh invites another and everyone has a great time but at the expense of the learning experience. Evening assignments will be given fast and superficial treatment. Distractions will be easily found.

It's easy for seminar leaders to fall in with a group like this, playing bridge or poker with them in the evenings, or a game of golf in the late afternoons. But there is a real danger in this. Leaders may unwittingly encourage fun and games at the expense of real learning. One of the associates in our firm is an avid bridge player but a very frustrated one because his wife dislikes the game. One time, when he found a trio of good bridge players in his seminar group, he eagerly filled out the foursome, joining them at the bridge table on successive extended evenings during the seminar. He realized later that his actions not only prevented his bridge companions from making a deep commitment to evening assignments, it also set a poor example for the other participants.

In other situations, participants might arrive with a greater seriousness of purpose. They may have a keener realization of the benefits to be obtained in relations to on-the-job performance and ultimate career advancement. The chances are good that they will reinforce each other's favorable attitudes as they work together. Although they may still enjoy a good laugh, they will do a much more conscientious job in their evening assignments and will contribute much more to group discussions.

By way of illustrating the importance of participant attitudes, I remember clearly one unusual experience I had involving a small, highly specialized electronic equipment manufacturer on the west coast. The president of the company had called us in to present our basic management program to him and his top management team. By prearrangement we stopped after every major segment of the program to lead a discussion designed to reach conclusions on how the material we had just covered should be built into the management processes of the company. The active involvement of the president and his demonstrated willingness to hear other people's ideas contributed to a most positive peer environment.

Postseminar Climate

Peer pressures after the seminar can also have a significant impact on the success of any seminar. They can contribute to reinforcement, or they can operate in the reverse way as well, contributing to various degrees of failure.

Let's look first at some positive situations. If the seminar graduates return to a work environment in which their new knowledge is actually being put to work by others, you'll probably get reinforcement on the job. It's even better if the participants' peers have been through the same program, found it useful, and have incorporated the new behavior patterns into their work habits. It's especially helpful if the authority figures within the group are counted among the successful users of the new behavior.

If you stop to think about it, you'll realize that the subject matter of the seminar plays a role here. If, in fact, it is realistically geared to the working environment, it's more likely that the people in the particular work group will accept and use it.

But the postseminar influence of peers can also be negative. If their fellow workers are not using the methods taught in the seminar, it is more difficult for the participants to do so. If the others make negative remarks about the methods they are supposed to implement on the job, only the most self-reliant and committed participants will resist the pressure.

How to Influence the Peer Climate

Given its importance then, how can you influence the peer climate? Success in gaining top-management support and the support of past participants' managers will help induce a favorable peer climate. But what additional approaches are available?

One especially helpful approach is to make a conscientious effort to understand the working environment of the participants of any program and to develop your seminar objectives and subject matter content based on this understanding. The more realistic and obviously useful the methods you are teaching, the more likely they will be put to work on the job by the participants and accepted by their peers.

You could use this approach with varying degrees of formalization.

Carefully designed questionnaires and structured interviews are worth consideration. But it's probably easier to have informal discussions with the authority figures in the particular population. Two-way communication is more likely to produce the realistic insights you need.

Probably the greatest influence training directors have on the peer group is the stream of people emerging from training seminars and returning to their respective places of work. They can literally act like missionaries in getting new values and new methods accepted by others. As in so many situations where you are trying to get people to adopt new behavior, they have to truly understand what they are expected to do and see how they can personally benefit from doing so. The larger the number of committed past participants in any work population, the more likely you are to influence and change the total work culture.

As we have seen, the total organizational environment is created by the aggregated impact of top management, the managers of any given seminar group, and by peers generally. Each of these three groups exerts a significant influence. None can be neglected, whether you are trying to maintain a favorable climate or to create one.

The organizational climate for training is a major determinant of overall success for any training function. It will necessarily differ from organization to organization. In some cases in which top management uses the training function effectively to introduce and implement major management initiatives, it will probably be very positive. In many others it will not be. It's also true that there are some real limits to what training directors can do to improve the overall climate, and it may take a long time. But notwithstanding the difficulties, it's well worth the effort.

3

How to Organize and Staff for Success

For medium- to larger-sized organizations the establishment of an internal training function is probably a necessity. The crucial importance of improving human productivity in the increasingly difficult environment in which most enterprises find themselves is generally well recognized. And it is well accepted that the training program will be far more effective both at top management and other organizational levels if it is conducted by an internal staff of qualified professionals.

It's possible to operate without a separate, formally organized, training staff. Many companies do, even some larger ones. Where we find no separate, formalized training function, it is frequently combined with other responsibilities in a human resources department or an administrative service group. There is a host of outside firms and individuals available to supply the actual training, but they need a point of contact.

In this chapter, you'll find some ideas and suggestions on how to organize and staff an internal training department. Without this kind of foundation to work from, you cannot succeed with your training seminars.

Rationale for a Training Staff

The need for organizing and staffing a training function tends to be evolutionary. In the early years of an enterprise, training and developing occurs almost exclusively on the job. It is viewed as the responsibility of individuals to get themselves trained. There is no formal training staff. When new people are hired, it is left to their immediate supervisors to train them in whatever skills are needed on the job.

For some organizations, this approach continues even as they grow to substantial size. Some very large professional service organizations, such as management consulting firms, accounting firms, and law firms, do not formalize separate, discrete training functions. The same is true with a number of fairly large advertising, banking, and public utility companies.

Nevertheless, there is a compelling case to be made for setting up a separate training function. The case becomes stronger as companies grow in size and as they find themselves in increasingly competitive environments.

Implementing Management Initiatives

In recent years, large numbers of leading companies have come to recognize the critical need for an internal training capability in order to succeed in launching broad management initiatives.

The outstanding example is total quality management. Management has to develop a deep commitment on the part of every employee to clearly delineate internal and external customer needs and meet or exceed those needs. Notions of "value added" have to be understood. A climate of mutual trust has to be created. Project teams have to be drilled in problem-solving techniques and statistical methods. All of these require the effective support of the training function.

The increasing use of management task forces often requires initial training to provide all team members with a common knowledge base from which to work. Almost always some kind of problem-solving model has to be understood, accepted, and used by them. If they are going to investigate organizational needs, they will need further training in organizational concepts and principles to work most effectively.

A prominent Wall Street investment banking firm which makes extensive use of project teams to develop and introduce new or improved computerized information services systems also provides training in interpersonal skills for team members. The firm recognizes that success in implementing change requires gaining the cooperation of other people. Management of the project is seen as involving the full scope of management skills on a small scale: planning, organizing, leading, and controlling.

Doing Research

An internal training department can perform a research function. It can explore the human resource development needs of the company to establish a surer basis for determining what training should be provided. It can keep in touch with the state of the art, i.e., what other companies are doing. It can maintain an information bank on available off-the-shelf training programs and program material and on outside consulting resources.

One of the leading New York commercial banks puts a high premium on keeping in touch with external resources. Its human resource development professionals are assigned different areas of the bank as "clients." They then research their clients' needs and match them up against external as well as internal resources available.

Developing and Adapting Programs

Sometimes training needs that have been developed through research don't seem to match up with any existing internal or external program. In that case, the training department can develop new programs or adapt existing programs to meet those needs. The developmental or creative challenge presented can offer a real motivational plus for training staff people. They are undoubtedly in a better position than an outside resource to relate training programs directly to the company's business and actual work environment.

In practice, we see this program development role most widely played in first-level supervisory programs. At that level, where the largest supervisory population exists, the economics are most favorable for the internal staff as opposed to external consultants.

Presenting Training Programs

For most companies, teaching—or more accurately, delivering training programs that result in desired on-the-job behavior change—is the primary function of the department. A company can gain great flexibility by having its own corps of qualified seminar leaders. Special programs can be called on short notice or rescheduled without the need to coordinate this with any outside consultant.

The economics favor the internal staff too. Ongoing programs can be staffed much more economically from within. At the same time, internal seminar leaders can learn from each other with a continuing up-

grade in quality. They are strongly oriented to succeed since their career progress depends on doing a good job—every time.

Evaluating Training Results

The training staff can also provide a means for constantly evaluating
the effectiveness of ongoing programs, making improvements as necessary. Seminar leaders themselves are constantly experimenting with different ways to secure better understanding of the subject matter. Participant evaluations and audits are further inputs. The evaluation
function extends to programs put on by outside consultants as well as to
the internal programs.

Providing Consulting Assistance

A training staff of qualified professionals can also provide advice and
service to managers at all levels on developmental needs and available
services. Generally accepted management theory makes line managers
accountable for developing their own people, with the training staff
available to offer help.

Much of this assistance is provided by the training department's ongoing programs. But from time to time, line managers need advice on
whether or not training will help correct some performance deficiency.
They may also need help in establishing viable individual development
plans for their people, or perhaps they may need to know how formal
training can assist in some operational change. In all these ways, the
easy availability of a training professional is of real value.

How to State the Training Mission

If you accept the need for an internal training function, the next step is
to delineate clearly and completely what that function is expected to accomplish. You cannot organize in a vacuum. You organize to accomplish something. The first step in thinking through how to organize and
staff the training function is to define its mission.

In offering suggestions on how to develop a satisfactory statement of
the training mission, I will draw extensively from concepts and methods
originated by Louis Allen which have been incorporated in the practice

of Louis Allen Associates, the firm which he founded.* At the same time, recognizing the differences in terminology that exist in the management community—especially planning terminology—I shall use terms for these concepts that I believe are most commonly used and most easily understood.

Regardless of the words used, the first step in setting up a training department is to develop a statement of overall purpose or continuing result to be achieved. I'll call it the "mission statement." The experience of many generations of successful managers leads to the conclusion that the mission statement should consist of four components that answer the questions why, who, what, and where.

Purpose Commitment. The first component of the mission statement describes the essential purpose or end result to be accomplished. It states *why* the training function exists. If it is doing its job, I would suggest that the training department should be contributing significantly to the productivity of human resources in the enterprise of which it is a part. Other conditions and efforts will also affect human productivity, such as the resources and equipment made available to people, so the training function cannot be held *fully* accountable for human productivity. But it can be held accountable for *contributing* to human productivity improvement.

Furthermore, the training department should be contributing more value to the total enterprise (even if that is difficult to measure) than it is costing. You can think of this difference as a *contribution* to the profits of the company, or to the basic purpose of the enterprise if it is nonprofit. You might phrase it this way:

> The mission of the XYZ Company training department is to improve the performance of human resources on the job and in this way to contribute to the profitable growth of the company.

Customer-Client Commitment. The second of the four components answers the question *who?* Who uses or benefits from the programs and services provided by the department? Or put in another way, Whose needs are being served by the department?

It's a key question. Until you identify whose needs are being served and until you define those needs carefully, you can't determine what programs and services you should be offering. Let me suggest that most training functions will have three categories of customers or clients:

*See Allen, Louis A.: *Making Managerial Planning More Effective,* McGraw-Hill, New York, 1982.

1. Top management, which will need the support of the function in evaluating and introducing broad corporate initiatives that affect or involve people. This group may also have a specific interest in the training of top-level managers, i.e., executive development.

2. Line managers at all levels, who will draw upon the department to help them discharge their responsibility for training and developing their own people.

3. Employees generally, whose knowledge, attitudes, and skills will be improved by participating in training programs.

Each of these classes of customer will have a different set of needs to be met. These needs should be periodically reviewed with key people from each customer group and redefined if necessary. We probably have to do some anticipation here. Forecasting future needs in these days of constant change will often be more important than analyzing present needs.

Product/Service Commitment. Once we know whose needs have to be met, and what those needs are or will be, we can think through what products and services have to be provided in order to meet those needs. We're not yet thinking about the *work* that must be done but rather about the end product or service to be provided.

For example, one way of stating the product line component of the mission statement might be

> To provide advice and counsel and educational services in the introduction of new or changed corporate human resource programs, and to provide an ongoing range of high-impact, participative technical and management training programs that meet identified needs.

Scope Commitment. The fourth component describes *where* the products or services are being provided. It sets the limits within which the training department functions. The scope component is especially important in large enterprises which may have portions of the training function decentralized into operating units. For example,

> To provide these programs and services throughout the whole company (or within corporate headquarters).

Putting this last component together with the other three produces a mission statement that covers all the essential dimensions. It might look like this:

The mission of the XYZ Company training department is to improve the performance of human resources on the job and in this way to contribute to the profitable growth of the company.

To achieve this mission it will provide advice and counsel and educational services that meet the needs of top management in the introduction of new or changed corporate human resource programs and will provide an ongoing range of high-impact, high-quality technical and management training programs and related consulting services, using both inside and outside resources, that meet the identified human resource development needs of managers and employees at all levels, throughout the whole company.

What Strategic Options to Consider

Once you have stated your mission, you have laid the foundation for a sound organization. You now have to proceed to the next step. You have to consider a series of strategy questions before you can determine exactly what work needs to be done and how you can fit that work into a sound organizational structure.

Here are important questions I would suggest. How complete an internal capability do you want to have? To what extent do you want to use outside resources? Are you going to decentralize any part of the function to lower organization levels? What broad type of structure do you want? Functional? Divisional? Matrix? What kind of balance is needed between specialists and generalists? How do you want to make effective use of teams? What values do you want to build in your people?

Some, and perhaps all, of these questions may be decided for you by the overall organizational climate in which you find yourself. The company may have adopted an overall management philosophy favoring self-sufficiency for all ongoing needs, decentralization into autonomous operating units, employee empowerment and self-managed teams.

But for the purpose of providing a complete perspective, let me assume that these questions have not been answered for you or that you have sufficient leeway to organize your own function. We can then examine these questions in terms of the options available and the criteria you can use for reaching decisions.

How Self-Sufficient?

The first question is the extent to which you should establish complete internal capability. Company practices vary widely here.

At one extreme are giant companies like General Electric, General

Motors, IBM, and Merck. They are virtually completely self-sufficient. At the other extreme are companies that have a single training director position with no staff at all. This appears to be true at the corporate level for American Cyanamid, CPC International, and United Technologies. These companies, however, will have training staffs in their operating units.

Most enterprises fall somewhere between these extremes. They maintain an in-house capability for some of their needs and draw on outside resources for the rest.

Training Workload. The kind of training workload that you forecast is one important criterion for deciding what is best for you. Here you have to look at the long term, difficult though that is. You don't want to be shifting your strategies every year. Probably the general guideline followed here is to build staff for your ongoing continuing needs and use program leaders borrowed from other parts of the company or outside consultants for everything else.

Let's be more specific. If you foresee that your workload will be sporadic, with only occasional peak demands, possibly mixed with highly specialized non-recurring requests, you are better off with a minimum staff. Otherwise you will find your people with time on their hands. They will want to keep themselves busy and are likely to be off in a dozen different directions of marginal importance. They will persuade themselves, and probably you, that existing programs need to be revised to become more effective. This is fun work and can fill up a lot of time.

Scope of Training Needs. Another criterion would be the required scope of training in terms of subject matter. The smaller the internal staff, the greater the likelihood that there will be limitations on the number of different courses that any one of them can teach at acceptable levels of quality; hence, there will be limitations on the total capability of the department.

Maximizing Relevance. Some training directors are adamant on the need for program leaders to be completely expert in the business of the company. These professionals want each program leader to be able to relate the programs they conduct specifically to the business experience of participants from all parts of the company. In their view, outside consultants can never know their company well enough to do this. It's hard enough to build this understanding into their own trainers.

On the other hand, there may be situations in which the borrowed trainer or the outside consultant can bring in a level of experience and knowledge that would be beyond that of the internal trainer. Executive participant groups are far more likely to accept the credibility of a professor from Harvard Business School, for example, than of their own home-grown professionals. We'll talk about this question in greater depth in Chapter 4.

Cost of Training. No evaluation of your options would be complete without considering cost. Establishing an internal capability, assuming there is an ongoing workload, will undoubtedly produce lower costs per participant. However, there are many hidden costs that are usually disregarded and special circumstances where it is economic to use outside resources.

One big cost that is often overlooked—in all likelihood the biggest cost of all—is the opportunity cost represented by taking people off the job and into the classroom. This cost would have to be measured by the salaries and other personnel costs of the participants. These are resources that are diverted from production to training. If you measured opportunity cost in lost production, the cost would be even higher. Even if they don't measure the cost this precisely, the managers of seminar participants have a direct appreciation for the lost productivity represented by their absences from the job.

Given the magnitude of this hidden cost, it's no wonder that line managers have been applying increasing pressure to shorten the length of training seminars. We have a basic management seminar that we use as a point of departure for developing customized programs for our clients. For many years, until only a few years ago, it was a 5-day program. Now it has been reduced to 4. And for many clients we have further shortened it to 3, and, in one case, 2 days.

If companies take this opportunity cost into account, which seems to be increasingly the case, the margin of benefit for full internal capability has to be less, at least as a percentage of the true total cost involved.

Outside consultants may cost more on a per diem basis but are still economic for handling peak loads, non-recurring needs, or programs requiring highly specialized knowledge and experience. It is often less costly to use (or modify) an off-the-shelf program provided by an outside vendor than it would be to develop such a program from ground zero.

What to Centralize, What to Decentralize?

The issue of whether to decentralize mostly affects larger training forces within larger organizations. Generally accepted management theory says that a staff service should be placed as close to the point of service as is economical. The options for application of this principle are fairly obvious: centralize the training function, decentralize it, or use some practical combination of the two. Let's look at some criteria that can help in making this decision.

Organizational Policy. Perhaps the most important of these criteria is existing company policy or practice. It would appear that the general practice in most large enterprises is to favor decentralization. Perhaps because of the influence of Peters & Waterman and also the growing acceptance of Deming's theories, the trend toward broad decentralization has been accelerating in recent years.* Without any strong corporate preference, training directors can examine the question on its own merits.

Commonality of Needs. Another consideration is the existence of a significant volume of common training needs. Needs that are often found to exist in all or most operating divisions are executive development, management training, computer literacy, and, to an increasing degree, establishment and maintenance of total quality-management programs. Some companies are reporting a growing need for remedial training as growing numbers of new employees are illiterate (at least in the official language of the company) or lack basic arithmetic skills. These too would cut across organizational lines.

Other needs might be specific to individual operating units. If these units are in clearly different businesses, as is often the case, they may require their own sales training and their own technical training capabilities. If they have different national cultures, as in the case of global enterprises, they are probably going to need their own training capabilities in other areas as well.

Geographic Dispersion. A centralized training staff can function most effectively if its clientele is geographically convenient. It's easier to keep in close touch with user needs and to carry out postseminar follow-up programs, and, of course, it is easier and less costly to establish and change seminar schedules.

To the extent that users of training programs and services are spread around the country or around the world, it becomes increasingly difficult to serve them from a single location. Large multi-national corporations have had some success in "exporting" seminars to branch locations

*Peters, Thomas J., and Waterman, Robert H., Jr.: *In Search of Excellence: Lessons from America's Best-Run Companies,* Harper & Row, 1982.

or other countries through traveling program leaders. Where this approach is feasible, it tends to overcome the problems of a centralized training function, but it may entail a lot of wear and tear on the training staff.

As of the date of this writing, the use of teleconferencing to bring people in different locations into a common seminar experience is still in its infancy. It will undoubtedly become more important in future years, further countering the geographic disadvantages of centralization.

Quality.   The effectiveness or quality of the training provided can be influenced by the decision on centralization or decentralization. If you have a large number of small staffs in scattered locations, overall quality can suffer. You will not be able to take full advantage of specialization. Each trainer will have to perform a broad range of duties. Those who may develop a high level of special expertise will not be able to share it beyond their own operating units.

Even beyond the sharing of special expertise, you lose the benefits of easy day-to-day cross-fertilization. Trading of ideas and experiences is a powerful developmental vehicle for fellow professionals. Successes and failures are not easily shared if your colleagues are scattered around the country, or around the world, instead of being in the next office.

Cost.   Cutting across all the criteria we have been discussing is the question of cost. Without question, a centralized function will be more efficient than setting up a separate capability in each operating unit. You'll get greater utilization of training professionals, and there will be less down time.

The central group need not require participants from remote areas to come to a central facility. They can schedule seminars at conference locations that are convenient to users in different geographic regions.

The question in any given case is whether decentralizing some part or all of the training function provides additional effectiveness that outweighs the extra cost.

Other Considerations.   In any particular instance there may be other considerations than those mentioned so far. Some divisions may represent recent acquisitions with well-established training functions, which might most conveniently be continued at the division level. On the other hand, if a new company is formed by merging two or more existing companies, there may be a special reason for setting up a single, centralized function. It could help to create a new common culture by providing opportunities to representatives from the different companies to associate with each other in common seminar settings.

Whether to Go Functional or Divisional?

Assuming the training group is of sufficient size to provide realistic options, a further question is whether to organize along divisional or functional lines. The question may be presented at the corporate level or within an operating unit.

These are the options. A *functional* organization can be created by grouping the work to be done by the *kind* of work to be done, or a *divisional* organization can be created by putting all the different kinds of work to be done in groupings established to meet the needs of different user groups. An organizational structure using some combination of these two can also be created. The categories of users around which a divisional form is structured can either be different organizational entities or different categories of program participants: executives, managers, technical people. See Figure 1 for examples of each.

Here are some considerations in weighing the issue of whether to go functional or divisional.

Cost. Cost is almost always one basis for reaching a decision. Frequently, but not necessarily, the purely functional organization will be more economic, either in terms of outright cost or cost related to productivity.

Specialization. The advantages of specialization also have to be considered. A functional organization will usually offer more opportunities for skill specialization. The type of skills necessary for excellent work in program development are different from those required for the most effective delivery of training programs. A person specializing in program development will bring a higher level of expertise to bear than would two people each spending half of their time on program development. And similarly for program delivery, one who specializes in seminar presentation develops greater skill than another who does it part-time only.

Accountability. On the other hand, the divisional structure should provide a more complete accountability for results. If the individual who develops a program also has to present it, there is only one person to claim the success or bear the brunt of failure. In a functional struc-

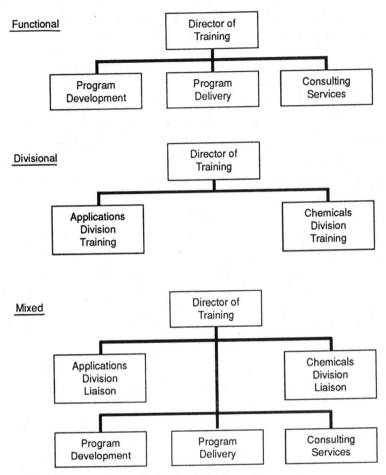

Figure 1. Functional versus divisional organization options.

ture, the one who presents the program can blame the program developer if something goes wrong, and the program developer can blame the presenter.

User Liaison. Divisionalization by user group or a mixed form with user group liaison positions (see Figure 1) would have to be favored, if different user groups have clearly distinctive training needs, or strongly believe this to be the case. Each user group has a clearly defined point of contact with someone in the training function who spends full-time responding to or advancing the interests of that group. The mixed form, with its liaison positions, is more appropriate for large organizations where the additional cost of those positions may well be worth the faster response to user needs.

The trend these days, regardless of the option selected, is to think of the staff as a *team*, participating in training decisions, working together, and helping each other. Rigid adherence to organizational boundaries is discouraged. Task forces that cross organizational lines are frequently set up to deal with significant issues. Each member of the training department is encouraged to feel a sense of responsibility for the total function.

How to Establish Positions and Relationships

With these basic organizational issues behind you, you are now in a position to think through the work that has to be done in the department and then to define individual positions and working relationships. Since management training is likely to be one of the subject matter areas on which you will be presenting programs, you may have to think of yourself as a role model. You ought to do for your own department what you are teaching managers generally to do for theirs.

To help you think through the work that has to be provided for in your department, we have shown in Figure 2 a typical breakdown of work done in a training staff. It may give you a starting point.

In defining individual positions to get this work done, we would urge that you follow these guidelines:

1. *Overall Objective.* You should start with the overall results to be achieved by the incumbent of the position. There is a human tendency to think too much of the work we do rather than the impact of that work. As an old story goes, Are you "laying bricks" or "building a cathedral"?

2. *Standards of Performance.* Just as we said earlier that the training function needed measurable standards of performance, so does each position. They provide a clear vision of the ongoing results for which the incumbent will be held accountable.

3. *Dimensions of Position.* An important parameter is to state the scale of financial and human resources that will be dedicated to this position.

4. *Principal Duties and Responsibilities.* The major categories of work to be performed, both management and technical/operating work, have to be clearly stated. Most position descriptions will include these, sometimes in far greater detail than we would believe desirable.

5. *Authority.* What decisions can the incumbent make without further clearance? Which require coordination or prior approval?

6. *Relationships.* With what other positions will the incumbent have significant interfaces and what is the nature of these relationships?

The examples of position definitions provided in Figures 3 and 4 follow most of these guidelines. You will notice, however, that position importance and position difficulty are included. These are needed in this company to tie the definitions into the salary plan.

In defining the position, it is well to consider the possibility of establishing pass-through positions that people would occupy for 1 or 2 years and then move on. It's a way of getting a continuous influx of new ideas, experience, and enthusiasm, a way to counter the risk of stagnation.

CONSULTING	Problem Definition
	Problem Analysis
	Presentation
RESEARCH	Training Needs Analysis
	Vendor Research
	Training Methods Research
	Program Follow-Up
PROGRAM DEVELOPMENT	Program Design
	Writing
	Audio-Visuals
	Testing
	Producing
PROGRAM DELIVERY	Discussion Leadership
	Individual Coaching
	Lecture
	Using Audio-Visuals
ADMINISTRATION	Program Procurement
	Program Scheduling
	Enrollment
	Securing Facilities
	Equipment and Facilities
	Participant Evaluation
	Attendance Records

Figure 2. Analysis of work done in staff training.

Figure 3. Position description and analysis form: manager, training and development.

GROUP: Heublein **DIVISION:** Staff **DEPARTMENT:** Human Resources

POSITION TITLE: Manager, Training and Development

REPORTS TO: Director, Training and Development

PURPOSE OF POSITION: (Why does the job exist?)

Design training courses which provide comprehensive instruction on skills development, sales methods, and marketing concepts. Facilitate and administer training via formal classroom and on-the-job training. Recruit and conduct screening interviews for sales personnel.

DIMENSION OF POSITION: (Personnel/Dollars/Units over which the position has controlling impact.)

Has control of designated funds for the planning, designing, and implementation of training programs for all sales and non-sales training.

PRINCIPAL DUTIES AND RESPONSIBILITIES:
1. Conduct thorough needs analysis of each position and use this data to design knowledge/skill training programs.
2. Administer the delivery of training programs to sales and non-sales personnel.
3. Recruit and aid in the selection of candidates for sales positions.
4. Design and develop new training programs.
5. Plan training methods and secure training materials.

POSITION IMPORTANCE:
1. **Decision-Making Authority** (Indicate the limits and controls on the position's authority.)
   Authority includes
   a. Instructional design
   b. Training priorities within assigned area
   c. Recruitment and selection methods
2. **Contacts** (State nature and purpose of internal/external contacts.)
   Frequent interface with senior sales and marketing managers. Also contact with non-sales managers. External contacts include recruitment agencies, suppliers, and consultants.
3. **Sources of Support** (Indicate what resources the position depends upon to overcome problems encountered.)
   Audio-visual department; human resource department; legal department.

POSITION DIFFICULTY:
4. **Major Problems** [Describe a few of the most complex problems critically involved in achieving the position's basic purpose and indicate how (programs/actions) they will be overcome.]
   a. Establishing and maintaining constructive communication channels with all levels of management.
   b. Identifying critical job tasks and providing relevant training programs to ensure competency.
   c. Monitoring transference of formal training back to the job.
   d. Providing timely reinforcement training programs.
5. **Specialized or Technical Knowledge/Skills** (Indicate knowledge/skills required to perform the position's basic responsibilities.)
   Sales skills knowledge; management skills knowledge; interviewing skills; affirmative action/EEO knowledge; instructional design skills; communication skills and training delivery skills.

Figure 4. Position description and analysis form: director, sales training and recruitment.

GROUP: Heublein   **DIVISION:** Spirits   **DEPARTMENT:** Sales Training

POSITION TITLE: Director, Sales Training and Recruitment

REPORTS TO: Vice President, Sales Operations, Sales

PURPOSE OF POSITION: (Why does the job exist?)

To increase the productivity of the sales force by *planning, organizing,* and *directing* the implementation of *training programs* which enable all sales and sales management personnel to exceed the sales and profit objectives established by the company, while operating within assigned budget guidelines.

DIMENSION OF POSITION: (Personnel/Dollars/Units over which the position has controlling impact.)
- Direct control of $565,000 in operating budget; five training managers, two secretaries, and one audio-visual productions manager.
- Directly responsible for design and delivery of all programs which result in the selection and training of all sales personnel within Heublein Wines, Spirits, I.V.W., Fine Wines, and Palace Brands. Total population in excess of 400 people.

PRINCIPAL DUTIES AND RESPONSIBILITIES: (Four to ten statements of accountabilities which can be observed or measured.)
- Identify the performance requirements of each position within the sales force which are critical to meeting job standards and design, and implement training programs which enable performers to meet job standards.
- Develop and implement knowledge and skill training programs which enable members of sales management to train and develop highly productive employees.
- Create succession criteria for each sales position and develop a system in which the criteria is used to promote from within.
- Develop group and individual skill programs which prepare employees to ascend to positions of greater responsibility.
- Train all sales managers in an interviewing and selection system which complies with all federal and state regulations.
- Analyze performance problems which exist in the sales force that are inhibiting productivity and design training programs to correct these deficiencies.
- Plan, design, and implement studies and audits which produce data concerning future human resource needs which will be required to capitalize upon marketing conditions.
- Monitor all training and development programs for cost-effectiveness, field compliance, and follow up to assure training objectives are being met.
- Ensure compliance with governmental laws and regulations, and company policies and procedures.

POSITION IMPORTANCE:
1. **Decision-Making Authority** (Indicate the limits and controls on the position's authority.)
   Full authority for all decisions involving the development and implementation of training programs for all field sales personnel. Shared authority with the Human Resource department for decisions involving career pathing. Full authority for all decisions regarding the production of all audio-visual programs designed for sales meetings, etc.

(Continued)

Figure 4. (*Continued*) Position description and analysis form: director, sales training and recruitment.

2. **Contacts** (State nature and purpose of internal/external contacts.)

   INTERNAL Frequent contact with divisional vice presidents, zone directors, regional managers, area managers, district sales managers, retail sales managers, and field sales representatives and sales specialists. Ongoing contact with vice president, sales operations; vice president of human resources; director, planning and analysis; director, training and development; marketing group directors; and director, promotion/planning and development.

   EXTERNAL Department heads of business schools, organizational development consultants, and appropriate support services companies. Close contact with distributor sales personnel in matters regarding training and development.

3. **Sources of Support** (Indicate what resources the position depends upon to overcome problems encountered.)
   Human resource department, legal department, promotion/planning and development department, audio-visual department, divisional vice presidents, zone directors, and external consultants.

POSITION DIFFICULTY:

4. **Major Problems** [Describe a few of the most complex problems critically involved in achieving the position's basic purpose and indicate how (programs/actions) they will be overcome.]
   a. Development of skill training programs which apply specifically to the various market challenges faced by the participants (i.e., chain-dominated vs. independent-dominated, control vs. open states). Most probable solution will be to conduct programs which limit participants to those with identical market conditions and sales opportunities thereby providing task-relevant training.
   b. Design and delivery of a highly professional distributor training program for sales representatives and sales management which results in improved execution at the retail level as well as heightened commitment to the sales of Heublein products. Solution will be to conduct a needs analysis of a sample of key distributors, use the data to structure the learning program, and involve local field sales management in the implementation and follow up in order to ensure distributor commitment.
   c. Development of a cost-effective succession planning program which will be used to identify and develop human resources to meet future sales management requirements. Proposed solution will be to utilize a job analysis of each management position to identify core skills and knowledge required for success, and design programs which will be utilized to develop potential candidates. A sophisticated assessment center program may be developed to identify candidates with the greatest potential for upward mobility.
   d. Develop and institute a regional field trainer program which will allow for the identification of job competency levels of field sales personnel as well as the ability to correct skill deficiencies with locally implemented training programs. Solution will be to train local managers in the skills necessary to measure on-the-job performance and, when required, administer training programs which result in increased productivity.

5. **Specialized or Technical Knowledge/Skills** (Indicate knowledge/skills required to perform the position's basic responsibilities.)
   Degreed individual with 10 years of successful design and implementation of

Figure 4. (*Continued*) Position description and analysis form: director, sales training and recruitment.

> adult education programs. Proven ability to select and develop a training and development staff and support services. Above-average interpersonal skills in group and one-to-one situations; sound planning and organizational skills; excellent analytical and problem-solving skills; ability to motivate others to utilize training provided; above-average written and oral communication skills; knowledge of EEO and Affirmative Action laws; knowledge of media production techniques; background in sales, sales management, and marketing. Appropriate sensitivity to organizational structure and individuals at all levels. Knowledge of audio-visual production, including studio design, program scripting, production and postproduction techniques.

Fixing the Salary Grade

In setting a salary grade for the position, you have to be guided by the latest compensation surveys. Our own observations suggest a fairly direct relationship between pay level and effectiveness. If a company is serious about wanting to improve the productivity of its human resources, it ought to pay enough to get the talent needed to do a better-than-average job. The American Society for Training and Development conducts salary surveys periodically that can serve as a useful point of reference in setting salary grades.

Establishing the Qualifications

Setting position qualifications, the proven skills and experience required to perform the job successfully, depends necessarily on the position to be filled. Nevertheless, here are some ideas of general applicability:

1. *Experience.* At least 3 to 5 years experience in training, including program development as well as presentation, except for entry-level jobs.
2. *Record of Success.* A record as an achiever—getting things done, and done well; and getting things done through others.
3. *Communicating Skills.* Considerably above average in both oral and written communications.
4. *Intelligence.* A quick and logical mind, with a better-than-average academic record.
5. *Personality.* A likable person, interested in and sensitive to other people, with a good sense of humor, a high energy level and considerable self-confidence.
6. *Potential.* Someone with the potential for advancement.

This last qualification suggested may not be wholly self-explanatory. You should guard against an individual's staying in the position so long as to "go stale." Fresh blood every 5 to 10 years can keep the function a vital one. Much can be said for using the position as a training ground for higher positions in the human resources field or as a means for rotation of people within that department.

Filling the Position

As in filling any position, you have to remember these well-established guidelines in staffing the training function:

1. Consider inside as well as outside candidates.
2. Get a large number of candidates, if possible.
3. Make a rough preliminary screening against the qualifications.
4. Hold a first interview.
5. Notify candidates no longer to be considered.
6. Make telephone checks with previous supervisors and past seminar participants.
7. Verify educational achievements and previous employment.
8. Audit platform skills.
9. Hold final interview, multiple interviews if possible.
10. Make decision.
11. Notify all candidates.
12. Develop plan for successful introduction of candidate.

Selecting your people, the last step in the process of organizing and staffing the training function, is of special importance. The success of the training seminars you put on will depend very heavily on the ability of the people you choose to develop the programs, conduct them, and provide back-up support. There are few, if any, "back room" people in training. They are all out there working with others in the company, representing the function almost every day. They will function more effectively in a soundly organized department. As a result, the training seminars you sponsor are far more likely to be effective in improving the performance and productivity of the human resources in your company.

4
When and How to Use Outside Resources

Training directors almost invariably supplement their internal training capabilities through the selective use of outside educational institutions, vendors, and consultants. They do so for some very practical reasons. Decisions on when to use outside resources, to whom to turn, and how best to work with them can have a major influence in getting the most improvement in employee productivity out of your training seminar dollars.

We saw in the last chapter how the question of using outside resources to extend the training department capabilities arises in the process of developing an organization structure. It will also arise in developing the training plan, considered in the next chapter.

The Pros and Cons

The question may arise broadly or in connection with meeting a specific development need. In either case, the first step in dealing with it is to decide whether to use outside resources at all.

The reader may feel that I am prejudiced in dealing with this subject, with some 32 years of consulting experience behind me. But in self-defense, let me point out that for 5 years I worked on the client side of this fence, both as president of Loral Corporation and vice president of finance of Allegheny Power System.

Perhaps more importantly, I have learned over the years that there has to be a good fit. What the client needs and what the consultant provides have to interface correctly. If they do, both parties can benefit. If they don't, both suffer loss. Yes, even if the consultants collect their fees, their reputations and future earnings capabilities depend on leaving satisfied clients behind.

The Potential Benefits

There are many reasons why so many training directors turn to outside consultants. Let's review them.

Extension of Capabilities. The most frequent reason given for using outsiders is to broaden the product line of the training department. If highly specialized expertise is required, it is usually less costly to meet this with qualified outsiders rather than staffing up internally, even more so if the need is sporadic.

Even for recurring needs, some companies prefer to avoid building in the fixed cost of full-time employees. In case of a downturn in business, they want to be in a position to reduce costs quickly and easily. They staff for the "valleys" in their training workloads and use outsiders to help them meet the "peaks."

Saving Time. Another benefit is to save program development time. If there is a clear training need and no existing in-house program to meet the need, an outside resource could be an attractive option. It offers the likelihood of an earlier start-up.

There is a potential danger here. A prominent New York commercial bank once purchased an off-the-shelf modular program on management leadership. It wasn't quite what the training director wanted, but she thought that her own staff could do some substitution and supplementation that would meet her needs. To free up her staff to do this, she skillfully negotiated an outright purchase from the outside vendor. The usual practice was for the vendor to supply participant workbooks as needed at a price that incorporated, in effect, a continuing royalty.

What she didn't anticipate was the creative momentum that the project developed in her staff. They found so many exciting ways to make the program more relevant to their target population that the vendor's original program was hardly discernible in the end product. She later admitted she would have been better off starting out from scratch. She didn't get the earlier start-up that she wanted, and it cost her a good deal more than she had expected.

Quality Assurance. If you can find a reliable vendor with the right program, many training professionals report, you have far greater assurance of program quality (and a scapegoat if you need one!). This isn't always the case, of course. You may have staff members fully qualified on a particular subject in whom you have complete confidence to develop a top-quality end product.

But the outsider has a track record that you can verify. You can talk to others who have used the program. You have the educational materials that you can study. You may even be able to audit the program. In short, you are dealing with a known versus an unknown program.

Credibility. An outside consultant can also offer greater credibility. It seems to be generally accepted that executive-level participant groups are more likely to accept an outsider than an insider. Particularly if the outsider offers impressive credentials. A faculty member from a prestigious graduate business school is far more likely to have an impact on such a group than an inside trainer with a lower title of rank.

The same is true for experienced professionals with front-rank consulting firms. They often have excellent credentials. They may also be able to call upon a wide range of experience with other companies. It is sometimes said that they may be more practical and less theoretical than the academicians.

Easy Discontinuance. Arrangements with outside consultants are generally terminable at any time, except possibly for some government contracts. Truly professional consultants know that the value of their services depends on a continuing relationship of mutual trust and benefit. If for any reason this relationship is broken, discontinuance may be in the best interests of both parties.

More Dispassionate Evaluation. As a final, and probably more arguable point, training departments may be more objective in evaluating programs brought in from the outside. They still have an involvement, since they perceived the need and brought in the external resource, but there is not the same emotional involvement that is likely to exist for programs developed internally. Failures attributable to the outside consultant are easier to identify and bear than their own.

Possible Disadvantages

Notwithstanding all these potential benefits, there are also some possible negatives. As in any decision-making process, both the advantages and the disadvantages have to be weighed in order to arrive at the best conclusion.

Expense.   Perhaps the primary negative is expense. Top names from leading business schools or experts with national reputations command per diem rates well into the four figures. Consulting firms are not far behind. They have to price their programs and services to recoup sometimes surprisingly high program development costs, as for example if video or multi-media techniques are involved. They also need to pay well to attract and keep the professional talent they need—especially in light of heavy away-from-home travel schedules.

Somewhat less costly on a per-participant basis are vendors' off-the-shelf programs conducted by in-house, certified trainers. The cost advantage increases as the trainee population exceeds roughly 40 people in number, assuming no additional costs for adaptation or customization. However, in recent years, there has been an increasing importance placed on programs that are company-specific rather than generic.

Perhaps the most cost-efficient approach is to purchase program segments from outside vendors and fit them into programs developed internally. This practice appears to have become quite common for securing video segments to reinforce internal programs. One prominent management development firm reports an increasing demand for joint development of management training programs. Some of the materials are provided by the consultant, and some are developed or provided by the internal staff.

Less Specific Business Relevance.   One training director put it to me this way: "The outside consultant can never have the same in-depth knowledge of our business. I expect my training professionals to be able to relate everything they teach to our own unique business environment. I want them to be able to do this for each major functional area in our organization. In this way, they can maximize their credibility and maximize the impact of whatever program they're presenting."

This view seems to be becoming more widespread with the increasing pressures to make "the business drive the training function, rather than the training function driving the business," as another human resources professional put it. The agendas of ASTD conferences are more and more giving recognition to the need for the training function to be a vital part of the business of which they are a part.

There is a great deal of merit in this view. Consultants, with some exceptions, are spread over many different industries and many different companies. They cannot gain the same in-depth knowledge and understanding of a particular business as the professional can who is devoted to it full-time.

At the same time, outside consultants frequently complain to each other that every client considers itself completely unique in all respects. A view not generally shared by the consulting professionals.

Loss of Control. A third disadvantage involves control. With the use of an outside resource, the training director no longer has the same direct, hands-on control. Even if nothing goes wrong, there is always the potential. Educational materials may not be received on time or the wrong ones may be delivered. Scheduling problems may prevent getting the right person from the outside firm to conduct the session.

Sometimes the outsider may make statements in answering participant questions that may be contradictory to what is being taught in other company programs. Or the outsider may fail to make appropriate cross-references to other company programs in leading group discussions. *← lack policy knowledge*

Risk on Relevance. Use of a standard program from an outside vendor usually represents some degree of compromise from the ideal. This risk can be minimized, perhaps even eliminated, by adapting and customizing standard seminars to specific internal needs.

In management seminars particularly, terminology problems may arise. There is, unfortunately, no universally accepted vocabulary of management terms. The problem is especially acute in the planning function. There are commonly used terms that are used differently in different companies, perhaps not even used at all. Here are some examples: vision, mission, philosophy, forecasts, environmental scanning, situation analysis, values, objectives, goals, strategies, standards of performance, performance measures, work standards, programs, schedules, budgets, policies, and procedures. It almost seems that writers of texts and articles like to invent, and define, their own terms. It tends to give them special visibility and may even assist in copyrighting their ideas.

What Outside Resources Are Available

If the issue is decided in favor of using outside resources, the next question is what outside resources are available. Here it helps to have developed a "network" of fellow professionals. The better your network, the easier it is to narrow your inquiry down to a relatively few possibilities.

Let's consider the various sources of outside assistance and what service they can provide.

Broadly speaking, there are three kinds of outside resources available: institutions, vendors of equipment and software, and consultants. The precise line that separates the three is somewhat blurred. Some educational institutions are home to faculty members who are independent consultants on the side. Some industry associations (a form of institution) have developed close relationships with specialized individual consultants who become an available resource to members of the association.

The three nevertheless have different orientations. For example, graduate business schools, such as Harvard or Stanford, tend to be more oriented to theory, research, and practices that have general application. Equipment vendors focus on their own products. Consultants tend to be concerned with what will actually work on the job for a particular client. Each of them fills an important niche in the total scheme of employee development.

Institutions

As to the first of these sources, there are established educational institutions offering courses in various subjects that training directors can use to meet specific needs. Not all these offerings can be classified as "seminars," but many of them can.

There are, to begin with, a number of very prestigious courses provided for higher-level executives, most notably the Advanced Management Program at Harvard and the Aspen Institute. They offer an attractive way to provide an enriching experience for the individual, high-potential executive.

Almost every industry association has as one of its objectives to provide educational services of one kind or another. You have to explore what's available in your own association. Frequently these services are embodied in big-name visiting speakers at general sessions of association meetings. But many smaller group opportunities on more specific subjects are also provided.

The College of Insurance, in New York City, supported by the insurance industry, offers an ongoing array of courses of importance to that industry. The same has been true for other industries, although usually to a lesser degree.

Equipment and Software Vendors

To an increasing extent as we hurtle ever faster through the age of electronics and technological change, we find that suppliers fill a crucial training need. In times past, a user's manual was considered sufficient for orienting people to a new piece of equipment, like a telephone instrument. Today, and even more certainly as we look into the future, it takes a good deal more.

The introduction of ever-improving software for desktop personal computers, more powerful work stations of various kinds, more widespread computerized quality-control systems, CAD/CAM technology, telecommunications—all these require some form of group learning experience. The manuals associated with many of these offerings are far too complex for neophytes to begin to understand. It requires training and retraining.

Consultants

The third outside resource, consultants, offers a broad range of sizes and types. Probably the largest number of professional consultants are individual practitioners, but there are also professional consulting firms that vary from the very small to the large, multi-national. Both the individuals and the firms tend to specialize by subject matter or clientele, although firms will naturally have a broader scope of capability by virtue of their larger number of professionals.

Individual practitioners, which include college professors consulting on the side, can offer a great deal. They are almost always less costly, except for the big-name professors from leading business schools. They may be more responsive to client needs because each client's business is much more critical.

But there are so many individual practitioners competing for business that it is quite difficult to find just the right one. Training directors are besieged by sales literature and telephone calls from these people, so much so that they have developed elaborate defenses to prevent the literature and telephone calls from ever reaching them! Invariably, a caller is advised that their target is "in a meeting," "away from her desk," "on the other telephone," or "out of town." This technique gives the training director the option of calling back or tossing the message slip in the basket.

The established professional firm will typically offer a broader range of programs and services and provide greater assurance of quality in both people and programs than the individual consultant. In using a firm, you are not completely dependent on any single individual. You have access to the pooled experience and skills of the whole firm. The additional cost that's usually involved has to be weighed against these advantages.

Scope of Services Provided

Ten years ago, the greatest use of outside consultants was in providing off-the-shelf programs and in seminar presentation. Now the scene has changed. Although still widely used in seminar presentation, the use of generic off-the-shelf programs has declined markedly. Instead, we find that the outsiders are doing much more program development and program adaptation. More frequently than in the past, they provide program segments rather than complete programs. The reason for this changing trend seems to be the wider use of well-qualified internal training staffs seeking company-specific rather than generic programs.

Program Presentation

Among medium- and smaller-sized companies particularly, consultants are widely used to conduct training seminars. The employee populations to be trained are smaller and the training workload irregular. Both are reasons favoring the use of outsiders. You don't have to burden yourself with the ongoing, fixed cost of a training staff.

Even among our industrial giants, outsiders are essential for important, non-recurring needs. For example, it's far more effective to use outside experts to train employees in the use of new equipment and systems. It's less costly to bring in the outside expert than it is to develop your own experts for such non-recurring needs.

For companies of all sizes, the use of outsiders seems to be favored for training top-level managers, i.e., executive development. The outsider has a great deal more credibility, if properly selected. The insiders with the necessary skills are usually of lower rank and often younger. They just don't have the same standing in the eyes of the top team.

On the other hand, the leading management development firms offer professionals with impressive credentials. Professors from leading graduate business schools, with their own special aura, are also frequently used for this population group. Although clearly coming within our definition of "seminars," these group experiences for executives are sometimes called something else: work conferences or executive action meetings. And they are usually far less directive than programs for lower-level people.

Another reason for using external resources arises when seminars are part of a broader corporate initiative that demands skills beyond those of the typical training function. Our own firm, Louis Allen Associates, is a case in point. More and more we are employing our educational services together with our consulting services. If we are engaged in helping a client develop an improved strategic plan, for example, our first step is to conduct workshops that create common understanding of the strategic planning process among the executives and later among the task force members who are involved. The same is true for improving organization structure, establishing improved planning and control systems, or pursuing specific profit improvement opportunities, all which also employ the task force approach.

Once we have used our educational capabilities to create a common knowledge base from which to function, our consulting services come into play. We provide leadership and coaching to the task forces as they make environmental, industry, and company performance analyses. We also help them interpret the results developed, develop detailed programs to implement the new strategic directions, and sell their findings and recommendations to top management.

Program Development

With the declining use of generic programs, outside firms have been moving increasingly into program development and adaptation. They may start out with one of their off-the-shelf programs, but they adapt and customize it to meet specific client needs. One leading firm that used to be a major factor in conducting its own management training programs, now considers all its educational materials as a database from which to draw in making up a company-specific program.

The degree to which standard programs are customized varies widely. It's usually worth at least some cosmetic changes to standard educational materials, which would be at one end of the scale. Covers, title pages, and mastheads can convey a clear client identification with little or no changes in substance. At the other extreme would probably be the use of examples drawn directly from the client work environment, cases rewritten for the same purpose, and terminology changes to accord with present usage in the company.

Contracting for program development tends to be expensive if established specifications are too rigid. With a little leeway, consultants can more easily piece together parts of different established programs, which can reduce the cost while at the same time providing quality reassurance.

Sometimes it's possible to negotiate a cost-sharing arrangement in which the new program becomes the property of the consultant for use with other clients. In these arrangements, the client may be able to recoup its share of development costs through a reduction in the per-participant charge customarily made for programs taken in-house and conducted by internal trainers.

The best results achieved from using outsiders for program development seem to come when there is a truly joint effort between the insiders and the outsiders. The insiders on the program development team bring a good understanding of the business and working environment. The outsiders bring special expertise in subject matter material and educational methodology. Together they can constitute a mutually reinforcing, broadly qualified team.

Packaged Programs

Even though they seem to have declined in overall importance, the day of the standard, generic program is far from over. Particularly when these programs are conducted by internal program leaders trained and certified by the vendor, they still offer important advantages. They can save program development time and expense. They permit an early start-up, and they are especially economic for large populations of trainees.

Excellent programs are available for a wide range of subjects. Some examples are sales training, problem solving, communications, and management fundamentals. Some of these standard programs are structured in a way that permits participants to bring in their own work situations and apply them to the concepts and approaches offered in the program.

Arrangements for purchasing these programs differ with different vendors. In some cases there is a one-time charge for the right to use the program and a fee payable for each participant going through it, for which educational materials are supplied. In others, there is only the continuing fee or royalty as participants go through the program. Users are typically required to sign an agreement not to reproduce the copyrighted educational materials but to buy them from the vendor as needed.

Training in-house program leaders may be included in the one-time price or may entail additional professional fees. Many vendors, perhaps most of them, will insist that the program be presented only by those that have been trained and certified by the vendor. This requirement is intended to ensure continuing high presentation quality and client satisfaction. It is probably a mutually useful arrangement for programs that are more leader-dependent.

Audit

Consultants are also available to audit and coach in-house presenters, usually in connection with a program they have provided. In most cases, this service has to be agreed upon at the time the program is purchased. Otherwise there are natural inhibitions. Consultants want their time to be specifically billable; they don't want to give it away. The in-house trainers, on the other hand, may feel their professional stature is being attacked if consultants are brought in to audit them.

Consultation

A further service occasionally provided is consulting assistance in making needs analyses and postseminar follow-up. Outsiders frequently have well-established methods to identify specific training needs. The service may apply broadly to the whole client organization in preparation for an annual training plan, or it may be to determine the individual training needs of a specific employee group in advance of a seminar. The service is performed via questionnaires which may be followed up by personal interviews.

On occasion, consultants are used to assist in the evaluation of seminar results. For example, one management development firm includes "action planning" as part of its most popular program. Participants bring a problem with them to the seminar which they analyze to develop the best solution. They each then develop an action plan around their solution to implement on the job. Follow-up by the consultant can determine, and sometimes measure, the results achieved through carrying out these action plans.

How to Select the Right Outside Resource

At one time or another, almost every training director will face the need to select an outside resource. How should they go about determining what outside resources to consider? How can they predict which one will prove to be the most effective? Here are some criteria to consider, together with suggestions on how to use them.

You'll find it to be very helpful to have your own set of criteria clearly in mind as you screen and interview potential resources. It will also assist in whatever independent investigations you want to make.

By the way, there are some individuals and firms that offer their services to help in this selection process. There are so many consultants offering seminar programs and services that this is certainly an option to consider. However, in my experience most organizations prefer to do it themselves, and many of them have established long-term relationships with some proven outside resource that makes it unnecessary to go through the complete selection process for every new need.

Here are some suggestions to use as thought starters in developing your own selection criteria.

Suggested Selection Criteria

Calibre of People.   Clearly the most important of all considerations has to be the established professional and personal qualifications of the individuals who would be providing the service. Notice that I included *personal* as well as professional qualifications. Of course, you have to satisfy yourself of their professional qualifications: their knowledge of the subject matter, their platform skills, their educational credentials, and the nature and scope of their prior experience. But the client-consultant relationship is a highly personal one. You have to feel right about the personal chemistry between the consultant and yourself and all the other people in your organization.

Quality of Educational Materials.   The quality and relevance of the educational materials to be used is also extremely important, whether these will be used as is or will serve as a basis for program development. Your concern should extend beyond the participant workbooks to include the leader's guide, handout materials, if any, and visual accompaniments as well. The workbook will give you the scope and nature of the subject matter covered, but in itself it won't give you a full understanding of the seminar.

All the educational materials should be reviewed to make sure of the learning method or methods employed. Increasing emphasis these days is placed on participant involvement. Self-discovery, either individually or in teams, is an excellent way to get a high level of involvement. It may take longer, and it provides less ego-satisfaction for the program leader, but it seems to produce more lasting results. It's probably most effective when used in combination with other approaches.

The length of the seminar is another important dimension. Notwithstanding the increasing recognition given to human resource development, line managers are rightly insisting that every day away from the job be truly worth it. Pressures are increasing to reduce the time demands for off-the-job training. A lot of new attention is being paid to accelerated learning. Bell Atlantic claims to have cut training time virtually in half with better results, through concentrated redesign of existing training seminars.*

If the proposed seminar will be conducted by in-house leaders, you have to satisfy yourself of the quality of the leader's guide provided. Is it organized in a way that is easy to use? Is it written in a simple, easily understood style? Does it provide for flexibility so that it can be used

---

*Gill, Mary Jane, and Meier, David, "Accelerated Learning Pays Off." *Training and Development Journal,* January 1989, p. 63.

with audiences of different levels of sophistication? Is it too detailed? Too brief?

The visual aids provided have to be evaluated as well. They perform a vital part of the learning process. The trend today is toward video dramatizations and interactive multi-media presentations. Ours is a television generation, which makes the quality of the video presentations important. If they do not measure up to what participants have become accustomed to through commercial television, they may impede rather than assist learning. They also have to be in keeping with the values of the employee population.

A case in point is the consultant who proudly demonstrated a program on leadership with award-winning videos to a wholesale grocery company. The prime character featured in the videos was a suave program leader—a handsome professional actor—dressed in a three-piece, tailored business suit complete with tie and matching breast-pocket handkerchief. "Our guys could never relate to that. They never wear suits at work, let alone ties. They just wouldn't believe what he says." Such was the response of the vice president, personnel of the prospective client company, who turned down the program.

Adaptability. A third selection criterion, adaptability, applies particularly to consultants rather than institutions and possibly equipment and software vendors. Those who have been involved in sales training know the importance of satisfying customer needs rather than selling a product. The concept can be applied as well to selecting consultants. A consultant's willingness to adapt materials to your needs can make that consultant clearly more valuable than another.

In years gone by, the cost of adapting standard programs was much greater than it is today. Participant workbooks and leader's guides are typically held in computer memories and easily adapted. This may become true in the future with visuals too. Even if cost is a factor, a readiness on the part of the consultant to discuss adaptations imaginatively can be a real plus. Often it's possible to find approaches that make the outsider's program more relevant without prohibitive increases in cost.

Scope and Depth of Available Resources. The depth and breadth of resources available is one clear advantage that an established firm has over the individual consultant. In the case of the professional who is part of a consulting firm, the client is not limited by the knowledge and skills of a single person nor dependent on the continuing health and availability of that person. Established firms typically ensure that at least a second member of the firm is known to the client and available to substitute if necessary. This second person also gives the primary consultant a resource to turn to for advice or simply to serve as a sounding board for ideas.

Then again, if the training director comes up with a new need, the established firm is more likely to be able to meet that need than is the individual practitioner. Once a training director has established a mutually satisfactory relationship with an outside firm, it saves a lot of time and trouble to turn to the same firm for other programs. The firm starts off with a good knowledge of the company and its people. You can also be reasonably sure that the additional program will be consistent with the first both in concepts and vocabulary.

Cost. An ever-present consideration is cost, particularly in the decade of the 1990s when industry generally is facing tougher worldwide competition than ever before. Training directors have to operate within established budgetary constraints. They probably never have enough money to do all the things they would like. They have to commit their available resources wisely to get the greatest return for their money.

In a very rough approximation, as the first four criteria above are given greater importance, the cost of using outside resources tends to increase. The selection decision, therefore, turns frequently to getting the best balance between, on the one hand, cost and, on the other, the calibre of the outside people involved, the quality of program materials, adaptability, and the scope and depth of resources available to the prospective consultant.

How to Research Your Options

As a practical matter, the most useful way to evaluate your various options is in your screening interviews. You can review the materials provided and ask probing questions to dig into the professional capabilities of the individuals who will be providing the services, who should be the ones you are interviewing. You are also going to get a first-hand feel for them as individuals. Do they come across as people you can work with? How adaptable are they? Would they have credibility with your various user populations? Keep your established criteria in mind as you do your probing.

But you probably should do some independent checking as well. How much will depend in part on the magnitude of the assignment you are considering. The best way to do so is through a personal audit. Sit in on one of their seminars and see them in action. It may present practical problems, such as finding the time to do it and making necessary arrangements, but it still provides the surest way to check out, for example, communication and discussion leadership skills.

The next-best approach is to contact those who have personal experience with the individuals under consideration. If an educational institution is involved, particularly if it's a prestigious one, the temptation is to accept at face value the individuals who would provide the service. Far better is to contact people who have previously gone through the program and gone through it with the same professors or teachers. In the case of consulting firms or individual consultants, present or past clients can be contacted without too much difficulty.

Most training directors maintain a network of professional relationships that can be helpful in checking out institutions, vendors, and consultants. Personal acquaintances are likely to be more objective than references provided to you, but make sure their opinions are based on personal experience rather than on hearsay.

How to Negotiate the Arrangements

If you have proceeded to the point where you have decided to use an outside resource and have made a selection against the criteria you developed, the next step is to negotiate the arrangements. See Figure 5 for a suggested checklist of items to consider. Some of them are worth special elaboration. You'll want to end up with a written set of arrangements. They can be in the form of a formal contract or in a letter signed by the consultant.

Staffing

Since the consultant-client relationship is an intensely personal one, make sure it is clearly stated who will provide the services from the consultant organization. It should be the person with whom you are negotiating or someone you already know and trust.

Copyrights

During the negotiation is the best time to get agreement on any rights you might want to have to reproduce and use copyrighted material. You may want to be able to incorporate extracts or ideas from these ma-

1. Clear and specific delineation of program or service to be provided
2. Program cost
3. Professional fees entailed
4. Expenses to be reimbursed
5. Other costs entailed (the facility, audio-visual equipment, shipping charges, etc.)
6. Commitment on named individual consultants to provide service
7. Participant evaluations
8. Participant completion certificates
9. Trainer certificates
10. Action steps to be taken
11. Schedule
12. Replacement of lost or damaged audio-visuals and leader's guides
13. Cost of future educational materials
14. Training future trainers
15. Rights to use copyrighted materials
16. Termination

Figure 5. Negotiating Checklist

terials into company manuals. Most outside firms will allow this if you give appropriate credit on cover or title pages.

You have to realize that these copyrighted educational materials have in most cases been developed at great expense. They represent the "bread and butter" of the consultant's business. It would be highly improper to reproduce and reuse these materials yourself or to copy the materials to avoid purchasing participant workbooks from the vendor.

A case in point is provided from our own experience. By accident, we happened to hear from an employee of one of our clients that one of our off-the-shelf programs was being conducted in the company. Checking our own records, we found that we had received no orders for participant workbooks, which meant that they were reproducing copyrighted workbooks that we had sold to them at an earlier time.

We were able to get hold of one of these photocopied workbooks and confronted the president of the company with the evidence. He had known nothing about it and was properly upset. He ordered full payment to us for all the workbooks they had made for themselves. He made it uncomfortably clear to the training director involved that such actions were not in keeping with the ethical standards established by the company.

Termination

In the mutual glow of agreeing on some important project together, it is easy to overlook the possibility that the arrangement may have to be terminated. Not all consulting assignments are fully successful. Also, unforeseen developments may make continuation of the program unwise or even impossible.

Some years ago, a consultant was meeting with a project team he had trained in connection with the installation of an improved planning and control system for the international division of a medium-sized company in the electric battery business. In the middle of the meeting, a messenger came in with a command from top management to appear immediately in the upstairs conference room for an important announcement.

A half hour later, the task force members returned with sheepish smiles on their collective faces. They had just learned that the international division had been eliminated, its functions being transferred to other product line divisions. The senior vice president who had headed up the division was given early retirement!

Evaluations

It may be desirable to ensure that each seminar will require participant evaluations and perhaps postseminar follow-up. If you have your own forms and procedures, get agreement on their use if the consultant is involved in any way. If the consultant has a standard approach, make sure that it is acceptable to you. Make sure that you will get copies of all completed evaluation forms.

Formalization

When you are satisfied that all the items have been covered, get the consultant to send you a written confirmation of the entire agreement. A written understanding will help to promote the harmonious consultant-client relationship that is most likely to produce the results you want. It can be disrupting to have disagreements over such things, for example, as who pays freight on educational materials.

These are just a few of the items listed on the negotiating checklist in Figure 5. You may want to add to that list. Whether you use mine or yours, the point is that a checklist will help you make sure that you will get the most from the money you spend on outside assistance.

At one time or another, training directors find that they will want to supplement their own capabilities with outside assistance. When that time comes for you, go back over this chapter. Review the reasons why you might want to use outside resources, what resources are available, what criteria to use in selecting from among them, and how to go about negotiating the arrangements.

5

How to Plan
for Maximum
Impact

Putting on successful seminars requires careful planning, whatever the mix between inside and outside resources. The importance of fact-founded, comprehensive planning is conscientiously preached in all management training courses. But most training directors do not practice what they preach!

In a survey of some 61 training directors, 21% of the respondents admitted that they had no "written statement of overall purpose or mission" for their departments. Only 15% reported that they had a written plan.* Informal discussions with many training directors since then persuade me that the situation is not much better today. They have budgets. They are required to have these. They probably have a calendar of course offerings. But they don't have the kind of comprehensive plan they promote for everybody else.

The arguments favoring some kind of formalized planning are overwhelming, but the practicalities of corporate life seem to win out over theory. It's difficult to understand why this should be the case. One reason, perhaps, is the need for a clearer, more practical step-by-step approach to the process. If so, this chapter may be of assistance.

---

*Munson, Lawrence S.: "Performance Standards: Do Training Directors Practice What They Preach?" *Personnel Journal,* May 1980, pp. 365–367.

The Rationale for Formal Planning

But first, let's look at the advantages of formalized training. Notice the use of the word "formalized" in describing planning. Virtually every action that we take is preceded by some planning, even if it is virtually instantaneous.

But in management practice it is generally agreed that if a plan is not committed to writing, it's not truly a management plan. It probably has not been thoughtfully developed, and it certainly cannot be shared with others. Within even a few weeks there will be differing memories of what planning decisions were made, and there certainly won't be a guide to day-to-day action.

Teamwork Encouraged   ownership

First of all, an effective planning process can help develop strong teamwork. Developing the plan in itself is an ideal opportunity to get the participation of the whole training team. If every team member has truly participated, you will win their commitment to the plan. The plan itself will represent a fully coordinated course of action that can avoid later confusion and discord. And, by the way, you'll get a much better plan.

The whole team can function more effectively together because they all know precisely what results have to be achieved and what everyone has to do to achieve those results. If Catherine's job is to process seminar enrollments and she is out sick, someone else can more easily step in. The plan lays out each team member's role and provides a convenient reference if someone has to fill in for an absent member.

Better Results   thought involved

Good planning will usually produce better results. If you and your team take time to think through all the things you want to accomplish over some future period of time, you are far more likely to focus on those that offer the greatest potential impact on overall results. You'll have to think through the different ways of achieving each major result and select the most effective course of action. Then you'll want to write it up in some way to help you make sure it really happens.

Take, for example, the manager who doesn't take the time to plan. He has to drive to a 9:30 A.M. meeting on the other side of town. The non-planning type is late getting up from the breakfast table. He thinks he knows how to get there and can't quickly put his hands on a map of the city to make sure. Time is short, so he can't take time to look around the house for it. He rushes out to the car, gets in, and is on his way.

Perhaps he is even congratulating himself on the very few minutes he spent between getting up from the breakfast table and shifting into high gear on the way to his appointment.

But, you guessed it, he finds he really doesn't know the way. He doesn't want to take time out to ask directions, but after a few frantic turnbacks, he realizes he has no alternative. It turns out that he has to stop twice to ask directions. As a result, he is 20 minutes late for his meeting and is all tensed up. He makes a poor presentation of the program he was trying to sell. His audience started out annoyed that they had to wait and ended up not accepting his proposal.

In this example, you would not expect the manager to develop a formal written plan covering his trip, but at least he ought to have jotted down the directions in his pocket calendar book along with the phone number he could call if delayed. He probably hadn't planned his presentation much better!

Relating this back to an annual plan for the training function, you have to take adequate time to consider and reach conclusions on a range of important questions. What went particularly well last year? Where were opportunities for improvement identified? What training needs did you have to postpone last year for lack of funds? Are they still pressing?

What operational, organizational, or technological changes are taking place that could affect the development needs of your clientele over the next several years? Which of the programs that you have had under consideration could have the greatest impact on improving the productivity of human resources in the company? How do your user groups perceive their needs?

What are your own capabilities in terms of subject matter competence, seminar leadership skills, and workload limitations? To what extent do you expect changes in your own staff? What are their development needs in view of the evolving demands for your services?

The precise questions will differ from one organization to another, but the need to identify what they are is universal. You will undoubtedly want your key users and your own people to help in the whole process. Their inputs can help you develop a much better plan than you could on your own. You will get greater reassurance of better results.

Better Use of Resources

Good planning will not only help you get better results, it will also help you use your available resources most efficiently in achieving those results. Planning gives you the time to think through what action steps you have to take, who is going to take those steps, what time frame is involved, and what resources are needed. Frequently you can identify alternative ways to achieve the results you want. Then, each alternative can be carefully weighed in terms of its effectiveness in achieving the desired end result, the chances of success versus the risks of failure, the side benefits or problems that could develop, and the cost of carrying it through to completion.

The analysis presented in the last chapter illustrates the point. Almost every training director faces this basic question: Should the training function be staffed to meet all foreseeable needs, and what mixture of internal and external resources should be used? The best answer has to come through thoughtful analysis of each particular situation and not through intuitive or opportunistic decisions.

Means for Building Support

The planning process gives you the opportunity to get members of higher management, as well as key users of the department's services, involved in the training function. Sometimes it is possible to formalize this involvement through a training committee or an advisory board with memberships drawn from top management and higher-level executives.

More and more forward-thinking companies are using the training function as a powerful ally in implementing companywide management initiatives. The widespread commitment in American industry to continuous quality improvement almost necessarily makes higher management a partner in developing training plans instead of simply a reviewer of proposals. The same is true for broad corporate programs to develop a changed corporate culture or establish an improved management system. This kind of higher-management involvement almost surely results in much stronger support for the whole training function.

The executive development function of United Technologies, headquartered in Hartford, Connecticut, uses this approach. The corporate director of the program is able to assemble the heads of all its operating units to brainstorm development needs and approaches. In the process, he gets a surer understanding of development needs as well as the commitment of the users of his services.

One of the prominent Wall Street investment bank houses uses the approach to develop and implement project management training. They call it "mining" the top IMS management team to determine the most important issues they perceive in getting the most effective results from the training. The training programs are modified accordingly, and the results are carefully tracked. Feedback to management provides for their further involvement and support.

Our own experience in helping companies develop and implement comprehensive systems of management also reinforces this idea. We usually see a top-management committee established to oversee the whole program. Top-level management system committees of this type have been used at various times by Union Carbide Corporation (headed by a vice chairman of the board), Merrill Lynch & Company (also headed by a vice chairman of the board), and Sea-Land Services, Inc. (headed by the then chairman and chief executive officer).

There is a special reason why key users should be included in the planning process. If the operating departments help determine the extent to which the training function will be used, then the support of these departments will be strengthened. With this kind of support, you shouldn't have much trouble filling your seminars. Without it, you may not be able to fill them.

Here's an important potential side benefit. Involving management and key users in the planning process should generate more and better ideas. With more input you have more suggestions to consider, and the result is better plans, provided you don't let the process run away with itself! Creative minds can easily develop a "laundry list" of ideas they want you to research and report back. They can have you so busy acting as staff to them that your planning is greatly delayed.

Smoother Operations

Good planning makes work easier to do. If you have a good plan, it becomes a continuing guide to action for you and each of your people. You don't have to rethink your options every day. If you have an approved plan, you don't have to reargue your case, or resell your management. It is right there for you and your people to follow.

By way of specific illustration, let's assume that you have scheduled eight computer literacy training seminars in groups of 20 participants over the course of a calendar year. You know that for each seminar there are certain steps that have to be taken, and you have determined from past experience the lead time you need for each. You know when to send out reminders and registration forms, when to follow up by telephone, when to send out materials to the registrants, when to produce or order educational materials, when to send these materials out to the registered participants, when to reconfirm with the facility in which the seminar is to be held, when to order or requisition the equipment you need, when to arrange any food and beverages for breaks and lunches, and when to do all the other things that have to be done.

All these steps can be entered into your computer system and processed to give you a master calendar of everything that has to be done. You and your people will be able to know each day of the week precisely what has to be done and who is going to do it. They don't have to ask you what they are supposed to do, and you don't have to tell them what needs to be done. If you're not yet computerized or your plan is not particularly complex, you can set up the same kind of day-to-day guidance manually.

Basis for Control

The same example leads directly into a further advantage. Having this kind of a plan gives you and each of your people the means for making sure that the things that are supposed to get done each day are in fact accomplished. Modern management doctrine recommends that we think of "control" in terms of information systems that enable people to evaluate and correct their own performance.

This kind of self-control works extremely well if you have capable and committed people. If you don't, you may have to provide daily checklists that people can initial as tasks are done. The checklists can be supplemented by weekly meetings that review for the benefit of the whole team what is planned for the next week and what problems, if any, can be anticipated.

Thinking more broadly, the existence of a plan not only provides a control on day-to-day activities, but, perhaps more importantly, it gives us the means for evaluating results achieved. Without some kind of formalized plans, you have no sure basis for knowing whether or not the results you and your people are actually achieving are acceptable or not. You're literally forced to use subjective judgment on the quality and quantity of results achieved. You almost have to control things by personal inspection—injecting yourself into all the operations of the department to check up on things. This approach could impose an extremely heavy workload on you. It will be resented by your people and lower their effectiveness, and may be problematic if your own manager's subjective judgment on what constitutes acceptable results differs from yours.

How to Deal with Common Barriers to Planning

Along with these benefits, there are a number of constraints that make it difficult to do a really good job of planning. These are the barriers that make so many training directors do a poor or incomplete job of planning. Let's look at the more important of these to see how valid they really are and what can be done about them.

Time Pressures

First of all, planning takes time—a lot of time—particularly if you don't have a good plan from last year to serve as a model and starting point. The time you need is not 10 minutes here, 10 minutes there, and 30 minutes on your commuter train. You have to set aside some solid blocks of hours. Some of this time will have to involve your people, which means fitting schedules for mutual convenience—another potential problem.

The training director with a heavy teaching schedule is at a particular disadvantage. You can't really do a good job of planning in the late afternoon or evening after a day of program presentation. You're too tired. The temptation to have a martini or two before dinner is all but irresistible, and you know what that does to your after dinner plans!

Take the case of a training director in a large insurance brokerage concern. When he first stepped into the job, there were already a large number of training programs in place operating under the aegis of a training committee that had been established by his predecessor. The new training director had come from a line position and had much to learn.

After almost a year in the position, he still hadn't found time to make a needs analysis and develop a plan. He was much too busy carrying out what was already in motion, responding to the requests of his training committee, and learning what he could about the training business.

A typical problem develops from a euphoria about some new training program that the training professional has developed and has met with an enthusiastic response. A training director, whom I helped to get a position with a large publishing company, developed this problem. He had produced a problem-solving workshop which was a winner. In no time he had almost completely filled up his schedule with this program. He put on one right after another.

About a year later I happened to run into the senior vice president, human resources, who had hired our trainer. When I asked him how everything was going, he responded "Henry is so busy putting on a program he developed himself that he's not managing the training function. What's worse, he doesn't seem to understand the problem when I try to explain it to him."

The same thing happened only recently to a good friend of mine who is in the corporate headquarters of a huge global enterprise. He and a colleague put together a program on strategic planning which is truly outstanding. Using a training room equipped with computer terminals to provide computer literacy training, the two lead a 3-day program featuring entrepreneurial decision making within the framework of the company's strategic planning processes. Teams of two engage eight other teams of two in a competitive game that is just as exciting as it is educational.

The program has been a tremendous success. My friend puts on roughly three programs a month, and there's still a long waiting list. Who could wish for anything more, you might ask. But when I asked him how he planned to bring the program to other areas of the company and what his plans were for the next program featuring the same technological approach, he looked at me blankly. He hadn't had time to think about these questions.

Poor Organizational Environment

Another problem can be the organizational environment. In order to make a thorough needs analysis, you have to involve many other people in the company. It cannot be done in an ivory tower. You have to get hold of the users of training services one way or another. They're in the best position to advise you of present and future needs.

But it is not always easy to get hold of these people. They have many other demands on their time. Many of which they perceive as having a higher priority than sitting down to talk with you. If the organization is in a constant state of crisis, or if everyone is short-handed because of a hiring freeze, it can be almost impossible to get others meaningfully involved in the planning process.

Top-Level Interruptions

Sometimes, unplanned top-management initiatives can keep the training function in a reactive mode. Much as we want to get the involvement of top management, it can be disruptive if it provides unplanned, impulsive directions.

A colleague of mine enjoys telling the story about a president who attended a public seminar on management in Baltimore because his wife wanted to go with him and see an art show that was being featured there. The seminar featured the subject of "human relations" at a time when the subject was treated somewhat superficially. The approach is now sometimes referred to as the "contented cow" school of behavior.

At any rate, the president was so carried away by the seminar that the first thing he did when he got back to this company was to announce at a staff meeting that he wanted every executive, every manager, and every supervisor to go through the program. And go through the program they all did!

Almost a year later, the president had an unexpected and not wholly satisfactory opportunity to observe the impact of the course on his people. He came across a foreman in his factory who was holding a worker by the throat and shaking him like a dog would shake a rabbit held in the same way. Livid with anger the foreman was shouting, "You did it wrong yesterday and you did it wrong again today! If you do it wrong tomorrow, you're fired...[long pause]...and how's your mother?"

Don't misunderstand me. Top-management involvement is to be welcomed. But if the president, or any other powerful top executive, makes a more or less general practice of unanticipated but major demands on the training function, planning becomes academic. In fact, it may become counterproductive. If carefully developed plans have to be abandoned, it becomes very frustrating. The more comfortable course is to minimize formal planning, keep on doing what you have been doing, and deal with each crisis as it comes along.

Shifting User Demands

Another constraint can be the complex of demands from users of your service. While we want these users to be actively involved in the process of needs analysis, the risk is that they can end up driving the training function. The training professionals can end up in a reactive rather than a proactive mode.

Coping with heavy user demands is particularly difficult for new training directors or for those who haven't established a strong position in the organization. They can easily become swamped by requests for service and be put in difficult situations. It's not easy to turn down or postpone your own customers. Still, I suppose it's better than the reverse position: trying to drum up interest in what you have to offer.

You can also argue that the need for planning is greater when you have active, competing demands. The forward-thinking training director can more easily persuade the line managers to participate in developing a plan that is within the capabilities of the department to carry out.

Budgetary Constraints

The existence of an annual budgetary process forces some kind of planning to take place. But it may delude people into thinking they are truly planning. Actually, the budget has to be viewed as the financial expression of a plan. The thinking and analyses that go into making a budget really represent the planning process, but these are often not recorded in any way. You have a budget, but you have to rely on your memory to recall the reasoning and discussions behind the numbers that are eventually finalized in the budget. Often the budget serves more as a control of expenditures rather than the continuing guide to action that a plan should be.

Then again, as the year plays itself out we may find that the company is not meeting its budget. Pressures arise then to try to preserve reasonably acceptable quarterly earnings results. What gets cut first? In many companies it's training. With the memory of prior experience in hand, training directors will develop great uncertainty as to what funds will be available. Rumors and expectations become more important as guides to continuing action than approved plans.

How to Identify Your Most Important Needs and Opportunities

The planning process begins with a series of inquiries and analyses before any specific commitments are made on a future course of action. We have to look at our own past performance in terms of strengths and weaknesses. We then have to project these into the future in the light of probable business developments, technological change, and our estimate on the extent of resources that we might have available.

Analyze Your Own Performance

It's not always easy to make an objective appraisal of one's own performance, but it is a necessary first step. If you have developed a teamwork approach in your department, you'll find that your team can be an effective support in this process. They will be looking at it from a variety of different viewpoints, which usually assists in reaching better judgments.

Here are some questions to ask. What seminars were well received and easy to fill? Which ones didn't measure up to expectations? What program modifications would appear to be necessary? What kind of feedback did you get from line managers? Are you doing a better job of meeting the needs of some segments of your organization than others? Are some functions not using enough of your services? Others too much? Are some of your trainers less well received? Does this indicate some need for internal training and development? How did your outside consultants perform? What programs did you have to postpone last year? Have they become more or less important in the light of a new year?

Keep Abreast of Business Plans

It has become a truism in training and development circles that the business should be the driving force in the development of training plans. This means we have to be privy to the business plans of the company. Ideally, we should have contributed to them.

An obvious illustration is the extent to which the company may be planning to emphasize total quality management and, within this broad subject, statistical control techniques. Such a course necessitates the support of the training function and has to be built into the training plan.

Another example would be downsizing of the organization, eliminating layers of management and empowering lower-level employees to take on greater responsibilities. Moves in this direction should be supported by the necessary training.

If the company is getting on the bandwagon of self-directed teams, it needs the backing of formal training. The teams need training in a variety of job skills to facilitate job rotation, in team and interaction skills to enhance productive teamwork, and in quality and problem-solving skills to participate in continuous quality-improvement programs.

Suppose the company is planning to introduce new programs such as flextime, incentive compensation, or some form of management by objectives. Here again the participation of the training function is essential.

Anticipate Future Developments

In addition to estimating the future impact of business plans, training directors have to predict the effect of other forces and trends that will represent the environment in which they will have to operate. Here we are making a distinction between factors over which they have little or no control, but which they have to anticipate, and those over which they *do* have control, for which they must plan.

General Business Conditions.

In most companies, forecasting future business conditions is made by the corporation for the whole company. Nevertheless, it is a necessary frame of reference. If no such forecast is provided, some reasonable assumptions have to be made. If a worst-case scenario is developed that could actually happen, we then should seriously consider contingency plans to deal with it. It could save a lot of agony later.

Available Resources.   Another key external factor to forecasting is the availability of resources—human resources and money. As we look at our present staff, we can expect some attrition. Perhaps we can even identify specific individuals due to be rotated out of the department or perhaps retired.

We have probably already gotten a clue from our own manager as to the availability of money over the planning period. In any event, we need to operate within the scope of reasonable expectations if the plan we propose is to have any chance for approval.

Technological Change.   The influence of technological change is a further factor to project into the future. What we are able to foresee may mean retraining for portions of our factory people or our management information staff. It may even affect the way we deliver training programs. See Chapter 7 for more discussion of this.

There is no clear-cut way to do this. You probably have to seek out the informed opinion of people who are knowledgeable in the different fields that are of concern. Your network of professionals in the field can come into play here. Vendors can also help. If you try to keep up to date with professional journals, that too can contribute to your thinking.

How to Forecast Your Workload

Coming closer to the heart of the planning process is the need to forecast the training workload that will be placed on your department. You need to forecast not just the total workload, which is translated into training staff positions needed, but also the nature and changing mix of user needs, which is translated into new or changed programs.

The workload that will be imposed by management initiatives will already have been determined by your review of company business plans. But you also have to consider all the other users of your services: the various company departments or divisions and various employee categories, such as those requiring remedial training, computer literacy training, and perhaps retirement orientation and training. Some organizations have systems in place to help provide this type of information. Others depend on various forms of research and analysis.

Computerized Systems

More and more companies are using computerized systems to project training workload information. One frequently used approach ties performance appraisals into comprehensive systems for storing and processing information on development needs. It seems like an eminently sensible approach. The data can easily be broken down into organizational segments and geographical locations, for further use.

Also helpful are systems that keep detailed records on individual training histories. By comparing the number of past participants in any program with the total potential population for that program, you can estimate remaining populations that may need to go through the program. The approach is especially useful for certain required courses and provides information that might not be generated by the performance appraisal system.

These systems can also store participant evaluations by individual program. Any trends that emerge can give clues to the need for dropping or revising programs or substituting new programs.

Screening Outside Seminar Requests

Consolidated Edison of New York City (and probably many other companies) gave the training director authority to approve or disapprove all requests for attendance at outside seminars. This approach not only helps prevent the company from spending money on marginally useful seminars, but, perhaps more importantly, it provides clues on the kind of training that people want. For example, an increasing volume of requests to go to outside assertiveness training seminars led to the establishment of an internal program to meet the growing need.

Questionnaires

A long-established method of determining future training needs is the use of questionnaires. They can easily be tailored to fit the needs of a particular organization, and they offer the means for statistical summation.

Shown in Figure 6 is a selected portion of the Allen Management Performance Survey, a questionnaire that is used to determine management development needs. The survey is based on the judgments of a broad spectrum of managers in different levels and functions of a company on the kind and quality of management methods actually in use in the company. The responses are then compared to the calculated means

How often are the following statements true throughout the organization in which you work? "Organization" means the overall organization, including the group in which you work.

- Read the response categories at the right.
- Then circle the number of the response that represents your best judgment.

	Never	Almost Never	Infrequently	About Half the Time	Frequently	Almost Always	Always
1. In this organization, people have clear and reasonable written objectives or goals	0	1	2	3	4	5	6
2. People understand and accept the objectives they are expected to accomplish	0	1	2	3	4	5	6
3. People understand how their own objectives relate to those of the overall organization	0	1	2	3	4	5	6
4. In this organization, before people take action to accomplish their objectives, they state in writing the sequence of steps they will carry out to achieve those objectives	0	1	2	3	4	5	6
5. When people change their objectives, they also change the steps they will take to achieve the objectives	0	1	2	3	4	5	6

Item	Statement	0	1	2	3	4	5	6
6.	In this organization, time schedules are used to make sure the work gets done on time	0	1	2	3	4	5	6
7.	The schedules are realistic; that is, they can be met if reasonable effort is made	0	1	2	3	4	5	6
8.	In this organization, people are required to prepare budgets of the money and other resources required before they are authorized to spend money to carry out projects or programs	0		2	3	4	5	6
9.	Before people spend money for a program or project, they must show in their budgets that there will be a worthwhile return from the money spent	0	1	2	3	4	5	6
10.	People understand and accept the budgets within which they are expected to achieve results	0	1	2	3	4	5	6
11.	In this organization, written policies are used to provide people with standing answers to problems that arise repeatedly	0	1	2	3	4	5	6
12.	The policies used to give proper consideration of the needs of people	0	1	2	3	4	5	6

© Louis A. Allen, associates, 1977 and reproduced with permission.

Figure 6. Excerpt from the Allen Management Performance Survey.

of the hundreds of companies in the Allen database. Presumably, the widest unfavorable variances represent the areas of greatest need.

Within recent years we have had widely divergent results from the survey. A survey undertaken for a large commercial bank in New York City revealed that the bank scored below the Allen norms on all counts! Needless to say, the top management of the bank was disappointed at the result but became convinced more than ever of the need for a broad management training program.

The other involved the Ralph Hart Division of Heublein, Inc., a leading wine and spirits company. The survey put the company *above* the Allen norms in every respect! The president of the division was naturally pleased. He used the results to focus on those areas where the margin of superiority was the thinnest.

The more usual approach to using questionnaires is to develop them specifically for the particular company involved. If you elect to use this approach, the first step is to design the questionnaire. It should be structured in such a manner as to give the respondent an understanding of the ranges of knowledge and skills to be considered and an easy way to differentiate priorities. Both of these features can be served by providing a relatively complete checklist with a priority code. At the same time, open-ended questions can help avoid too tight a structure, which would discourage independent thought.

In setting up your checklist, make sure you are providing the means for determining the needs of different population groups. You need to differentiate between those groups concerned primarily with technical skills and those with management skills. The latter category can be usefully further subdivided into different management levels, as for example, (1) presupervisory, (2) supervisory, (3) managers, and (4) executives.

Once you have developed your questionnaire, you need to develop a covering memorandum with explanations and instructions. The whole package should be tested out with selected individuals. You want to make sure it is easy to understand and use. You will often get some useful ideas for improvement.

Interviews

Another frequently used approach, interviews, is often used by way of follow-up to a questionnaire. It offers the advantage of two-way communication so that matters of mutual interest can be explored in greater depth. It can also be used to strengthen interpersonal ties with key user groups. However, unless a pattern interview is used, interviews alone will not produce statistical summaries that assist in drawing overall conclusions.

Interviewing takes time though—a good deal more than questionnaires alone. Some time can be saved through the use of telephone interviews, but they are far less effective than personal meetings.

The effectiveness of the interviewing method depends very much on the self-discipline and skills of the training professionals. A written interview schedule should be set with a checkoff system as interviews are actually held. It will also be very helpful to work up a simple interview outline to make sure all the important points are covered in each contact. Careful notes should be taken immediately after each session to minimize the chance of forgetting. Unless these steps are taken you won't get the most out of your interviews.

Advisory Panels

Various organizational techniques are also used to provide the necessary inputs on future user workloads. Training committees are frequently used for this purpose, an approach that offers several real advantages. It is quick and relatively inexpensive, at least in out-of-pocket expenses. It tends to build the support of line managers represented on the committee. They become positive influence centers throughout the company. In addition, this approach certainly offers a direct channel of communication that makes the training function responsive to the needs of various elements of the organization.

There are disadvantages too. There is some loss of control by the training director. A committee can sometimes be carried away by its own presumed expertise and enthusiasm into unsound conclusions. The approach is not truly fact-founded. It depends more on the subjective judgments of the group.

A middle road is to make sure that the committee is advisory only in nature. The training director is still to be held accountable for the kind and quality of programs and services to be provided and therefore must have the authority to make final decisions. A skillful training director can steer the committee away from unwise conclusions and use committee sessions to educate committee members on the training function.

How to Structure and Write
Your Plan

Although the primary focus of this book is on training seminars, it is convenient to think of the entire training plan in considering how to go about the planning process. Seminars will constitute a major element of the plan, but a truly comprehensive plan will have to encompass other avenues for human resource development.

As already mentioned, our experience indicates that most training directors don't do much more planning than is required for the annual budget and to produce a calendar of program offerings. In an effort to encourage more training directors to improve their planning practices, let me set forth some specific suggestions on how a practical and useful training plan can be developed.

General Guidelines

First of all, there are some general considerations or guidelines that have to be understood and followed. The form of any training plan will be influenced by individual preference and established company practices, but, in any event, these fundamentals should be followed.

Clearly Business-Driven. The plan should clearly indicate that it is based on an analysis and projection of the needs of the business.

Based on Assumptions As to the Future. At an early place in your planning document, you should collect whatever assumptions you have made as to future conditions and trends. All the analyses previously reviewed about evolving business conditions and technological change should be summarized. Doing so will be a constant reminder of the frame of reference used in developing the plan. Presumably, if something should happen to change that frame of reference, the plan should be changed as well.

For many companies, a key assumption will be the expected rate of growth. If a sharp rate of growth is expected for a number of years into the future, an increasing demand for training of all kinds can be expected. An age group forecast of your employee population, within that overall growth forecast, may reveal many types of special needs, for example, retirement counseling.

Many companies are forecasting significant changes in the makeup of their employee groups. One training director found that she had to provide a questionnaire in seven different languages to allow employees to respond to an employee attitude survey in their native tongue. And the survey was conducted in a suburban area in New England!

Experience Based. Similarly, the most important conclusions reached from your analysis of previous experience should be documented in the plan. What strategic directions have you chosen as a result of evaluating the weaknesses and strengths of the training function? Frequently, the plan itself will be the easiest way of documenting your findings and conclusions.

Developed with Participation. Your plan will be improved by enlisting the active participation of your people. They will add ideas and insights, and in the process they will become committed to the plan. If practicable, the participation of important users should also be secured.

Time Span Beyond 1 Year. Your planning horizon should stretch out longer than a single year. Training needs don't fit nicely into 1-year packages. Some important management initiatives, such as management system implementation or total quality management, will extend over a period of years. It is particularly useful to make note of future needs that have to be postponed beyond the budget year. It helps condition management to these unmet needs.

Coordinated with Management and Users. Formalization of a training plan provides an opportunity to get members of top management and key user groups involved in its final review. Getting these people to "sign off" on the plan can help prevent future problems. They are not likely to attack it later for not meeting their needs.

Clearly Cost-Effective. There has been a greater effort in recent years to measure the effectiveness of formal training against the cost of the training. And "cost" is more and more being considered to include the opportunity cost of taking participants away from their jobs. It is measured by their salaries while undertaking the training. Training directors who are not part of this movement yet will probably be affected in the future.

I can appreciate this effort to get at the true cost of training, but I have long believed that when people are initially employed, it should be understood that part of their ongoing employment will be dedicated to training and retraining. I worry that unwise decisions can be made in this way.

When it comes to travel costs, on the other hand, I believe firmly that they should be included in the overall cost of training. They are directly related to the training, even if they are paid by the using departments. For companies that are spread out geographically, these expenses can be considerable.

Far more difficult in this equation is estimating the overall value or benefit to be realized through the plan. Because it is so difficult, it is often not done at all. Sometimes assumptions can be made on the basis of previous surveys of results achieved. Also some specific types of technical training can be more easily measured, such as improvements in productivity.

Managers as a whole have been so brainwashed by the accounting profession that they are very loathe to make any quantitative estimate of benefit if it has to rest on assumptions. This is not meant as a criticism. The discipline provided to use by the accounting profession is of tremendous value, but in this one respect it may be unnecessarily inhibiting.

For example, a clearly conservative assumption may be quite acceptable. If we can calculate the impact of getting sales trainees out in the field selling, why can't we estimate the value of getting them productive 2 weeks sooner through training? For another example, an obviously conservative estimate on productivity gain through a computerized system can be readily translated into added production, revenue, and profit. In either case, value assumptions provide a better frame of reference than nothing at all.

How to Use Objectives

Fundamental to any training plan is prescribing the end results that are to be achieved, which is another way of saying developing objectives. It is so fundamental, that long experience suggests the need to differentiate different kinds of objectives that meet differing needs.

Although terminology will differ from company to company, we see the usefulness of differentiating three different kinds of objectives:

1. The *key objective,* more frequently termed the "mission," is the comprehensive, overall continuing result to be achieved. For a simple example, it might be something like "to contribute to improving the productivity of employees on the job." We would recommend in addition to such an overall result a statement that identifies the customers or clients whose needs are to be met and a description of the products or services being offered to meet those needs.

In Chapter 3 we described how to develop a mission statement and standards as a preliminary to organizing the training function. These should now be included in your training plan.

2. *Continuing objectives,* or continuing results to be achieved in each critical area of performance within the scope of the key objective. A simple example might be "to provide supervisory training programs that meet the needs of first-level supervisors." We would recommend that every subcategory of work, or separate function, within the training department have such a continuing objective.

3. *Specific objectives,* on the other hand are time-limited. They have a target date, for example, "To develop an improved supervisory training program by December 31, 19xx." These objectives are frequently called "goals." Some organizations will add a measurable outcome as part of

the specific objective, as for example, "To reduce maintenance costs 10% by December 31, 19xx."

How to Use Measurable Standards

Our view is that each of these different kinds of objectives should be accompanied by a set of measurable standards that are built around the most important dimensions of success. A single measure doesn't really do the job. You can reduce costs by 10% if you sacrifice quality or eliminate maintenance, but if you cover all the critical facets, you prevent distortions like this. They should be clearly measurable. You should be able to know without question whether actual results measure up to your commitments.

A sound set of standards attached to an objective provides a clear vision of the end result. And we all know that when this happens, the odds of achieving the objective are significantly improved.

Assume, by way of example, that you have a specific objective to develop a revised first-level supervisory training program so that you have the means to strengthen supervisory performance. Let's say also that you want to do so by December 1 of this year. Our point is that this objective doesn't become sufficiently measurable until you think through the most important dimensions of a successful result and establish a measure for each dimension that will constitute acceptable performance.

Here are some measurable standards that might accompany such an objective. The desired *behavioral changes* are probably the first dimension to be stated, not only the changes but how they will be measured. Should these behavioral changes be self-evaluated or evaluated by the participants' managers? Do all participants have to demonstrate the desired performance, or will we be satisfied with 90% of them?

The precise *subject matter coverage* should also be prescribed. A list of subjects might do it. The program either includes all those subjects or it doesn't, which makes the standard measurable. It doesn't have to be quantitative.

The *basic design* should also be prescribed. Perhaps it would be in terms of the adult learning method employed, the proportion of time spent in application exercises versus straight lecture, the number of days of duration, whether or not it is modular to permit flexibility in scheduling, or whatever is appropriate to the individual case.

The *cost* of achieving the objective should always be considered but will not necessarily be one of the critical dimensions of a successful result. If the cost is not great, or if the objective is mandated, cost may not be critically important.

I know what you're thinking. If you have gotten the behavioral changes you wanted, isn't that enough? Surely that describes the desired end result. Why are other standards needed?

The answer is that they help create full understanding among those who will be working together to achieve the end result. If you, as training director, plan to delegate the achievement of the objective to someone in your department, you'll feel a lot more comfortable with full mutual understanding of all these standards.

The example just given involved a specific objective or one with a target date. The same idea applies to the key objective and continuing objectives. The difference is that the set of standards you develop are also ongoing. Like the objective they accompany, they have no target date. They apply today, next week, next month, and on into the future until changed.

The Seminar Schedule

Backing up your various objectives should be a listing of the seminars that are scheduled, together with the time and place of each offering. In order to facilitate registrations, you should publish a separate promotional piece describing each of the seminars in terms of behavioral objectives, subject matter, duration, methodology, and cost, if any, for the registrants. These can then be made into an appendix to the training plan.

Departmental Projects

In addition to the seminars you will be offering, you probably have some research projects, program development projects, internal training programs, or other projects you want to undertake during the period covered by the plan. Each one should be headed up by a specific objective with accompanying standards and backed up by a set of program steps with a stated accountability and time frame for each. Your best estimate of benefits and cost for each should also be expressed.

How to Format Your Plan

There appears to be no single best format to use in finalizing your training plan. The subject is wide open for individual preferences. But we suggest in Figure 7 a broad outline that can serve as a starting point or frame of reference. It might be particularly helpful if you have no established precedent from which to work.

1. *Overview or summary.* A brief summary of the plan tied into the realities of the company's business; assumptions made as to the future environment; highlights as to what's new or different from previous plans; preview or outline of the materials to be covered in the plan. ~~write last~~

2. *Key objective or mission.* A reminder that puts the rest of the plan in proper perspective. Include the set of standards that you have developed for your key objective. Highlight any changes and why they were made.

3. *Projects.* Separately describe each of the research projects, program developments, or other projects being undertaken. Provide a specific objective with standards for each backed up by a program, schedule, and budget. Highlight the benefits to be realized and the cost of each.

4. *Seminars and workshops.* List and comment on these, noting any significant changes to preexisting practices. Consider use of an appendix if this section would get too bulky.

5. *Evaluation.* Explain methods to be used to evaluate results of the plan or parts of the plan.

6. *Budget.* A summary of proposed expenditures to carry out the plan should be provided at the end in whatever detail is required by the company.

Figure 7. Training plan format.

A good framework doesn't necessarily mean a good plan, but it does provide a "track to run on" that could facilitate good planning. And good planning takes a great deal of analysis, discussion, and participation along the lines reviewed in this chapter.

In thinking about format, remember that you want your plan to be a working document for your people and a selling document for management and users of your services. Use a team approach in finalizing your plan. You'll find that it helps you come up with a document that communicates clearly and accurately.

6

How to Design
a High-Impact
Seminar

How much of the success of a seminar is due to the material and how much is due to the seminar leader? This is a question that experienced professionals ask themselves from time to time. It's human nature for the seminar leader to feel an inward glow of personal triumph at the burst of applause after closing the program. Yet, on reflection, many practitioners, perhaps most, will admit that 80% of the credit goes to the material and only 20% to the program leader.

Opinions will differ on this, of course, but think about it for a moment. With good material the chances are that an average presenter can be quite successful. On the other hand, with poor material even the most highly gifted professional will have trouble pulling off the program. The way for a poorly designed seminar to be saved is for the program leader to do some impromptu program redesign from the seminar platform.

A distinguished colleague once told me, "When all else fails, put them into small teams to share their experiences and ideas. That will liven them up. And by the time they're ready to report out to the whole group, you have had a chance to collect your wits and decide how to save the situation."

A good working knowledge of seminar design is useful in several ways. The most obvious one is the development of a new seminar to meet some newly defined need. Even if someone else is developing it for you, you probably want to provide some preliminary coaching and direction and then agree on a detailed action plan. You may even participate in the program development effort, and you certainly have to be able to evaluate the end result.

Other ways that a working knowledge of seminar design will be useful are in redesigning an existing program or in evaluating a program provided by an outside vendor. All the training seminars that you sponsor have to rest on a sound design in order to be most effective.

In many ways, program development or redesign can be an extraordinary opportunity to provide a sense of satisfaction to truly creative people, and it offers a means to make a lasting contribution to the development of human resources in your own organization. In fact, it can be so personally rewarding that there is a temptation to do too much of it! You have to make sure that the expenditure of effort, which can be substantial, is really worth the result you are striving to achieve. You don't want to use a large piece of steamroller equipment to crack a walnut!

Defining the Real Need

The starting point in the design process is to determine the real need. There is a temptation in some quarters to turn to training whenever there is some performance deficiency or some need to change existing practices. And the training department, in turn, is often only too eager to use its unique capabilities. If the need has been identified by top management or a strong line executive, it is particularly tempting to accept it on face value.

That's why it is important to evaluate the reason for considering a new or revised training seminar. A performance deficiency could be due to many other causes than a lack of understanding or skill in performing certain work. It may be that existing procedures need to be revised, or there may be organizational inadequacies. Perhaps working conditions need to be improved. Furthermore, especially so in recent years, self-development through computer-assisted instruction or otherwise may be a more time-efficient substitute for traditional seminars in some situations.

This observation may explain why many training functions have established a consulting as well as an educational role. A prime purpose would be to get reassurance that there is a need, that it has been properly identified, and that training is an appropriate response to the need. Bankers Trust Company in New York is one of the companies that has developed such a consulting capability within the training function.

Let me give you an illustration of what can happen if you rush into a training seminar as the solution to a problem. A prominent accounting firm had a training committee of top executives which came up with a need for creating a better understanding of time management in members of its professional staff. Eager to demonstrate a prompt response to this request, a newly formed training department went to the outside for help. The training director developed certain specifications for a 1-day workshop and contacted a number of firms to make proposals based on them.

The firm that was selected undertook considerable modification of its standard time-management workshop, introducing a considerable amount of new material at the request of his sponsors. But after one marginally successful and a second disastrous pilot session, it was concluded that it would have been a much better use of the time of the professional staff to have written guidelines available for them to study as their schedules permitted. Investing a full day in training represented a substantial loss of billable time.

Setting the Program Objective

Let's say that the need has been established and it can be effectively met by a training seminar. Now we have to go about developing a program to meet the need. Even if we start with an existing program that has to be modified, the steps are essentially the same. The first one is to define your objective. What are you trying to accomplish and for what population group? Are you going to train certain operators to become skilled on a new piece of equipment? To provide a refresher course in management leadership to experienced middle managers? To improve the communication skills of sales representatives? To give a project team the problem-solving and teamwork skills they'll need to undertake a continuous improvement project? You have to define your training objective and the target population group.

The reasons are fundamental. Without such a definition, a *written* definition by the way, you have no sure basis for determining subject matter content and education approach. If the participant group does not consider the subject matter relevant to its needs, you are not going to be successful. The participants will not respond to the material presented, and they surely won't show the improved performance on the job that you are trying to secure.

Furthermore, you have to know your target population group to be able to design the proper educational approach. If your approach is too simple for the group, it could easily be frustrating for them. If too sophisticated, they may not follow the flow of ideas and not learn from the seminar.

To be more specific, you have to determine the degree of skill building needed as compared to theory. Although improved performance on the job may be the objective of most training seminars, sometimes there is a heavy overtone of general education for purposes of perspective and broad understanding. Some of the better-known programs for top executives have a very strong orientation away from skill building and toward creative thinking or philosophic concepts.

You can carry the analysis a step further and identify different categories of objectives. The principal focus of this book is individual behavior change on the job, but there may be other objectives. Awareness may be the principal objective in certain safety training programs. Sometimes the focus is on changing the culture of an entire organization. In other cases, it may be simply to provide a vehicle for networking and team building.

In each case, the objective would have a significant impact on the design of the program. If it's behavior change, you probably want to provide opportunities to see the desired new behavior in a video dramatization and provide classroom opportunities to practice the new behavior. If it's to create knowledge and awareness, you may want to include progress checks on knowledge acquisition. If it's team building, you'll have to place a heavy emphasis on team exercises, preceded by instruction on how to function effectively as a team member.

This line of thinking underlines the importance of a carefully developed training plan, discussed in the last chapter. If you have one, you have probably already defined the behavioral objectives of the seminar you are developing and of the target population. If you don't have one, you need to do so now.

Analyzing the Setting

Another preliminary consideration is the overall setting within which the program will be presented. You have to be aware at the outset of interfaces with other programs and existing practices in order to avoid possible confusion or resistance. At the same time, you might be able to create interest in some other program you offer by appropriate cross-references. Or perhaps more importantly, you may have to position the program logically within the entire family of programs you are offering.

The bitter experience of a project manager of a large management development program for a major department in a large eastern state is a sad example of failure to be sensitive to these interfaces. In the second year of the program, he brought in a second outside consulting firm with impeccable credentials. He attempted to introduce portions of an established off-the-shelf program provided by that firm. Unfortunately, the vocabulary and approach provided by the second vendor contradicted in some very important respects that which had already been provided to the same target population the year before by the first vendor.

It was very embarrassing for all concerned when the first participant group refused to go along with the second vendor's program. The group was supposedly being trained to conduct the program in-house, but the seminar leaders-to-be knew they would not be able to present it successfully because of the conflicts and confusion.

You also have to consider the physical setting. For example, if the program is to be given at a sleep-away facility, you are well advised to consider some team assignments for the evenings. You can cover a lot more ground that way and also promote some productive interaction among the participants. We tend to favor team exercises rather than classroom activities. Some participants may need the stimulation of interaction with their peers after a heavy dinner, and perhaps a few cocktails, to maintain a high level of interest.

If the plan is to use a resort site for the program, you will create a lot of frustration if you don't allow for some use of the recreational facilities that are offered. There are several ways to do this. You can plan the session for the start or the end of the week and arrange for use of the golf course, tennis courts, or other facilities the day before or the day after the seminar. If you are planning an all-week session (few people do these days), give some consideration to an early afternoon adjournment on Wednesday to let people recharge their mental batteries with some sport or exercise.

Aside from the physical aspects of the setting, you may have to consider the psychological. Is the company still trying to merge different cultures from a recent acquisition or merger? Has there been or threatened to be a major downsizing? Is there a new chief executive who might be interested in participating in the seminar in some way to get a chance to mingle with his new people? Is the company experiencing some tough competition that is creating apprehension as to the future? These are a few of the less tangible issues that you might have to take into account.

Determining Subject Matter Content

Once the objective has been clearly defined and the overall setting understood, the subject matter content can be developed. A useful approach is to block out the broad subject matter content in a full-sentence outline, leaving ample margins and space between lines for reworking. You put this in the left-hand column of a three-column worksheet, headed "Subject Matter." You then use the second column, headed "Treatment," to indicate whether the subject will be covered by a video, a case, application exercise, group discussion, or otherwise. The third column, headed "Time Allocation," is reserved for a rough preliminary estimate of time required for each subject.* Here are some ideas to consider as you develop the subject matter.

Fixing Scope and Depth

The depth and breadth of subject matter treatment will be largely determined by the needs analysis and stated objective, but other considerations may have to be reviewed.

Minimizing Time Away from Work. One of these is the increasing pressure that line managers seem to be exerting to minimize time away from the job. It has produced a new buzz phrase: accelerated learning. Of course, in any program development effort you want to make sure that every hour invested is truly worth it.

The worst thing that can happen is to have too many participants report back that the course could have been just as effective if it had taken 1 day less. You'll always get one or two fast learners who will make this complaint on their evaluation sheets—usually counterbalanced by those who would have liked an additional day.

One way to deal with the constraints of time is to provide for preseminar assignments. These can simply be text material to be read or cases to be read and analyzed in preparation for discussions at the seminar. There are some indications that computer-assisted self-instruction is being used increasingly to prepare participants in advance. There is much to be said for this practice. It reserves for the seminar that which a group experience can do best: providing interaction and sharing of ideas and insights among participants.

Different Learning Tracks. Another situation you may have to face is a target population group that is not truly homogeneous. In such a case, the subject matter may have to be structured in a way that takes account of the different levels of understanding and sophistication that may exist from group to group. You may need to provide in your leader's guide a plan for dealing with a fast-track group and one for a slow-track

---

*See also Bunch, John: "The Storyboard Strategy." *Training & Development*, ASTD, July 1991, p. 69.

group. Core material may have to be supplemented by optional team exercises or subjects for group discussion.

Logical Sequencing

Learning is greatly facilitated if the subject matter is presented in a logical, easy-to-follow flow of ideas. The process should begin by providing a broad frame of reference and then proceed from one idea to the next in a logical sequence that builds one idea upon the other much as a bricklayer goes about building a wall — one brick at a time.

It often helps to provide a quick overview of each main topic as it comes along, providing a bridge from the last topic and mentioning the points to be covered under the new heading. Then as each subsidiary point is reached, the participants are better able to put it into perspective.

Participants should be provided with something familiar and well understood to which they can relate each new idea as it comes along. For a simple example, farm children quickly grasped the functioning of the human heart when it was compared to a water pump.

The best way to be sure of a logical sequence is to take your full-sentence outline of the subject matter and read it aloud to someone else — or to your own image in a mirror if no one else is available.

When McKinsey & Company first started recruiting for its professional consulting staff directly from graduate business schools, the management group of the firm was very surprised to discover that top graduates from the most distinguished educational institutions could not write an acceptable business report. They had to be put through an intensive course in report writing, conducted by an outside consultant retained for this sole purpose.

The central focus of the course was the need for a single theme or "angle," around which to structure the ideas or proof necessary for a persuasive presentation. The structuring was done in a preliminary outline composed of complete sentences. The same is true in developing an effective training seminar. The theme is the behavioral objective which establishes what material is relevant, and the outline provides the overall design.

Planning the Learning Methodology

A basic part of program design is to establish a frame of reference in regard to a proven adult learning process. Such a reference guide will be essential when you go about developing the educational materials.

After all, you are trying to get people to learn something. It only makes sense to adopt an approach that will make it easy for them to do so. A proven adult learning process should be followed, but it should not be followed with such unwavering precision as to become monotonous.

A few years ago, I audited a seminar leader who failed to observe this caution. At eight different points in the 3-day seminar he was presenting, the participant workbook provided a number of management principles, each set relating to a different aspect of management. As each set of principles came up, he would assign each one of the principles to a different team of two participants. He asked each team to restate their assigned principle in their own words and provide an example of how a manager could use the principle on the job.

The technique itself is not a bad one. It provides for some interaction in small groups. It tests understanding and gets some degree of simulated application. But because it was done the same way every time, the group came to expect it and got bored with it. "Oh, not again!" they would say, as our leader continued on his enthusiastic way.

To my knowledge there is no complete unanimity as to the most effective learning process. Some educators strongly favor the case method, getting participants to draw conclusions from some real or simulated situation presented to them. This can bring about a great deal of active participation. It also seems to be true that when people think something through for themselves, they are far more likely to remember it. But it can be very time-consuming, and at a time when many companies are stressing accelerated learning to minimize time away from the job, this can be problematic.

My own experience suggests that this so-called "discovery method" of learning is an extremely effective approach with more experienced groups who have some background upon which to draw. It can also be used as an occasional change of pace. But for most groups I recommend this six-step approach:

1. *Motivation.* The first step is to secure a positive motivation toward learning what is being offered. You can't assume that because they're there that they want to learn. Chances are most of them have been told to be there! You have to make them understand how they could benefit personally from learning and using the ideas and information to be presented. Not only at the outset with respect to the total seminar but also to each new subject as it is being presented.

2. *Explanation.* Then the ideas should be presented clearly and in a logical sequence so the process of learning can begin.

3. *Demonstration.* To get greater and clearer understanding, the sem-

inar leader should do or perform that which is to be learned or provide an example or illustration to demonstrate the idea.

4. *Self-evaluation.* The participants should then be given an opportunity to assess their own understanding of the materials presented. For example, you can use a self-evaluation worksheet, or you can provide for testing questions to generate a group discussion.

5. *Application.* The learners should then have an opportunity to apply the ideas in some way, through individual or team application exercises, cases, and ultimately on the job.

6. *Feedback.* Participants need to have some way of knowing whether they are performing properly. Without some kind of feedback, they cannot know what they are doing right that should be continued and what they are doing wrong that should be discontinued. The seminar design should provide for this needed feedback.

Considering High-Tech Program Delivery

These days, and even more so into the future, you have to think about the use of emerging technology in training.* If your company has already invested in some equipment and developed some know-how, it's a somewhat easier question: To what extent can you use that technology to deliver the seminar we are developing? Or is it time to take a further step into high-tech training? If your company is still on the sidelines, this may be the time to consider making the plunge.

In considering any of these questions, it is helpful to have a frame of reference as to the different aspects of conducting seminars that the new technology is affecting:

1. *Super audio-visual support.* One area of important development is providing far more versatile, higher-impact audio-visual support of seminar subject matter. Computer-controlled techniques offer a wide variety of visual imagery, live or still, with or without audio messages, all under the control of the program leader. The ability to respond to the unique needs of different seminar groups is vastly multiplied. In a way, you could think of this development as a high-quality image projector, with access to computer-stored information and video cassettes.

---

*For a full treatment of this subject see Hannum, Wallace: *The Application of Emerging Training Technology.* American Society of Training and Development, 1990.

2. *Direct, intensified participant involvement.* The ability to provide direct interaction between the computer and different teams and even different individuals offers a new wealth of opportunities for intensified participant involvement. The most obvious and most exciting one is simulation. Others are access to information and self-testing without interrupting class activities.

In simulation, participants are grouped into teams and are asked to assume roles mirroring the real world. As they progress through the simulation, they develop the desired skills in a highly stimulating, often competitive, environment. The use of computers permits simulations that are far more sophisticated and realistic than would otherwise be possible.

Very possibly the most explosively growing application of computer simulations is in self-instruction. Just the other day I learned to my astonishment that one of my professional colleagues had a program that was teaching him to fly commercial jet aircraft at home on his personal computer. He calmly related that he had spent 1½ hours the weekend before in a most realistic simulation of a flight from Atlanta to Tampa! He was on lesson 21 out of a total of 215!

3. *Breakdown of geographic barriers.* The third area of development opens up new opportunities for the delivery of training seminars: teleconferencing to reach widely dispersed training populations, especially those with concentrations of people too sparse to collect into a traditional seminar setting.

I remember only too clearly the complaint of one training director. His budget for the year was rapidly disappearing because of the cost of transporting people to seminar sites and maintaining them while they were there. I felt particular empathy for him, since my professional fees were coming out of the same budget!

4. *Work station training delivery.* At first look, the fourth area seems to offer competition to the traditional type of seminars: bringing training directly to individual work stations. Yet, it offers possibilities that could add to the effectiveness of training seminars.

Preseminar, self-instruction assignments could bring all seminar participants to a common, high level of understanding before they assembled together in the seminar. In this way, the seminar environment could be used for what it does best: provide a forum for group application experiences and group discussion. The net result would be to reduce the need for lecture at the seminar and very possibly shorten its duration.

The technology could also provide easy postseminar access to the body of knowledge presented in the seminar. People could access it right at their work stations to refresh their memories.

Providing for Ample Participation

Let's get back to the seminar we are now designing. Whether or not we plan to use the new technology, we have to provide in our design for as much participant involvement as practicable. The more you can get participants to relate what they are learning to their own jobs and to share their ideas and experiences with each other, the higher the levels of interest and motivation. Periods of straight lecture should be limited to no more than 10 minutes at a time. Even then, the presentation should be punctuated by relevant examples and perhaps humorous asides. Here are a number of ways to get participation.

Preseminar Assignments

In assignments distributed to the seminar participants before the session, they can be asked to read and develop answers to questions on a case they know will be discussed at the seminar. They can make a preliminary evaluation of a problem to which they will apply a problem-solving method to be taught in the class. They can be asked to take some kind of self-evaluation test to alert them to areas of greatest need, or they can be asked to list their expectations of the seminar. All these techniques help to get the participant involved at a higher level than will simply reading text.

Icebreakers

At the very start of a seminar, an exercise to break inhibitions and encourage participation can be most useful. Usually these are left to the judgment of the seminar leader, but, if used, perhaps a half hour or more has to be allowed in the first day's schedule.

One easy icebreaker I have used with considerable success is to divide the whole group into teams of two, each team member interviewing the other for 5 minutes to get the information necessary to introduce the other to the whole group. The exercise seems to work best if the discussion leader challenges each interviewer to be a "probing reporter" and to find some especially newsworthy aspect of each others' background. It is somewhat time-consuming, but it is an easy way for strangers to get acquainted and a good way to get them accustomed to taking speaking roles during the seminar.

Probably the easiest and most common icebreaker, and one that is most time-efficient, is simply to ask the participants to introduce them-

selves. It helps to put a short outline on the easel pad for them to follow: (1) early family background, (2) short career history, (3) present
responsibilities, (4) expectations of the seminar.

Cases

Well-designed cases relevant to the materials being covered are an excellent way to get a high level of involvement, particularly if they permit differing points of view to be developed. The usual approach is to assign the
same case to teams of four or five people, giving them at least 10 minutes
to work on it. Let them know in advance how much time they have. After
they have completed their assignments, have them elect one of their members as team leader to report back to the group as a whole.

Ideally, cases should be set in working environments to which the
participants can relate, but, as a general rule, actual cases should be
avoided. They might introduce personalities into the discussion, or perhaps some of the participants themselves were involved with a case. If
so, they may happily introduce a whole lot of factual material of interest
to them and perhaps the rest of the group, but this material may ob-
scure the main points to be made and extend the time allowed for discussion of the case.

Because four or five people are typically involved, you may want to
plan for the teams to leave their seminar seats and meet around tables
provided elsewhere in the meeting room. If the case is sufficiently challenging to require 25 minutes or longer, separate, break-away rooms in
which the teams could meet is highly desirable.

Application Exercises

Relating freshly learned ideas to structured problems or situations is
virtually an essential part of the adult learning process. It is most effectively done in subgroups or teams of two or three, because of the interaction provided, but can be done individually. Typically, the subgroups
or teams are made from people sitting together, which eliminates the
need for them to move from their seminar seats. They just form a
group where they are sitting. After the allotted time, feedback is obtained from the teams.

Group Discussion

Sharing of ideas and insights through a general discussion involving the
whole group of participants is another way to get participation. The dis-

cussion can be started through questions posed by the seminar leader, or it can come about as a result of feedback from cases or exercises assigned to teams.

Some of these questions may be included in the participant's workbook. In any event, the leader's guide should supply the seminar leader with specific questions that may be used to generate group discussion.

Group discussion is more efficient in use of time but doesn't get the same scope of participation as cases and application exercises.

Games

Competitive games between individuals or teams are time-consuming but are very exciting to the participants. You have to allow enough time for the game to run its course. You don't want the participants to be frustrated because they feel they are being rushed through the exercise, which means you can't use very many of them in the same seminar.

In the Situation Leadership seminar offered by Hershey and Blanchard the high point is an extended game in which individuals move pieces along a monopoly-like board. Two spaces forward if you choose the best answer out of four choices, one space for an acceptable answer, but minus one space for a clearly wrong choice.

Heublein, Inc., uses the game approach in one portion of its basic management training program, Effective Management. In an evening assignment, teams are asked to develop an "action plan" in accordance with guidelines presented in the seminar during the day. The next morning, each team critiques the action plans developed by the other teams, earning 2 points for correctly identifying certain "common mistakes," 1 point for each "improvement opportunity," but minus 1 point for a clearly incorrect challenge.

Role Playing

Asking participants to assume certain "roles" is another means for getting people involved. Role playing can be built directly into the design of the seminar, or it may be an impromptu decision of the seminar leader.

In the former case, the workbook would contain background information on the situation to be presented. It would then provide specific background for each assigned role, not to be read by the one assigned to the other role.

Role playing can be done within each small team or before the group as a whole. Using small teams will provide the broadest kind of participation and at the same time will be less threatening to the role players, but it's more difficult for the seminar leader to follow the role playing process and to provide meaningful feedback.

In the informal type of role playing, the program leader might say, "Alice, would you play the part of the manager in a difficult performance review session, and Bill the part of the employee. Try to show us, Alice, how you might go about giving some negative feedback while maintaining an overall positive view of the employee's importance to your department."

Simulation*

With the increasing use of computer technology, simulation is becoming more available as a means for intensifying participant involvement, as already noted.

For example, Swiss Bank Corporation has developed a computer model that permits various executive groups to simulate the worldwide operations of the bank.

For another example, a major worldwide oil company offers a course at its corporate headquarters in Westchester, New York, that makes extensive use of simulation. Teams of two compete with all the other teams making entrepreneurial decisions that are reflected by the computer into financial results. The competition is keen to see which team ends up with the best balance sheet at the end of 2½ days. The experience is so exciting that there is a long waiting list to take the course.

Testing the Design

In a sense, the final design of any seminar is incorporated into the educational materials that constitute the program. In many instances, however, it is helpful to have a design outline to review with potential users of the program and with other training professionals before the participant workbooks and leaders' guides are developed. It's much easier to make changes.

The three-column worksheet mentioned earlier is one of many ways to lay out such a program design. You can use it to put together the essentials of your overall design, together with time allowances and educational treatment for each major subject matter heading. It will provide the frame of reference needed to develop the final educational materials, covered in the next chapter.

*See Galitz, Dr. Lawrence: "The Case for Simulation Training." *Banking & Financial Journal*, Philip Thorn Associates Ltd., vol. 5, no. 2, p. 10, June 1989.

7

How to Design a Quality Workbook and Other Aids

Once you have your seminar design and it's been reviewed and improved by user representatives and professional colleagues, you are ready to develop the materials needed to present the seminar. You have to develop the educational materials needed by the participants and those needed by the program leader.

Participant Materials

The primary educational vehicle is what is provided to the participants, usually some form of workbook presented at the start of the seminar. Frequently, the workbook is supplemented by some form of preseminar assignment and some reference text.

The Participant's Workbook

The people going through a seminar need written materials that clearly present, explain, and illustrate the ideas introduced in the program. A full-sentence text outline of the subject matter is typically provided, together with background information for application assignments and role-playing exercises, cases, checklists, and possibly progress checks or self-evaluation tests. There may also be logic diagrams, models, and other illustrations to assist in understanding.

Not every seminar setting requires a formal workbook. In some situations it may be inappropriate. Other materials available in these instances would be a simple agenda, an outline of discussion, or perhaps just an empty pad for note taking.

You wouldn't want a workbook for a loosely structured team-building workshop. Here, the participants determine their own agenda and the discussion leader "processes" group thinking on an easel pad. I've seen some very effective sessions in which the participant group brainstorms to create a long list of ideas for, say, improving an organization's effectiveness. Then they select the three or four most promising ideas and break into teams to analyze and come up with recommendations as to each of these.

Formal workbooks would also be inappropriate for an executive briefing involving a small group of higher-level executives. Most of these executives dislike a formal, workbook-structured training session. They don't want to deal with make-believe cases and work exercises. They much prefer a kind of "work conference" in which an "Agenda and Discussion Outline" is used instead of a three-ring binder workbook.

Sometimes it's useful to provide a folder with pockets into which you can insert relevant materials. The left-hand pocket could contain an agenda or discussion outline, and the right-hand one could have specific materials relevant to the discussion that could be referred to as appropriate. This approach has the great advantage that it can be used when there is a short lead time. You can put a session together on relatively little notice.

Nevertheless, by far the most common and probably most useful learning aid is the participant workbook, which is typically provided at the seminar rather than before. I tend to favor the three-ring binder type because of the easy way it can be used to incorporate handouts. Here are some specific suggestions.

1. Make sure the title of the seminar appears on the cover as well as on the title page within the workbook.

2. Use the company's logo and color scheme (even on vendor-provided workbooks) on the cover and within to give it a more clearly relevant appearance. You may want to use a company masthead on each of the pages making up the workbook.

3. Include the date, to clearly identify different editions of the same seminar.

4. Include a table of contents in a format that provides a preview of the material to be covered.

5. State the objective of the seminar at the outset, in terms of what the participants are supposed to get out of it.

6. Use tabs that will tie back to the table of contents to separate the individual sections.

7. Put application exercises and cases in the text at the place in the sequence of instruction where they are to be used. An exception to this may be made where the same workbook is to be used with population groups of different experience levels. Here, it provides greater flexibility to have at least some of the cases and exercises in the appendix where they can be used or omitted as appropriate for different groups.

8. Reserve the appendix for extended examples or bibliographies that are not a direct part of the learning experience being presented.

9. Use correct-and-edit exercises to assist in the learning process (examples with deliberate mistakes the participants are required to identify and correct).

10. Put the text material in the form of an expanded outline rather than a complete text. Hit the highlights. Avoid long sections of text material. Reserve these for an accompanying text (see below).

11. Include questions to be used as a basis for group discussions, with ample space after each for participants to write down their own ideas and take notes on group discussions.

12. Use both sides of the page, leaving adequate space for note taking. Wherever possible, pages that relate directly to each other should face each other, for example, guidelines to be followed in writing an objective on the left page, and examples to be evaluated against these guidelines on the right page.

13. Start major subject matter sections on a fresh page.

14. Avoid providing "suggested answers" or "school solutions" to problems assigned to participants in the workbook. A few creative people will page forward and find them, with the result that their teams will not benefit from thinking the problem through for themselves.

Packaging Options

Participant materials can be assembled or packaged in a variety of ways. The simpler, less expensive techniques are appropriate for special nonrecurring seminars.

Bound. The pages of textbooks or booklets provided with standard off-the-shelf programs are typically bound within a more-or-less permanent cardboard or heavy paper cover. The rationale is that no changes are expected in the materials over long periods of time and they will be used by large populations. Bound materials are preferred by outside vendors for another reason: they provide better copyright protection.

Loose Leaf. Three-hole-punched pages in a loose-leaf binder are probably the most popular design for participant workbooks. They are widely used for both internally developed seminars and those provided by outside firms.

The loose-leaf format offers great flexibility. Additions and eliminations can be easily made, especially if pages have two numbers: the first identifying the section within the workbook, the second the page within that section, for example "2-9." Individual pages can easily be changed, either to update them or adapt them to different groups. Handout material can be prepunched and inserted by the participants directly into their own workbooks.

Loose Pages. Handouts, by their nature, are prepared in loose pages and distributed to participants at the appropriate place in the course of the seminar. It offers the seminar leaders certain flexibility; they can elect whether or not to use the handouts and nobody knows the difference. Sometimes it's important to hand out materials that are developed for an entirely separate purpose, such as performance appraisal forms or interview forms. These might not conveniently fit into a workbook format. Then again, loose pages offer a fast way to pull together a presentation for a particular meeting.

However, loose pages are easily lost or their sequence is disturbed, which make them less useful as a later reference. If it's important to have a record, the sponsor of the session should gather the pages together and staple them to a covering memorandum summarizing the purpose of the meeting, the attendees, and any conclusions reached.

The Preseminar Assignment

Giving assignments to participants in advance of a seminar has a number of potential advantages, in addition to securing participant involvement as noted above. The assignments have to be well designed, though, and participants have to really do them. Usually, they are packaged in a booklet that can be taken apart so that the pages can be inserted in the participant's workbook at the seminar.

Raising Knowledge Levels. Advance reading assignments can raise knowledge levels and reduce the need for lecture at the seminar, leaving more time available for interaction among participants. However, the reading assignment should not be too long or too difficult. My own preference is to keep the amount of reading down to less than 15 pages, as a rough rule of thumb.

If the reading assignment is too onerous, many people will end up not doing it, which will cause an unwelcome disparity in knowledge levels among the participant group. What happens is that the few who gave it their all will tend to dominate group discussion. If the seminar leader allows this to happen, the others will be left behind. On the other hand, if the seminar leader sets the pace for those who haven't done the reading, the few who did will get bored. In either event there is a loss of effectiveness.

Preanalysis of Cases. It's particularly helpful to include in the preseminar reading any cases that will be covered on the first day of the seminar, with questions the seminar attendees have to answer. Giving them time in class to read cases tends to interrupt the active flow of the program. It's much better to be able to put them into teams at once and have them discuss the cases in small groups. The sound of teams sharing ideas is much more exciting than the deadly silence that falls on the group as they read a case individually in class.

Establishing Relevance. If possible, the preseminar assignment should require participants to relate the text material provided to their own jobs. In this way, they will see the relevance of the seminar, and their motivation will be enhanced. A series of questions, with spaces to be used for the answers, is a good way to do this. Using questions in this way is also a way of making sure that they really understand what they read. They may have to go back over the text to answer the questions, which provides some useful reinforcement.

Building Expectations. You can sometimes increase the interest level of the participants by asking them in advance to write down their expectations for the seminar. If you do this, then the seminar leader should collect these expectations at the start of the seminar. If some of them are not going to be met, it is best to set the matter straight at the outset.

Self-Assessment. Sometimes it's possible to design a self-evaluation instrument and include it in the preseminar assignment. If participants can identify their own most important improvement needs, it will heighten their interest when these topics are covered in the seminar.

Reference Texts

Some seminars are rich enough in subject matter to warrant the use of reference texts in addition to workbooks and preseminar assignments. The text material can be separately bound or appended to the participant workbook.

Advantages.   Here are some reasons for doing this.

1. It helps keep detailed text material out of the workbook, which can then be simplified and focused more on work exercises, cases, and visualizations.
2. It provides a convenient way for participants to review material during the seminar and amplify their understanding.
3. It can be used for evening assignments, to reduce the need for lecture on the succeeding day. The presenter can review the text material assigned by posing questions and generating group discussion.
4. It is a more convenient and more complete continuing reference than the workbook, which is structured to assist learning. If bound separately, the textbook can fit easily into bookcases provided at participants' work stations.
5. It is almost essential, if the seminar is designed primarily around cases and self-discovery since the workbook will not be a useful future reference.
6. Texts that represent copies of authoritative company manuals or standard operating procedures tend to have an added importance in the eyes of participants.
7. Texts can select the few most important visualizations used in the workbook, give them added significance, and make them more easily accessible.

Disadvantages. Notwithstanding these advantages, there are other considerations which would argue against the use of text material in some situations.

1. Text materials may be costly to produce if not already available. They would probably not be suitable for small participant populations.
2. Every time a change is made to the workbook, you have to check the

text for conformance. Because of the relative ease of making workbook changes and the greater difficulty of revising text material, this is a real danger. There are many more times than I would like to admit when I simply could no longer use a text because of inconsistencies with new material in the workbook.

3. The texts may add appreciably to the bulk of the seminar materials, which could be important in some situations. I can remember sitting up all night in LaGuardia Airport in a blizzard, surrounded by so many boxes of educational materials that I could not conveniently take refuge in a nearby airport motel during the time before the storm completely closed in the airport.

4. It opens up the possibility that a few participants would throw themselves into the text materials covering the next day's session and dominate the discussion.

Other Participant Materials

There are other items for use by participants that are not strictly educational but can add impact to a seminar.

One dedicated training director I know is always shopping around for interesting but relatively inexpensive gifts to give to seminar participants. He was good enough to include me in his largess when I was the program leader. I still find myself using some of these gifts with a positive feeling: a pen-highlighter combination, a case for toilet articles, a key chain, a paperweight. Perhaps it contributes in some way to his relative success in filling seminar seats.

Other training directors and some program designers include things like memory cards or coffee mugs with reminder messages as a regular part of their seminars.

A roster of the participants in each session is always appreciated. It makes it easier to get to know your classmates and to develop a lasting network.

A biography of the program leader or guest speaker can also add to the success of a program. People have an interest in knowing the background and training from which their discussion leaders speak. It helps them in asking questions and may add to their readiness to accept the materials being presented.

Leader's Materials

Fully as important as the materials provided to the participants are those made available to the seminar leader. These can be particularly crucial in training seminar leaders to conduct a new seminar, and they can serve a continuing reference need as well. Generally speaking, there is at one extreme a detailed, formalized leader's guide produced in a separate booklet or binder. At the other are a variety of techniques used by individual trainers.

$2\ Types$

① **The Formal Leader's Guide**

In the initial design or in any major revision of a training program it is probably necessary to provide seminar leaders with a formal, detailed guide for conducting the program. As seminar leaders get to know the program, they will almost inevitably substitute their own informal system. Programs purchased from outside vendors will routinely be accompanied by prepared leader's guides that may be fully as impressive as the participant workbooks.

There is probably less in the way of usual practice when it comes to developing leader's guides. Perhaps it's because the program leader and the program designer are often the same person, in which case there is less need for a complete formal guide. But where there will be many seminar leaders, with some continuing need to orient new leaders, and the program is expected to endure for many years, the formal guide is probably essential.

The formal, detailed leader's guide should include the following:

1. An introduction, which orients the leader to the behavioral objective, the target population group, and the background leading up to the development of the seminar. It should also summarize the subject matter and day-by-day schedule.

2. A preseminar checklist to help the program leader get everything ready in advance. It should include reminders as to name cards, rosters, room setup, audio-visual equipment, and video.

3. Suggested remarks to introduce the program as a whole and to make transitions from one major subject to the next.

4. A prescribed sequence of subject matter, keyed to pages in the participant workbook, with a recommended time allotment for each subject and estimated time of day for starting and completing each one.

5. Suggested questions to use to start group discussions, together with anticipated responses.

6. Cues for using audio-visual aids and for making case and application exercise assignments.

7. Suggested solutions for cases and application exercises.

8. Examples and illustrations for use in making different subject matter materials relevant to the group.

9. Evening assignments.

10. Suggestions on summaries for each day and for the total program.

Informal Leader's Guides

You probably need something more formal and detailed to train seminar leaders at the outset in a new or substantially revised program— something that can also serve as the official leader's guide. But sooner or later individual leaders will develop their own informal guides that are less bulky and are tailored to each individual.

Cue Cards.   One such approach is the use of cue cards. The cards can be 3 × 5 or 5 × 8 inches (or the metric equivalents). Cards can be used inconspicuously, can be easily revised and resequenced, and are not too bulky to transport. You are, however, in deep trouble if you lose a card or if you drop your deck of cards on the floor, but if you feel comfortable using cue cards, go right ahead. I find them more useful for presentations to larger groups than I do for training seminars.

Crib Notes on Transparency Frames.   Another technique, if you use overhead projectors, is to put crib notes on the frames of the prepared transparencies. It is convenient and quite unobservable. It is especially useful as a reminder of ideas to use for elaboration of the subject matter covered by each transparency. But it probably cannot be used as a complete leader's guide because the notes are tied to specific visuals.

Separate Bold Outline.   Another device is the use of a broad felt-tipped pen, or equivalent, or full-page-size paper. This offers the advantage of being able to write your notes more boldly than you can on a cue card or margin of a transparency because there is more room to do so. You can place your outline on the leader's table and read it from a distance of many feet. The individual pages can be three-hole punched and put inconspicuously within the pages of a participant's workbook. Changes are easy to make by obliterations and additions to individual master pages, which can then be photocopied.

Marked-up Workbook.   My own preference is to mark up a participant's workbook and, if useful, to insert some pages within it. I put my time schedule in pencil, usually showing on each workbook page my desired starting and ending times. Since my time cues are entered in pencil, I can change them easily if starting times are different for different groups.

I have my own abbreviations for group discussion (GD), team exercise (T/E), individual work exercise (IWE), and use of an audio-visual aid (A/V), which I also enter right into the workbook at the proper place. I even indicate appropriate places for some of my favorite stories, with a few key words to remind me of salient points.

The two main reasons why I like this system are that it saves space and I always know what page in the participant's workbook I'm on. I may have to remind participants what page in their workbook they should have open before them.

For the experienced professional who is thoroughly familiar with a seminar, a brief outline of topics and scheduled times may be sufficient. But heed this word of caution. It is easy to become overconfident.

A very experienced professional colleague of mine told me how embarrassed he was once for lack of sufficient crib notes. He was embarked on a spirited presentation on the subject of human motivation and behavior when his mind suddenly went blank. Momentarily, he was at a loss to accredit theory X and theory Y to Herzberg or McGregor! My recommendation is to err on the side of preparation. Have all the specifics readily available in case *your* mind goes blank.

Audio-Visual Aids

It would be a rare training seminar today that would not be accompanied by audio-visual aids planned and designed as an integral part of the program. In addition, seminar leaders will introduce their own visual aids via the easel pad or using blank acetate sheets on an overhead projector. These supplementary visuals will add value to a program, but a standard set should be established for each seminar.

When to Use

The purpose of using audio-visuals is to facilitate and reinforce learning. They should be used only when those purposes can be served. They can communicate desired behavior or the consequences of improper behavior, a complex of interrelationships, or an understanding of a person's own interpersonal skills in a far more powerful way than words alone. They can set the stage for meaningful discussion and can add visual interest or impact and accent a change of pace. Here are some ideas based on my experience that can be helpful.

Learning Behavior. It used to be a great wonder to me that children seem to learn skiing so much more easily and quickly than I did, when I took up the sport at the ripe age of 27. But the answer is very simple. Children can model their behavior after the ski instructor much more easily than adults. They don't have to intellectualize it, as we do, and they have no fear. They watch the ski instructor do it, and they do it the same way.

It's the same idea in employee training. If the trainees can see the *correct* way of doing something, it's a much quicker and more effective learning experience than reading or hearing words describing that behavior. The technique is especially useful in demonstrating the operation of equipment, making a sales presentation, or performing a variety of management tasks, e.g., how to conduct an employment interview, correcting employee performance, on-the-job coaching.

Dramatizations of improper performance often excite high participant interest but run the risk that the poor performance vignettes will be remembered better than the positive ideas being presented. Even today, I vividly remember a videotape I saw some 5 years ago of an American businessman trying to sell his company's services to a Mexican entrepreneur at a restaurant in Mexico City without first creating proper rapport. But I don't remember how you were supposed to create that rapport!

Demonstrating Relationships. Audio-visual images can demonstrate relationships that are not easily or quickly understandable through words alone. There are many familiar examples of this. A histogram or bar chart can quickly demonstrate the major cost components in some operations. An organization chart is a fast and easy way to show a complex of reporting relationships that would require laborious text to cover the same ground. Flow charts, models, graphs, pie charts, and diagrams can present a complex of relationships at a single glance. These can be presented via the video means with a narrator or by projected still images with the program leader providing the audio portion. The latter approach has the advantage of flexibility. The pace and accompanying commentary can be adjusted for different groups.

Emphasis. Audio-visuals are also used to add emphasis to important ideas. You not only hear an idea from the seminar leader or narrator, but you can see the words presented on the screen, for instance, an important definition or management principle. You can still see it after the spoken words have been completed. It gives you further time to reflect on it and perhaps relate it to your own experience.

Staging Team Exercises.   The video technique is particularly useful in setting the stage for team exercises and group discussions. What did Derrick do right? What did he do wrong? How would you have done it?

Testing Self-Knowledge.   With the advent of computerized techniques we may be able to make greater use of self-testing in the course of a seminar. Participants would access the computer and get feedback on their own screens. It is commonplace today in self-education or computer-based training. In some areas it is being used in seminar situations. Direct interaction with the computer may well become routine in the conduct of training seminars in future years.

Orienting the Participants.   Audio-visuals can also be used to clarify the organization of subject matter in a seminar. "In this afternoon's session, we shall be covering seven guidelines to more effective communications," the presenter or narrator might say. The seven guidelines would be visually listed. Then as each guideline is discussed, it could be underlined or highlighted on the visual so that the participants know the precise subject matter being discussed as well as the overall framework into which it fits.

Providing Changes of Pace.   Too much lecture, too patterned a use of group discussion or team exercises, too much of any one approach can result in the loss of participant interest. Yes, even too much computer-driven video! I suspect that as more training directors become equipped and proficient in the use of new technology, there will be a temptation to use too much of it.

CRITIQUE

Practical Suggestions

Here are a few practical ideas I have gleaned from my own experience and from discussion with other professionals that could be of interest to you.

1. *Support Your Program Leader*.   There is no substitute for the skilled program leader who is constantly assessing the capabilities and needs of each seminar group and who is adapting the presentation to meet these needs most effectively. Your audio-visual content should support your discussion leader and not provide a straitjacket. If you structure too much audio-visual material in an effort to get the same message across to the total target population group, you may lose the

benefits that a flesh-and-blood discussion leader can provide. You may also create a negative motivational climate that could affect your ability to maintain a top-quality training staff.

2. *Use Your Videos for Action Sequences.* In the early years of video—particularly the home-grown variety—there was a tendency to put a presenter in front of the camera to lecture. It became known as the "talking head" school of video. But without the magical interplay between audience and speaker, it takes an unusually gifted orator to capture and hold the interest of trainees. And there are precious few of these. The point is to use this medium where it clearly has the greatest impact: in dramatizations involving real people and perhaps moving imagery a la Walt Disney.

3. *Keep Your Sequences Short.* If you are using dramatizations to set up a team exercise or group discussion, keep them short—in most cases no longer than 10 minutes, preferably 4 to 5. It's not so much that you will lose your audience, though that is a possibility, but it will be difficult for the attendees to remember them well enough to engage in useful discussion with their teammates.

4. *Test for Audience Response.* Before Marvin Bower, managing director of McKinsey & Company, sent out a firmwide memorandum on any subject, he would show a draft to the three or four most cynical associates in the New York office. Almost invariably they would identify something in it that could easily be misinterpreted, which he would then rewrite.

The same idea applies to making videos, with particular reference to casting. A prominent corporation in downtown New York City, providing computerized services, chose one of their most attractive woman employees to play a certain part in a program they were developing. Much to their astonishment, she did not project the kind of person she really was. She came across as a lady of the streets! Fortunately they found this out in a pilot run of the program, so they were able to change it, but at considerable expense.

5. *Use More Visualization, Less Text.* The unique advantage of visual aids is to get quick understanding of ideas that cannot as easily be described in a sequence of words. In designing visual images, therefore, be sure to exploit this special benefit. Keep any text simple and concise. Reserve the fuller treatment for the participant's workbook or seminar reference text.

6. *Make Each Visual Count.* I attended a presentation by a prominent consulting firm once in which the consultant used a series of flip charts, mounted on an easel. As he turned from one sheet to the next, you could see that each page was filled from top to bottom with text in outline

form. There was so much on each page that it became clear it was an outline developed for the convenience of the presenter. He didn't need any notes. They were all on the flip charts for everyone to see! He later handed out copies of all these pages and that was his report!

To be sure, the example was a presentation rather than a seminar. But I have seen seminars, some of them from well-known firms, which were accompanied by a stack of overhead transparencies, each filled with text covering virtually every point mentioned in the participant's workbook — usually verbatim.

It's as simple as this: you don't need a visual for every single point to be made in the course of a seminar. You have to be selective, or else you're drowning the participants in a sea of information, and doing so in a monotonous way that will surely encourage some of the seminar goers to lose interest.

Video Cassettes, Computer Software, and Other Technologies

There is a wide variety of audio-visual systems available today, which means you have to choose your system, or combination of systems, in order to know what materials to provide for your seminar: video cassettes, computer software, overhead transparencies, 35mm slides, wall charts, etc.

In off-the-shelf programs provided by outside firms there is a great dependence on standard audio-visuals, most frequently video sequences, to facilitate the use of a program by many leaders to large populations. It is a way of ensuring that essentially the same message will be given to all participants.

With the vastly expanding possibilities being made available through emerging training technology (see Chapter 6), audio-visuals have become more than a support to the subject matter of a seminar. They may be the major educational vehicle themselves, as in the case of computer-based simulation and games.

The investment required in the equipment and software and the army of training professionals who have to learn to become comfortable with the new technology, both suggest that it may be many years before it is widely used in industry generally. Or so it seems to this observer, even though the larger industrial organizations throughout the world seem to be accepting it at a fairly rapid pace.

So let's review what's available today, recognizing that in the future the various elements may be put together into comprehensive, computer-driven systems that will add greatly to the total impact provided.

Video Cassettes. Probably the most widely used technique in recent years has been the use of video cassettes with a video cassette recorder (VCR) and a TV monitor, used increasingly with large-screen projection. It seems to have almost completely supplanted 16mm sound motion pictures for many obvious reasons. You don't have to dim the lights to see the presentation. It's much easier and less costly to make your own video sequences, using a video camera; and qualified professionals are readily available to help you do this. The projection is virtually noise-free, and the cassettes are much more portable than the old 16mm reels.

Most outside vendors have adopted this medium as their primary audio-visual aid. Prominent individual lecturers have also gone on videotape to extend themselves into new markets.

Powerful as this medium is, you do face a dilemma. This is such an age of television, that participants will unconsciously set high standards for any video dramatizations and sequences used. If you try to do your own scripts and use your own people in key roles, you may not measure up to their expectations. On the other hand, hiring a producer, scriptwriters, and theatrical professionals could push your program development costs into many hundreds of thousands of dollars.

But there may be a solution. There are outside professionals who can help you produce video sequences quite inexpensively. I collaborated with one of them recently. He is extremely shrewd in selecting company employees who will project well on screen. They play the same roles that they play on the job and don't have to memorize any lines. After a brief orientation, he takes and retakes each short scene until he gets what he wants, coaching between takes as necessary. His success is due in large part to his skillful editing in the final production process.

The main disadvantage of video has been the difficulty of changing the sequence of the images, but with the new computerized technology that disadvantage seems to be disappearing. Program leaders will have a much greater capability to determine their own sequencing.

The Overhead Projector. Probably still the most widely used visual aid is the overhead projector, which projects only still, visual images. Its many strong advantages seem to outweigh its disadvantages.

It has great versatility, good definition, and can be operated directly by the program leader who supplies the audio accompaniment. There is usually no need to dim the normal lighting in the room. Direct eye contact with the seminar participants is maintained, and presenters can easily change the sequence of the transparencies or return to one previously shown. You can write on blank acetate sheets in much the same way as you would on an easel pad.

These advantages outweigh the relatively few shortcomings of overhead projectors. But for the record, here are its demerits. First of all, it does not project photographic images. This is its most important disadvantage as compared to, say, the 35mm slide projector.

Another limitation is that the image projected on the screen will be larger at the top than at the bottom — the "keystone" effect — because it will be farther away from the light source than the bottom of the screen. It *is* possible to use an attachment to tip the top of the screen forward, but for some reason these attachments are not routinely available at most seminar sites.

A related problem that sometimes develops is a difficulty in getting the image level on the screen. Any minor difference in the distance between the projector and each side of the screen will raise this problem. You have to keep adjusting the angle of the screen or the projector to get a level image. Some projectors are equipped with a control that makes it easy to raise one side of the unit to adjust the image. If not, you sometimes have to slip pads of paper or books under the unit until the image is level. If you are the type of person who goes around the house straightening pictures on the walls, you may find this problem particularly annoying.

For very large groups, most overhead projectors will not throw a strong enough image to fill up a large screen, which is another disadvantage as compared to 35mm slides. But in a seminar setting, we are usually talking about small enough groups so that this is not a serious disadvantage.

Another problem is that the upright arm can interfere with the vision of some participants. There are models available that permit you to fold the arm down when the projector is not in use, which is greatly to be desired. Otherwise, your only recourse is to remove the equipment when not in use.

Finally, in setting up the screen you have to position it to avoid any ceiling lights. These can obliterate the projected image. Sometimes you'll need to call the maintenance people to unscrew a ceiling light bulb.

On balance, however, the overhead projector is a very satisfactory, relatively inexpensive method for adding visual support to a presentation. It will continue to be widely used even though it will be displaced in many companies by computer-driven systems.

The 35mm Projector.   A 35mm slide projector equipped with a carousel slide holder is another visual aid technique, but one that is more appropriate for large audiences than for the typical seminar group. It provides a superior image and, unlike the overhead projector, will project photographic images—and do so with great clarity and definition. Furthermore, 35mm slides can be produced at far less cost than prepared overhead transparencies.

However, the machine has to be placed a great distance from the screen. You have to use a long extension cord if you want to position yourself before or near the screen, or else you have to have a projection booth with remote controls, which can add considerable expense. In either event, the presenters need to have a method for knowing exactly what slides are coming up so their remarks will be synchronized with the slides.

A further real disadvantage is that the lights in the room have to be dimmed in order to get the greatest clarity in the projected image. This feature is the reason why this technique is not widely used in conducting seminars. If you have to be constantly running back and forth to a light switch on the wall, it can be both bothersome and disconcerting. Sometimes there is no middle ground because of the existing lighting system in the seminar room. You either have to have too much light or virtually none at all. The latter situation makes it difficult for participants to take notes (and easier to sneak in a short nap).

Easel Pad.   No seminar leader can function without a large-size (usually 30- by 40-inch) paper pad mounted on an easel. It has so many uses. You can record key points brought out in group discussions, which adds emphasis to each point and gives the group an opportunity to reflect on it. You can tear pages off and tape them to the wall for continuing display. You can flip back to previous pages to make a cross-reference. You can write down assignments made to subgroups or evening assignments. Comparisons or relationships can sometimes more easily be explained through diagrams on the easel pad.

Because of its great versatility, the easel pad seems to have largely replaced the blackboard and, to a lesser degree, the plastic composition board—both of which have to be continuously erased and thus cannot store information for later reference.

Wall Charts and Display Boards.   Wall charts and display boards probably have to be used in conjunction with other media. They are too bulky to carry the entire visual aid load, but they can add importance to key points. They can also provide a continuing reference.

For example, if participants are engaged in an extended problem-solving exercise, it can be a great help to have the seven steps of the problem-solving process displayed on the wall. Everyone can easily see it and can refer to it at will.

Rear-View Projection.   Most of the techniques reviewed that involve the projection of images can be used in combination with rear-view projection facilities and equipment. That is, they can be placed in a soundproofed room behind the screen — not in the seminar room at all. The one exception is the overhead projector, which has to be operated directly by the program leader in order to benefit from its great versatility.

The effect can be very dramatic, especially with the use of projected video images and extra-large screens. But it is expensive, requires considerably more floor space, and if something goes wrong, the seminar leader is not in control.

I was using a series of 35mm slides once in a training center that featured rear-view projection and the use of two projectors that would alternately fade in and fade out. The local equipment expert proudly showed off the equipment to me and loaded my slides alternately onto the two projectors.

What I didn't know at the time was the critical issue of which projector would start first and should therefore have slides numbered 1, 3, 5, 7, etc. When I launched into my presentation, I quickly realized that the sequence appearing on the screen was 2, 1, 4, 3, 6, 5, etc., which greatly confused the audience as well as the presenter. But the control panel I was working had no means of correcting this! All I could do was to proceed without the benefit of my slides.

In any event, as you plan and develop your participant workbook and preseminar assignment, your leader's guide, and audio-visual support materials, you have to make them all fit together in a coherent whole. And you have to fit it all into the time schedule fixed in the seminar design. The best way to do this is through practice presentations made in the course of training your seminar leaders, which is covered in the next chapter. These people will come up with a large number of suggestions, some of which you will want to use to make your seminar materials even better.

8

How to Get the Most Out of Your Seminar Leaders

An effective seminar leader is the next link in the chain of prerequisites for a successful training seminar. The best-designed seminar with top educational materials is nevertheless subject to this further variable: the knowledge, attitudes, and skills of the seminar leader. Whether you use members of your own staff, non-training department employees, or consultants, you have to be concerned with selecting, training, and motivating them to continued peak performance.

The emphasis among these three concerns will differ depending on the resource you are using. If you or some qualified person on your staff will be the seminar leader, you will be less concerned about the material in this chapter on selecting seminar leaders. You've already gone through the selection process.

Training and motivating will be of greatest importance when you are using non-training department employees on a part-time, special assignment. Chances are you don't know them too well, and success in their special assignment is not crucial to their future in the company.

Qualified consultants should come ready-trained. And in most cases they will be properly motivated, since their professional careers depend on their continued excellence. This will be particularly true if they have

participated in the program development, which often is the case. They
want as much as you do to see it be a resounding success.

Why You Have to Select Your
Seminar Leaders Carefully

One way or another, selecting the right person as seminar leader is a
necessary starting point. Some people can do a superior job. Some are
merely adequate. And some simply cannot lead stimulating seminars.
Somehow we have to end up better than "adequate" and as close to "superior" as we possibly can.

Anyone who has had experience in training people to conduct seminars will tell you that there can be a wide gap between the best and the
least qualified of any group. I have had a great deal of experience
teaching client personnel to put on Allen seminars. It is a matter of
great concern to me, because of my reputation and the firm's, that I
don't entrust our programs to leaders who lack the ability to make them
"sing."

To illustrate, I had to train two people from two different client organizations in one of our programs at the same time, a while back. Both
were experienced in various personnel functions, including training.
Both were attractive, articulate, and seemingly self-confident. But when
I put them through some "dry runs" or practice presentations, it turned
out they were worlds apart.

One of the two obviously enjoyed being "on stage." Her words came
easily and clearly, her eyes confidently seeking out members of the
make-believe audience. The other was unbelievably inept. He had trouble finding the right words to express his ideas. He rambled. He let his
eyes wander around the room and, at one point, even focus on the ceiling! He simply could not be qualified as a trainer for our program.

For another example, a newly appointed "training specialist" proved
to be clearly inadequate as a discussion leader. He had been transferred
from field sales and was being trained in one of our programs as a first
step in his new job. After discussing the problem with his new boss, we
all decided—including the training specialist—that we were fortunate to
discover his inadequacies at the outset. It could have proved to be a serious problem for this individual, and his career, if he had been allowed
to continue in his new job to become a highly visible failure.

Sometimes the problem is not one of ability but one of attitude. The
problem occurs in two ways. One recurring situation is the disinclina-
tion of experienced trainers to go through a leader training program. It
is "beneath them." They think that all they need is a good leader's guide

and they can put a program over because of their great platform skills. Unfortunately, that is usually not the case.

The other kind of attitude problem is evidenced by the lack of commitment of a professional trainer to a program procured or developed by a predecessor. There is no emotional ownership. By way of recent example, a training director inherited an off-the-shelf program purchased by her predecessor with some left-over budget money. Quite naturally, she viewed the program as someone else's. If it doesn't go over, she will feel it is the fault of the program. She will not perceive it as her own lack of commitment.

What to Look for in Your Seminar Leader

What criteria should you use, then, in selecting your seminar leader? Here are some ideas I have accumulated from personal experience and observation and from discussions with other professionals in the field.

Credibility

First of all, the person you put before trainee groups should be someone whose position, background, and/or personal impact predisposes these groups to accept the ideas to be presented to them. The outside consultant usually carries high credibility, but it's worth checking. In choosing from within, give preference to line managers and higher-ranking people. The need for credibility is more difficult to satisfy with higher-level participant groups, which probably explains the proportionately greater use of consultants at executive levels as compared to lower-level groups.

Personal Effectiveness

The personal impact of the seminar leader is a second important criterion. It is closely related to credibility but nevertheless has a somewhat different focus. Those who are perceived as "winners" or "comers" will tend to be more successful in gaining the full acceptance of trainee groups. And, by the way, these people usually have the same perception of themselves. "Presence" and "bearing" are hard to define, but you can tell them when you see them.

Remember the television debates between Jimmy Carter and Ronald Reagan in 1980? Mr. Carter appeared worried and ill at ease. Helped no doubt by his acting background, Mr. Reagan projected an image of relaxed self-confidence. The difference in personal impact surely must have had an effect at the polling booths.

Commitment

Look for people who have a high, positive motivation toward training, people who enjoy getting up in front of other people. Most people find the experience stressful, but the kind of person to look for is one who literally "blossoms" in front of others.

The wrong way to go about the selection process is seen in the experience of one large, commercial bank in New York City. The bank deliberately chose as the instructor for each separate session of a modular training program, the officer of the bank who most needed improvement in the subject matter of that session! In other words, the worst delegator had to teach delegation, and the worst communicator, communicating. The idea was they had to learn their subject completely before they could teach it. But being selected in this autocratic way did not ensure the personal commitment of each instructor. It was no wonder that the whole program received a mediocre response.

Discussion Leadership Skills

The ultimate success of seminar leaders will depend on their skill in drawing people into group discussions and in guiding these discussions along productive paths. Look for prior successful experience. If this is not available, here are some personal attributes that I have generally found in people who become effective discussion leaders; some of these can only be fully tested in the leader training process.

1. Oral communication facility
2. Presence in front of groups
3. Sensitivity to people, being able to "read them"
4. Being a good listener
5. Adaptability
6. Native intelligence, quickness of mind
7. Sense of humor
8. Warmth of personality

Knowledge of Subject Matter

Although not always essential, some degree of knowledge and experience in the subject matter is certainly a plus. It not only facilitates the leader training process, it gives the seminar leader personal experiences and insights to share with participant groups, adding both interest and credibility.

If you are looking for someone to do management training, look for individuals with actual management experience. If you are looking for someone to teach written communications, look for someone whose writings have been published.

By way of analogy, I know of some university professors who lack all the generally accepted hallmarks of effective oral communication but whose reputation in some field is so great as to hold students literally spellbound.

How to Train Seminar Leaders

Once they have been selected, seminar leaders have to be properly trained to ensure the success of the seminar. The extent and intensity of this training will vary, depending on the subject matter and the preexisting knowledge and skills of the leader selected. The danger here is to assume too much. It is far better to err somewhat on the side of too much training, being sensitive on occasion to protecting the egos of those trainers who may consider themselves already fully qualified.

Scope

The scope of leader training provided, at least to non-professionals in the field, should include the following.

Subject Matter Content. Your seminar leaders should know the subject matter of the seminar so well that they exude confidence. They don't have to worry about the next subject coming along, so they can concentrate on the reactions of the participant group. They know they can deal effectively with any question that might be posed.

Adult Learning Process. They should also be made to understand what is involved in the adult learning process so that they can properly fulfill their role. If they understand that the first step is motivation, they are much more likely to stress the importance and relevance of each new subject as it comes along. If they understand the significance of testing, application, and feedback, they are far less likely to resort to pure lecture to secure understanding. They will seek out contributions from the group and provide opportunities for participants to demonstrate the quality of learning that is taking place.

The Seminar Design.   Only with a sound understanding of the seminar's design can your seminar leaders make sound adaptations to meet the needs of different participant groups. The leader's guide serves as the primary educational tool during leader training and serves as a primary reference thereafter.

Discussion Leadership Techniques.   Your future seminar leaders should know how to use open questions and directed questions to initiate group discussion. They need to know how to encourage the sharing of relevant experiences while at the same time exercising control over the direction and extent of the discussion. They'll need to know how to deal with those who dominate discussions, those who don't participate, those who may talk to each other during group discussions, those who challenge the leader, those who are always late getting back to class, etc.

Management of Audio-Visual Aids.   As computer-driven systems are used increasingly to provide simulation or simply to reinforce subject matter understanding, trainers need to become versed in operating these systems. Even simple video systems can present problems to the uninitiated.

Administration and Logistics.   Particularly important for non-training department, part-time seminar leaders is a complete orientation on administration and logistics. How are participants selected? What is the schedule of seminars? How are schedule changes to be made? Who is in charge of securing the facility, making room reservations, arranging for equipment, getting participant workbooks to the seminar site? How about name plates? Participant rosters? How do you deal with people who have to miss portions of the class? All relevant questions of this nature should be covered during the leader training session.

Method

The method to be used in training seminar leaders will vary, depending on the type of seminar, the subject matter, and the number and preexisting qualifications of the seminar leader nominees. The greatest care and attention will be required for new trainers or line managers on part-time assignment. To a greater or lesser extent, you have to consider the appropriate use of self-study, workshops, self-evaluation, auditing others, and learning by doing. Usually some combination of these will be most appropriate.

Self-Study.   In the final analysis, learning comes from within. People can be helped to learn in many ways, but it is really up to them. Self-study or self-development, using materials that you can provide, has to be a primary means of training your seminar leaders. They have to be provided with appropriate leader's guides, in some cases computer-based training modules, and pertinent texts. If you have a group of trainers, you can suggest to them that they form study groups to reinforce each other's learning.

Workshops.   Group sessions with practice presentations and critiques represent another useful method, a prerequisite where groups are being trained. Practice presentations with videotaping and playback and group critiques take up the major portion of these workshops.

The group critiques have to be managed carefully so as to build and not weaken the participants' self-confidence. Get your trainees to critique themselves before you turn it over to the group or offer your suggestions.

It's a good idea to coach the group at the outset on how to provide and accept suggestions that are constructive. "Try it again, Bill, and this time come through with greater confidence" is much easier to take than, "You didn't seem to have a command of your material." Impress on them the importance of selecting a very few points for improvement — the most important ones — after each practice presentation. And, of course, be a role model yourself.

Learning by Example.   In training new members of our own professional staff, we have found through the years that they can learn a great deal by auditing experienced professionals. Your seminar leaders can do likewise, if the program they are supposed to lead is already up and running. It is an especially efficient method if you have only one person, or possibly two people, to train. It doesn't involve additional time demands on any of your people, since presumably they would be giving the seminars anyway.

But there is a caution here. Your trainees should not model themselves too closely on someone else. They should recognize that they have to develop their own style — one that is comfortable for them. A good example is the use of humor. Some people have a great gift for knowing when a funny story would provide a needed break in the action and for putting it across successfully. Others have trouble with jokes and should avoid them. A punch line that gets no laughs can be an embarrassment to the leader and to the participants.

Learning by Doing.   Seminar leader skills are developed, in the final analysis, by practice in conducting seminars. Just as golfers develop skills on the practice tee or on the golf course, seminar leaders become proficient by actually conducting seminars. Practice presentations during the training period can simulate conducting the seminar but obviously are not the real thing. You don't have an eager group of trainees looking up at you expectantly.

We would recommend that you give each seminar leader a live audience as soon after the formal training as possible. You might consider dividing a presentation up among two or three newly trained leaders to reduce the element of stress on any one of them. It also helps to audit one of their early efforts to provide constructive criticism, with a special eye to building their confidence.

How to Motivate Seminar Leaders

Now that you have tour-trained seminar leaders, how do you ensure their continued enthusiastic commitment? If you have a sound seminar design and good educational materials, you have enhanced the probability of success for your program leaders. You will have given them the opportunity to experience the thrill of success, which in itself is a powerful motivator. If you have selected the right people and trained them well, they will get great ego gratification provided by the esteem of successive seminar classes. Nevertheless, it is important to be alert for possible signs of lessening commitment. Keep in mind some of the motivational factors that might be involved and help your people understand and benefit from them.

Growth and Development

The opportunity for growth and development is one of them. It may well be what attracted your people to become seminar leaders in the first place. Much of this learning will come naturally, but it helps to make sure your people are aware of their growing capabilities.

Every teacher will admit that learning within the seminar room is a two-way street. It provides a learning opportunity for the leader as well as for the attendees. Sometimes this learning comes via direct contributions from the participants who may have some special experience of knowledge to share. Other times it comes from difficult questions which force the leader to new depths of understanding to respond meaningfully to them. Some seminar leaders find a special challenge in constantly exploring new ways of teaching difficult or complex ideas. They respond well to opportunities to trade these ideas with others who are presenting the same program.

Ego Gratification

"I look for people who went out for dramatics in school and college," commented one training director. "It's a clue that they really enjoy being 'on stage.'" The quote highlights the second motivational factor: ego gratification or the emotional need to experience the favorable response of others.

The analogy to dramatics is a good one. Those who are patrons of the live stage talk about the magical rapport that builds between players and audience. The favorable response of the audience acts as an emotional stimulant to the actors and actresses. Even though the same line may have been given hundreds of times before, there is a new freshness, a new spontaneity that comes directly from the action and reaction that takes place across the footlights.

Some of the best trainers I know have huge ego needs. They need to be continuously fed by the appreciation and response of participant groups. These people will tell you that the same electric rapport that develops across the footlights in a theater also develops between trainer and trainees in a seminar. They sometimes make a game of it, with successive classes—to see how long it takes them to "win over" each one.

Achievement

A third motivational factor, a sense of achievement, is also present in a seminar setting. Some of it is intangible, coming out of a realization that the participants are in fact learning. Some of it comes verbally from the participants themselves, either directly to the leader during the course of the program or in written evaluations at its close.

Professional trainers also find a sense of achievement in testing and making modifications in the way they present certain subjects. So long as these variations do not affect the integrity of the seminar, they should be encouraged and given adequate recognition. Sometimes the modifications can be built back into the official leader's guide or communicated in some way to the other leaders of the same seminar.

Hardly a seminar session goes by without some participant asking the presenter: "How many times a year do you give this program?" It seems difficult for participants to realize that each class is different, made up of different personalities with different backgrounds and experience, interacting and reacting in different way. Group discussions take new twists, new questions are asked, and modifications are always being tested out by the presenter.

Recognition

The fourth motivational factor, recognition, is probably more directly under the training director's control than the other three. Therefore, it may be the most important. By recognition, we mean more than the response of the seminar participants, although that is also important. Rather, we are referring to the type of recognition that a training director or company management can provide.

One of our associates has for some years conducted a specially designed management program for higher-level managers in a prominent publishing company. It had become customary for the president of the company to join the group for cocktails and dinner. On this particular occasion our associate was unable to attend the social function, although he had been presenting the management program. However, he learned afterward that the president had singled him out, by name, for some very complimentary remarks during the course of the evening. (I suspect the president knew that his comments would get back to the seminar leader.)

The example suggests one important way of providing recognition, but there are others. Don't underestimate your own influence as training director. "I notice that you again topped all presenters in the participant evaluations you got last week, Muriel. That's really great. It's important for the participants in our programs to find them to be a positive experience. I especially liked one of the 'open end' comments about the fine way you got everybody to participate in group discussions."

Don't overlook opportunities to make special presentations to top management or to make special mention in newsletters or the company's internal publication. Awards and certificates of special achievement can be given. A letter from the senior vice president, human resources—or from the president of the company—can sometimes be used with good effect. But in all instances, these measures have to be sincere and in response to specific demonstrated accomplishment.

This type of recognition can help to maintain the continuing commitment of your trainers. But the other motivational factors—growth and development, ego gratification, and a sense of achievement—are very much dependent on selecting the right people to present the seminars and giving them the training that will ensure success.

9

Setting
the Stage

The best-designed seminar conducted by a skilled program leader may nevertheless fail if the seminar setting is wrong. Decisions involving the seminar room and layout are the most important, but the geographic location and supporting services and facilities have to be considered as well.

The subject has been overlaid with a new complex dimension as teleconferencing is beginning to take hold. In some cases, we may be talking about a complex of locations, geographically dispersed, and possibly in different time zones. A new constraint has been added as well: the availability of teleconferencing equipment. The centrally generated program has to be received and projected on a suitable screen, and the questions and inputs of remotely located participants have to be transmitted back to the program source.

These needs may complicate decisions on the setting, at least initially, since we now have to consider the setting for the transmission of the program and multiple settings for the remote participants. Once a satisfactory network has been established, it can presumably be reused as needed. Some experts in the field are predicting a greater use of company conference rooms, linking various company locations together, which can be used for a wide variety of meetings as well as for training seminars.

Empire Blue Cross/Blue Shield has electronic links with its various locations in New York State which are already in frequent use for purposes of business conferences. Plans are under way to use the same network for training purposes. Systems such as this will doubtlessly become commonplace in the years ahead for organizations that are spread among multiple locations. As mentioned earlier, some of our universities are already offering televised seminars to remote audiences. Stanford and M.I.T., and doubtlessly many others, are also doing so.

If you have already entered the age of teleconferencing and established a network that meets your recurring needs, you'll find that you'll be skimming much of this chapter. If you have not yet done so, you'll find some ideas that may be useful in setting one up. Yet, I suspect that there will continue to be large numbers of companies and other organizations who will be using the more traditional approach to seminar sites. In any event, here are some ideas gained from actual experience which should prove helpful in finding the proper site for your seminar.

Why the Setting is Important

A good environment can't ensure success, but a poor one can mean failure. If the participants can't see well, can't hear well, or are physically uncomfortable, they're not going to be able to learn very much. The same result comes about if the total setting is psychologically depressing or if there are distractions. Here are a few cases in point.

The training director of one prominent electronics company, headquartered in Massachusetts, for reasons known only to himself, seemed to take delight in finding unusual places for holding seminars. One such site was a religious retreat located on a hill in a suburb of Boston. You might think that the overall spirit of peace, quiet, and spiritual dedication would be a plus, but you would be wrong. The sleeping rooms were small and bare, reminding one of cells in a medieval monastery. There was barely room for one straight-back chair, one plain dresser, and a narrow bed. The walls were painted an off-white, toward-tan color and had nothing on them—not even a religious picture.

The only place that teams could use to meet on their evening case assignments was a large reception lounge on the ground floor. It worked reasonably well for this purpose on the first night—each team congregating in a separate corner of the room—but on two successive evenings, the lounge filled up with people noisily enjoying each other's company as they gathered for an evening religious service. There was a brief respite during the service, but afterward they were all in the lounge chattering happily with each other. The noise level was amplified by echoes from the uncarpeted floor and bare walls. Here and there, hardly observable within this milling mass of people, a participant team could be seen huddled together trying to discuss a Universal Products Company case.

On another occasion, because of airport connection problems, the seminar leader arrived 2 minutes late for a seminar scheduled to start at

easy access
personal accom
space

9:00 A.M. in the Hilton Hotel at O'Hare Airport outside Chicago. She arrived to find twenty large individuals seated classroom style in a room that was no larger than a standard guest room with beds removed. It seemed to her that the oxygen in the room was close to being completely exhausted, replaced by the carbon dioxide emanating from all those lungs in a small room with a low ceiling.

The client coordinator had brought an overhead projector and screen, as planned, but because of the small size of the room they had to be positioned so closely together that the projected image was no larger than a standard letter-size sheet of paper.

Fortunately, the hotel was able to provide a larger room, but a half day of the seminar was lost securing and moving into that room. Many sarcastic remarks were made when the seminar leader brought up the subject of "planning" during the seminar!

How to Select the Location

Geographic location is the question that usually is presented first in planning the seminar setting. Though geography may not be as important as the seminar room itself, you usually have to make decisions on overall location before you can identify and evaluate available alternatives on individual facilities, seminar room, and supporting services.

Choosing the geographic location may end up as a matter of established precedent or personal preference, but there are some factors worth considering before you make an intuitive decision. It may be time to rethink past practices and personal bias.

If your company has its own training facility, you probably want to use it. Many corporations have made substantial investments in a corporate training facility and equipped it to meet the specifications of the training function. If you're with one of these companies, the question you face is the extent to which you want to bring in participants from other corporate locations to the corporate facility, or whether you want to use other locations to reduce travel expense. You may want to consider teleconferencing so that groups of trainees in other locations can participate in the seminar at the same time.

My own bias, for what it's worth, is to use teleconferencing when the training situation is not heavily dependent upon interaction among the participants. You wouldn't plan a management training seminar for 40 or 50 people in the same room because there wouldn't be an adequate opportunity for each person to get actively involved. So why would you do it for 40 or 50 people spread over three or four locations?

If you don't have a company facility, you come squarely face to face with

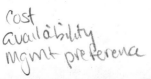

the question of location. Do you want to hold it sufficiently near company headquarters so that you can arrange for high-ranking executives to meet with your participant groups at an evening social hour? That also poses a temptation for those participants whose offices are at company headquarters to get in an hour or two at their work stations before the seminar begins and at the end of each day. In most cases this effort will detract from the learning they are expected to get at the seminar.

A location reasonably convenient to the largest component of the target population is usually the determining factor. It tends to reduce travel costs and time away from the job. If most of the attendees can commute in the way that they normally would, you have found a cost-effective solution.

But there may be other considerations. If you have just opened a new plant or a new laboratory, you might want to use the seminar as an easy way to give people a chance to visit it. If you have just acquired some new businesses, you might want to get your new management population to have an opportunity to visit the corporate office and get to know people there.

We can't leave the question of location without some mention of "outdoor training."* It is also variously termed "adventure training" and "experimental training." The essence of this relatively new movement is to expose groups of trainees to a series of activities, often involving an element of risk, that are usually aimed at team building and enhancing decision-making skills. The debriefing sessions conducted by trained behavioral specialists are important parts of the experience.

Participation in these programs is highly stimulating and the movement has generated a loyal core of adherents. I have not personally conducted any such session, but based on my experience as a participant and inputs I get from other professionals, I believe it will have a limited though continuing role in the total training effort over the next decade. It appears to have a relatively narrow focus in terms of training objectives and is quite expensive in terms of both money and time away from the job.

How to Choose the Facility

Once you have selected your geographic location, you need to find a suitable facility in the area for the dates you have set up in your training

---

*See the March 1991 issue of the Training & Development Journal published by the American Society for Training and Development. It has three articles on outdoor training beginning on pages 50, 58, and 63, respectively.

schedule. There are quite a few different kinds of facilities that are likely to be available. You'll need to evaluate them in terms of cost, travel convenience, and quality of service. You'll see in Figure 8 a comparison of different types of facilities with my own view of the advantages and disadvantages of each. Let's consider each type for a moment.

Company Training Centers

In most cases, company training centers, if you have one, offer the best solution. Some are located in or close to the company headquarters, as in the case of Johnson & Higgins and Swiss Bank (New York branch). Others are removed from the company offices to reduce the risk of interruptions or the possibility that participants will be trying to hold down their regular jobs—before and after seminar hours.

In all likelihood, the training function has had an active role in setting specifications for the floor layout and installed equipment. The centers have been designed and built to facilitate learning. They should be ideal for your purposes.

Facility	Cost	Service	Access	Overall
Company conference center	No out-of-pocket cost	Good, but not lavish	Good	If you have one, use it
Company conference room	No out-of-pocket cost	Full services not required; breaks only	Excellent	Least costly, but potential too great for distractions and interruptions
In-town hotel	Expensive	Good	Excellent	Quite acceptable, if affordable
Conference center	Expensive	Excellent	Good	Ideal, if affordable
Suburban motor inn	Fairly expensive	Good	Good to excellent	Quite acceptable, more easily affordable
Remote retreat	Usually reasonable	Fair	Usually not too easily accessible	Varies

Figure 8. Comparison of different seminar facilities.

The more remote training centers often have sleeping accommodations, which makes it possible to make better use of evening assignments, particularly team exercises. There is a great sense of comraderie, and the commitment of the participants tends to be intensified by the greater and more informal opportunity they have to react with one another.

There is one small problem I have encountered with company training centers. They can induce a "rest and recreation" attitude on the part of attendees, which will lessen their commitment to learn. And yet, if they are too Spartan, employees may not be eager to go there.

In any event, as the pace of training escalates, we are likely to see more and more company training centers.

Company Conference Rooms

A company's own multi-purpose conference room in its regular place of business has no equal in terms of low cost and convenience. Commuting habits don't have to be changed — at least for the local attendees. Transportation and sleep-away costs are either completely avoided or reduced to a minimum.

But these benefits are largely counterbalanced by a number of real disadvantages. For one thing, some of the participants will find their regular offices nearby and succumb to the powerful temptation to keep an eye on how things are going. The result will be that they're late in the morning, late getting back from breaks, and exhausted from trying to do two things at once. They may miss whole blocks of time because of some emergency — real or perceived — that they uncover.

Another disadvantage is the convenience of these participants to their managers and colleagues. They may be called out for meetings or waylaid during breaks. All of which is a major distraction not only to them but to the other participants.

In-Town Hotels

Generally the in-town hotel offers easy transportation, attractive facilities, and good supporting services, although the extent of these advantages will differ from city to city and town to town.

But in major metropolitan centers like New York City, the cost can be very high, particularly if sleeping accommodations are needed. Also, if you are only scheduling one or two seminars, you do not represent especially attractive business for the hotel and may not get the service that you would like. Often, the seminar room will be used for other functions in the evening which means it probably won't be set up exactly right the next morning. Also, there may be some enticing evening distractions.

Conference Centers

Establishments that cater especially to organizations conducting training sessions for their employees are also an available choice. Understandably, they pay a great deal of attention to creating a favorable seminar environment. The meeting rooms are typically soundproof. The chairs provided are usually more comfortable than those provided by hotels. They don't have to be stacked for easy storage to make way for an evening non-seminar function. Lighting controls are provided that permit easy adjustment to different requirements. Temperature and ventilation controls are either accessible to the seminar leader or quickly adjusted as needed.

By way of example, in the eastern part of the United States there are the Harrison Conference Centers in Glen Cove, Long Island, and Southbury, Connecticut; the Tarrytown Conference Center in Tarrytown, New York, and many others. In other parts of the country there are the Southern Conference Center and Lanier Conference Center in Atlanta, Georgia; and the Woodlands Conference Center in Houston, Texas, to name only a few.

Suburban Motor Inns

The suburban motor inn has become a very popular location for holding training seminars, particularly for companies headquartered in the suburbs themselves. There is usually a fairly large selection to choose from in any desired geographic area and most of them feature easy transportation to a nearby airport. Generally, they offer attractive facilities and good supporting services. They tend to be less expensive than the in-town hotel and more interested in seminar business.

But suburban motor inns have disadvantages too. Their seminar rooms have to be used for multiple purposes: receptions, cocktail parties, or hospitality suites. As a result, many of them tend to favor movable partitions for walls to provide flexibility. But I have yet to find a room with movable partitions that was truly soundproof and have rarely found a sales representative who didn't say they were.

Then again, chairs may be designed for easy stacking instead of comfortable sitting. Lighting may be more appropriate to a social occasion than to a seminar and very likely will not be sufficiently under the control of the seminar leader. The rooms may be used in the evening for other events, which means that participants cannot leave things in the room, name plates will be disorganized, and the room will not be properly set up the next day.

The suburbs are not free from evening enticements. Almost without exception, a rock band with full electronic amplification will be playing from 9:00 P.M. to 1:00 A.M. or later. Many of these suburban inns have become lively social centers for the surrounding communities.

Remote Retreats

Some companies prefer getting their people away from civilization so that they can immerse themselves more completely in the business of learning. The remote retreat offers the least possibility for interruption and the greatest opportunity for mutual commitment and networking. That is, unless it is also a resort area that offers an enticing variety of athletic and recreational facilities.

One large publishing company that I know used to favor a motel in a remote location along the ocean in New Jersey during off-season. The motel looks right over the ocean but offers nothing by way of exercise or entertainment. Walkers and perhaps joggers can find an outlet for their energies—as can those who seek their fellowship at the bar. But the rather large proportion of younger people who are physical fitness–oriented miss the lack of exercise equipment and a swimming pool.

Charming as some of them can be, these remote retreats can present further problems. Transportation can be difficult. As a result, time away from the job can be increased simply by the amount of time it takes to get to and from the seminar site. Also, the quality of supporting services can be risky. If the facility is truly remote, there is a strong likelihood of limited menus, no valet service, few telephones, and certainly no room service.

Resorts

The use of resorts is generally reserved for off-season because of the cost involved. If the seminar is given at a time that is not completely off season, you probably need to provide time to take advantage of the golf course, tennis courts, and other recreational facilities. You'll find that many of these resorts are eager to develop off-peak revenue and will treat you well.

How to Select the Seminar Room

The selection of the seminar room is far more important to the success of the seminar than the geographic location and type of facility. The room in which the actual training will take place has to meet the physical and psychological needs of the participants and the leader.

In a very real sense, these needs resemble Frederick Herzberg's maintenance or hygiene needs with respect to motivation. If not met, these needs can have a negative influence, but they probably don't have a significant positive influence. Similarly, meeting the participants' physical needs probably won't contribute much to the learning process, but it can most certainly prevent distractions that could detract from the success of the seminar.

Physical Considerations

The minds of seminar participants cannot function with full effectiveness if their bodies are uncomfortable, for example, if they are too warm, if they are breathing stale air, if they are seated too close together, or if they are seated in uncomfortable chairs. Then again, they cannot learn at all if they cannot see or hear what is going on.

Temperature. Every experienced seminar leader knows the importance of being able to control the temperature. As the thermometer rises above 72°F, there is an increase in lethargy and drowsiness and a decrease in the quality of group discussion. Seminar leaders prefer the temperature to be slightly on the cool side, but please don't go below 66°F—or you again begin to lose the group.

All of this underlines the importance of having a room in which the seminar leader can measure and control the temperature. Remember, though, in regulating the temperature, that it is easy to go from one extreme to the other. If the room gets too warm, the tendency is to push the temperature control sharply toward cooler and to forget it—until it gets uncomfortably cool. This tendency to go to extremes is one reason that many facilities make the control accessible only to their own engineers.

Ventilation. Closely related to temperature is the need for circulating air. If the proportion of stale air goes up, the concentration and involvement of the group goes down. This consideration used to be far more important when cigarette smoking was freely allowed in seminars.

The need for fresh air favors larger rooms, higher ceilings, and, again, means for the seminar leader to control circulation — even if by so simple a means as being able to open windows. Fortunately, circulation is not usually a major problem in most modern facilities.

Vision.   Lighting and room size should be such that everyone can easily see the instructor, projected visual aids, easel pad or chalk pad, participant materials, and each other. Lighting controls should be conveniently located near the seminar leader's table, especially if the lights need to be dimmed to accommodate the projection equipment being used.

At one time, one of our clients featured the Engineers Club in New York City for holding their seminars. It was not what you'd call a modern facility, but it had a lot of old world charm. It wasn't until I saw so many references to the problem in the participant evaluations that I became aware that my face had been in shadow during the whole program. I never realized that this was a factor to consider until then. But when I thought about it, a lot of meaning comes across in facial expressions and eye-to-eye contacts. Without these, something is lost. No movie director would run the camera unless the faces of his main characters were clearly in view.

Hearing.   Making sure that everyone can hear what's going on is usually not so much of a problem with acoustics as it is a problem with interference. That's why I distrust movable partitions. They are never sufficiently soundproof to keep out the noise of a lively seminar going on behind them.

Unfortunately, noise interference is not always avoidable through careful planning. At about 9:00 A.M. one morning, a work crew with pneumatic drills attacked a sidewalk in need of repair directly under a second-floor seminar room at the Nassau Inn in Princeton, New Jersey. The noise was deafening, although intermittent. The arrival of these workers was something that could not have been anticipated when the facility was booked 6 months earlier, and it's not easily stopped when it happens. Although the incident became the subject of some good-humored comment, it nevertheless interfered with the learning process.

Sitting Comfort.   There are three different aspects to the problem of sitting comfort and they are all important, especially since most seminar attendees are unaccustomed to long periods of sitting in a classroom situation. The first is elbow room. Crowding people too closely together is to be avoided. Each person needs at least 2½ feet of space, preferably 3 feet at the seminar table.

The second is knee room. In setting up the room, try to avoid having people sit right up against table legs. It will be just your luck to have the long-legged basketball types get those locations, and they'll fidget their way through the whole day!

The third is comfortable chairs. Ideally they should come with ample cushioning and springs. A plain wooden chair can become exceedingly uncomfortable over the long haul. I remember when I was president of Loral Corporation being invited to an orientation session by I.B.M. There were only about eight chairs in the room—easy chairs that swiveled around at will. They were positioned seemingly at random within an octagonal room the walls of which turned out to be screens for rear-view projectors. The whole effect was overwhelming—and exquisitely comfortable.

Sometimes, in spite of adequate chairs, we encounter people with a physical problem that makes sitting for long periods actually painful. This was explained to me by the chairman of the board of a large, new client, who had a bad leg. Every so often with an engaging smile, he would stand up for 5 or 10 minutes at his place around the table. Even though we all understood the reason behind it, it always came as a bit of a shock. The first few times, I thought he was getting up to make a speech. But no, that wasn't the case. He simply had to stretch his leg. I was careful on succeeding days to place his name card at one end or other of the U-shaped table so that it was easier for him to get up.

Actually, one of the reasons I favor frequent team exercises is to give the participants an opportunity to move around a little, even if it is only to move their chairs back and form a circle away from the seminar table. People can get tired sitting in the same position for too long.

Psychological Considerations

Influences on the mental outlook of the group are almost as important as sheer physical comfort. The seminar room should be attractive and pleasing rather than discordant, and the whole setting should be free from distraction.

Decor. The overall color scheme and decoration plan can have an influence on the attitudes of the participants. Of course, peoples' tastes will differ. You can't always please everybody. It's probably best to avoid extremes of design and color, but don't bother to hire your own design expert. Your own judgment on what is reasonably attractive is sufficient.

Space. Rooms that are too small or that have low ceilings can induce a feeling of psychological imprisonment in some people. You are better off to err on the side of spaciousness and higher ceilings. More space in the room makes it easier to give people enough space at the seminar table and to form breakaway team meetings without the need for separate breakaway rooms.

I can only recall one time that the seminar room was actually too large. It was a huge ballroom with a stage at one end, which of course we didn't use. Even at that, it worked reasonably well. We put the U-shaped table at one end of the ballroom, with a number of circular tables for breakaway subgroup meetings spread around at the other end.

Noise.   Noise can be a mental distraction as well as a barrier to hearing. One of my professional colleagues shared an experience in point with me. At 3:00 P.M. during a seminar he was conducting, sounds of dance music could be heard floating up from a ballroom located below the seminar room. It was off-season in one of those resort locations. The motor inn was holding a tea dance for the enjoyment of a large population of retired citizens from the neighborhood. They were obviously having a great time; but some of the familiar dance tunes started a few trainees to tap their feet in time and their minds to reminisce. The music wasn't loud enough to prevent anyone from hearing the seminar leader, but it was a real mental distraction.

Visual Distractions.   Visual distractions can also get in the way, which is one reason I disfavor windows in the seminar room. The participants love them though. They like to look out. It gives them less of a feeling of captivity, I guess.

But listen to this story. It could happen to you, although probably not in such a dynamic fashion. The setting is a resort hotel on the Isle of Capri. One whole wall of the seminar room consisted of double-paned glass, overlooking a beautiful swimming pool complete with deck chairs and attractive plantings. It was in fact a pleasant and restful outlook for most of the first morning. But about 11:00 A.M. a group of young women in their teens descended on the pool wearing bikini bathing suits! There was absolute chaos in the all-male, away-from-home seminar group.

How to Set Up the Seminar Room

You've already heard me refer to a U-shaped seminar table, which is greatly to be preferred with groups that number from 8 to 20 or even 25 participants. The reasons are simple. All the participants are facing each other, which greatly facilitates group discussion. They can also see the instructor at the open end of the U and the place cards identifying everyone by name (see Figure 9).

For groups of seven or fewer you don't need the U shape. A circular, oval, or rectangular table can be used, with the seminar leader seated at one end. It gives a more informal, intimate feeling. You probably have to have any projection equipment on separate tables or stands away from the conference table so that there is an unobstructed view of all participants during periods of discussion.

For groups larger than 20 or 25 there are two options, if you can't conveniently break the group up into separate seminars (which is to be preferred if you can do it). One is to position the class around round

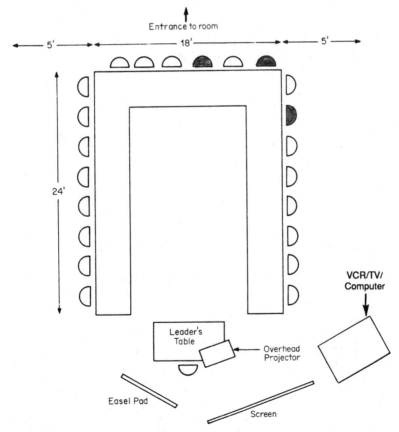

Figure 9. Preferred setup for a 20-participant seminar.

tables, each table becoming a separate team for team exercises. The second is to line them up in rows, classroom style. Sometimes you can find ways for participants in the first row to turn around and form a team with others in the second row. But, the first option is better if you can arrange for a lot of team exercises.

The rationale behind the equipment layout is to create a better learning environment, for which there are few absolute rules — especially now, when different configurations of computer-driven systems are coming into use. Seminar leaders have to position these in a way that is convenient for them to operate, ideally without interfering with the vision of the participants and without turning their backs on the class.

Overhead projectors can be conveniently placed on the leader's table, if it has a collapsible arm, or on a separate table that can be moved to prevent the upright arm from interfering with the view of the leader, if it does not. The projection screen can be placed behind the leader. If convenient, it is preferable to place it slightly to one side to permit the leader to step away on the other side to more easily get out of the field of vision of participants looking at the screen.

The easel pad should be positioned in accordance with the leader's hand dominance. A right-handed leader will want the pad on the left to make it easier to face partially toward the class while using the easel. A left-handed leader will prefer it on the right.

Lecterns are to be avoided: they encourage stand-up lecturing and excessive use of notes. They discourage informal give and take.

How to Ensure Acceptable Supporting Services

If you have found the perfect seminar room and arranged for the right setup, you still have to consider the surrounding facilities and services. The overall atmosphere of a place, the attitude of its staff, its scenic outlook, the quality of the food served, the comfort of its sleeping accommodations, and the availability of physical exercise and recreation — all of these can play a part in making the seminar a pleasant experience. But the more you insist on top quality, the more it's going to cost.

Problems with a facility are more likely to occur if it is not a conference center or a well-established hotel chain. Here — obtained from bitter experience — are the kinds of problems you may face.

1. Slow meal service, making people late for the afternoon session

2. Break service not on time, with disappointed trainees milling around the halls

3. Telephones ringing in the seminar room, interrupting the flow of discussion

4. Not enough public telephones near the seminar room, with lines forming and people returning late from breaks

5. Rest rooms inconveniently located

6. Sleeping rooms too near the loud rock music in the bar

7. Poor food quality or too limited a menu

8. Insufficient physical exercise facilities

9. Too few recreation facilities

10. Uncooperative staff

11. Poor message service

12. No credit cards accepted

Many of these problems can be avoided by a personal visit to the facility and by checking with others who have used it. It's surprising how attractive even dreary places can be made to look in brochures. A seminar just the right size and shape may have a pillar in the middle of the room.

Securing the right facility within the funds available is a challenge that involves geographical convenience, some degree of isolation from participants' ongoing job responsibilities, pleasant surroundings, adequate supporting services and—above all—a seminar room that encourages learning. In Figure 10 we have provided a checklist that can help establish the proper setting for your training seminar.

THE ROOM
  Lighting
  Ventilation
  Temperature
THE LAYOUT
  Number of places set
  Spacing of participant chairs
  Arrangement of tables
  Table and chair for leader
  Space for breakaway groups
  Water glasses and pitchers
THE EQUIPMENT
  Positioning of screen and overhead projector
  TV/VCR setup
  Computer setup
  Extension wires taped down
  Spare bulbs
  Location and type of easel pad
THE MATERIALS
  Participant workbooks, rosters, and place cards
  Overhead transparencies and blank acetate sheets
  Felt-tip pens for overhead and easel
  Leader's biography
  Handouts
  Wall charts, maps, exhibits
  Pointer
  Pads and pencils
SUPPORTING SERVICES
  Time schedule for breaks and lunch
  Location of breaks
  Menu
  Telephones and telephone messages
  Rest room locations
  Appropriate dress in dining rooms

Figure 10. Seminar checklist.

10

How to Manage the Seminar Delivery

Up to now, we have been concerned with all the things that have to take place in advance of the seminar. In this chapter and the next two, we are on the firing line. We have come in our narrative to the seminar itself. We need to consider now all the things that have to go right during the delivery of the seminar to give it maximum effectiveness.

The focal point now shifts from the training director to the seminar leader, who may often be the same person. Here is the payoff. If everything has been done right to this point, the odds greatly favor success. But the chances are that not everything *has* gone right, which provides a continuing challenge to seminar leaders. Now they have to manage the delivery of the seminar, including groups of 15 to 25 trainees who themselves represent a mixture of experience, personalities, and motivation.

The managerial role of seminar leaders in delivering the seminar can easily be overlooked. Their role as communicators, covered in the next chapter, is more dramatic and visible. But think about it. They have to *plan* and *control* the progress of the seminar. They have to *organize* people into subgroups or teams and *delegate* work to them. They have to *select* people to answer questions or otherwise participate in the seminar. They have to *motivate* people through encouragement and recognition. And they have to manage the provision of supporting services.

Why You Need to Double
Check All Arrangements

Presumably, most of the planning has already been done when seminar leaders arrive at the seminar site to deliver the program. But nevertheless, experience tells us that you have to make a last-minute check to fine-tune the plan and make any last-minute improvisations.

There is much to do. The setup of the seminar room is seldom just right: the arrangement of tables, the number and spacing of chairs, the placement of equipment, the availability of your educational materials, the temperature and lighting. Adjustments often have to be made to the planned schedule and subject matter to meet the special requirements of each group of participants.

Seminar leaders who fail to check the arrangements before starting the seminar quickly learn better. No matter how reliable the administrative back-up, there are always problems. Hopefully the mistakes are little ones that are easily corrected (but see Chapter 12 for some big ones): too many or too few chairs, no table for the program leader, open end of the "U" facing the wrong way, not enough room behind the speaker to position the screen and overhead projector properly, VCR or computer equipment that doesn't seem to work, no spare bulbs for the projector.

How to Double Check the
Arrangements

Ideally, you should check everything the night before, but this is not always possible. The setup crew usually doesn't do the room until very early the next day. Electronic equipment and projectors are kept under lock and key somewhere.

But you should be able to reassure yourself on the educational materials. It may be difficult to fight your way through well-intentioned but unresourceful employees, but most facilities will have an assistant manager, maintenance worker, or engineer hidden around somewhere who can help you. If you persist, you can find one of them to help you locate the educational materials and have them brought to the seminar room. If you can do this the night before, you'll sleep better.

Even if the setup crew has done a good job the next morning, there are important preliminaries beyond its capabilities. Educational materials, rosters, and place cards have to be distributed to be ready for the participants when they arrive. The screen, projectors, VCR, and computer equipment have to be carefully positioned and tested. Your video cassettes have to be properly inserted, your courseware has to be turned on, and your overhead transparencies have to be at hand in proper sequence.

You should have everything in place by the time the first participant arrives. It is always a little disconcerting when early arrivals find you rushing around to put things in order. I usually put the early birds to work distributing educational materials, and they are always happy to do so.

In the rush of getting everything in place on time, it is easy to forget something. I would strongly recommend that you have a seminar checklist prepared in advance. You'll want to make your own, but to give you some ideas you can use as a starting point, refer to Figure 10 in Chapter 9.

Why You Should Know Your Participants and How to Do So

The more you can learn about the individuals who will be in your class, the better off you will be. But if you're a busy person, much of this has to be done at the seminar itself. You'll need to know their general level of knowledge and experience with respect to the subject matter you will be presenting in order to set your pace and difficulty level. How will this group react to your favorite stories? How can you rework the stories to make them more appropriate?

One example comes to mind from an early point in my presenting career. I had to substitute on fairly short notice for another seminar leader in presenting a program on management leadership to a group of higher-level executives in a large retailing company. Although I was still somewhat of a novice, I thought the program went reasonably well. However, I learned later from the other seminar leader that the group had not responded well to the examples I used. They were too heavily drawn from my own personal experience in other industries. I had not reworked them to become more relevant to retailing executives.

Sometimes you even have to watch your language mannerisms. Some years ago the American Tobacco Company was pushing the slogan "Lucky Strike Extra," which somehow crept into my own vocabulary to mean anything provided that was beyond expectations. I didn't realize how much a part of my language habits the phrase had become until I caught myself about to use it in a seminar with executives from R.J. Reynolds!

One well-known device for learning about the individuals in your group is to get them to introduce themselves to the rest of the group.

You'll find it helpful to put a short outline on the easel pad for them to follow in doing so. Feel free to interrupt in an interested way and ask questions as necessary to bring out more information. I often start off with my own background to help the group get the idea of what I want.

Another device is to ask questions, informally during breaks or even during the seminar. "How many of you are familiar with the thinking of Abraham Maslow on this subject?" is a question I often ask in introducing the subject of motivation. If I see a room full of hands, I know not to elaborate on his theories. There's nothing worse than telling a group about things they already know.

How to Plan Each Day's Schedule

Another important checkpoint is to think through the schedule for each day in advance. The preplanned schedule may have to be adjusted for a variety of reasons. Local conditions or the preferences of the class may suggest changes in starting and finishing times or more extensive evening assignments, which then have to be reflected throughout the preestablished seminar schedule. You may want to introduce more application exercises for groups that seem to be slow in getting actively involved, which probably means changes in time allotments elsewhere. Maybe you have a subject left over from the day before which has to be covered.

Starting Time

I was well along in my career before I learned that not everyone is a morning person like me. I remember so clearly a session I was conducting for a fairly senior group of managers for a major defense contractor. The group voted 19 to 1 to start at 8:30 A.M. The one dissenter did not make an impassioned plea on his own behalf, so we went ahead with the 8:30 A.M. starting time, all of us, that is, except our individualist! He would calmly walk into the room at 9:00 A.M. and take his place at the seminar table. The rest of the group refused to give in to him and he refused to yield to them, muttering something about his "morning constitutional." And so it went for the rest of the program!

As you may guess from this anecdote, my style is to let the group agree to vary the preestablished starting and adjournment times without changing the total classroom hours. Since that one experience, however, I now require the acceptance of all participants before changing the announced hours. It can sometimes happen that such a change can cause great inconvenience for one or two people who may be loathe to resist the will of the majority.

If the seminar is set in a facility in which all the participants have sleeping accommodations, you can usually start as early as 8:00 or even 7:30 A.M. How early you can start may depend on how early and how efficiently breakfast is being served. The pay-off for an early start is an earlier adjournment, which could have special value in a setting that offers a wide range of recreational opportunities.

On the other hand, if there are a number of commuters in the group, you probably have to conform to their accustomed time schedule, particularly if car pools are involved.

Breaks

On the subject of breaks, I believe I am in the minority. Most seminars are designed around a single 15-minute break in mid-morning and similarly in mid-afternoon. I followed this schedule for many years until I met one of those unforgettable people that make a significant impact on your life and thinking.

He was a vice president, operations, for a major machine tools manufacturer who had come up through sales. He provided me with the most carefully thought out checklist for planning and conducting successful sales meetings that I have ever seen. (Unfortunately, I lost it several years later in the course of one of my office moves.)

One of his theories was that adults (particularly sales types) can only be expected to sit still and remain alert for a period of roughly 1 hour. This idea ran counter to many years of experience I had had using the more usual approach. However, I gave it a try and got rave reviews for it!

Ever since (except for special situations, like executive work conferences), I have divided the morning into three periods of roughly 1 hour each, separated by 10-minute breaks, and similarly for the afternoon. You'd be surprised how well it works. The only problem is getting them back at the end of the 10 minutes, a problem for which I have developed several approaches which can be used together.

1. When I announce the break schedule, I make a special point of stressing the importance of time discipline.

2. I also indicate that we have a lot of material to cover, hinting that losing time getting back from breaks may mean adding time at the

end of the day. (This shouldn't be made to sound like a threat or you
risk some loss of rapport.)

3. When the 10 minutes are up, I go out into the hall or wherever most
   of the group has congregated and get some of the leaders to round
   up the rest.

4. I start the next period precisely on time, with a voice loud enough to
   be heard by the loiterers.

5. I start the next period with a funny story—one that has some relationship to the subject at hand, hoping that they will voluntarily be
   on time next time to hear my next story.

While we're on the subject, let me share some ideas with you on what to
serve during breaks. What seems to work well is to have coffee, tea, and
muffins or small danish pastry items available half an hour before the session starts, which can then be replenished as necessary for the later breaks.
In the afternoon, many people prefer a plate of fruit rather than pastry,
and soft drinks in addition to the usual tea and coffee.

Lunches. Lunch should be scheduled in a way that breaks the day
evenly into two halves. For some reason, many trainers think routinely
that lunch should be from 12:00 noon to 1:00 P.M. That may be fine for
many programs. But if, for example, you start as early as 7:30 A.M., you
are condemning your trainees to go for 4½ hours before refueling! It
could also mean a disproportionately shorter afternoon session. If you
start early, you need to plan for an early lunch.

Group luncheons with a predetermined menu or served buffet style
will facilitate discussion and interaction around the subject matter
covered in the morning. They also take up less time. Use of a predetermined menu has the further advantage of avoiding a heavy noon
meal, which can have a deadening effect on the early afternoon class
work.

By the way, you may have to take a strong stand with the hotel or
conference center on this. They make money by selling you a multi-
course, substantial noon meal. But be firm. After all, they are there to
serve you, not vice versa.

If participants are allowed to order individually from the menu or if
they are left to their own devices for lunch, you may have trouble fitting
lunch into a 1-hour time frame. That's why we recommend avoiding
these alternatives.

Adjournment

Ideally, seminars should allow 3 hours of classroom time in the morning and the same in the afternoon, exclusive of breaks, for a total of 6 hours of training. This can be extended to 3½ hours or more, depending on the culture of the particular company. There is a limit to what even a dedicated group can absorb.

In effect, therefore, the adjournment time is set by the starting time and lunch schedule. But once set, I am a firm believer in keeping precisely to the schedule.

Evening Assignments

Evening reading assignments have the advantage of reducing the time that would otherwise be spent in straight explanation or lecture on the succeeding day. They also help the people with little knowledge or experience to get enough background to take a useful part in group or team discussions the next day.

If the participants are staying overnight at the facility, they will welcome an organized opportunity to mix with their colleagues by way of team application exercises or cases. It's a way to keep the fun lovers out of mischief as well.

McGraw-Hill used to schedule a series of seminars at Point Pleasant, New Jersey, during the off-season. There was literally nothing to do in the evenings except drink at the bar, unless you had enough energy to drive an hour and a half to Atlantic City. The use of challenging cases assigned to different teams gave all the participants—even the less outward-going among them—incentive to associate meaningfully together during the evening. And, importantly, it gave them a chance to talk about and work with ideas that were directly relevant to the subject matter covered in the seminar.

My preference is *not* to schedule formal sessions involving the whole group during the evening. After an already long day, they will not be functioning effectively. This is particularly so if the host facility is featuring a "happy hour" before dinner, offering two drinks for the price of one.

Be careful that overnight assignments are not too time demanding. I remember conducting a seminar in Boca Raton, Florida, at a hotel amply possessed with athletic and recreational activities. The group was kept so busy they couldn't really enjoy these, which prompted one member to write on his seminar evaluation, "Why do you schedule these sessions at a resort location like this and then give us no opportunity to take advantage of the golfing, tennis, and other activities available?"

There are times when clients may insist on evening classes as a substitute for time away from work. I ran a series from 4:30 P.M. to 8:00 P.M., with supper brought in, for a Wall Street arbitrage firm that couldn't take its traders or support people from their work stations while the east coast exchanges were still open. I'm sure they resented it, although they didn't dare to say so. And I doubt that they got very much out of the seminars.

How to Work Your Time Plan

Your daily plan is useful only to the extent you keep checking your progress against it. Having planned the time to be given to each subject, you have to control the pace of the seminar against the plan, and you have to control the group to keep their discussions relevant and useful. Your control has to be exercised unobtrusively and with a reasonable degree of flexibility. You want to encourage free and easy participation. Constant interruptions and reminders that "we must be moving on now" will discourage participation and develop frustrations.

The rule for keeping to your time plan is simple: keep constantly aware of the actual time as compared to the time planned. Place a watch with a large face on your table to which you can casually refer without anyone noticing it. The watch should have a face with numbers large enough to be read from several paces away. A pocket calculator with stop watch and alarm beep capabilities can be helpful in timing team exercises; especially if you are visiting from team to team and are away from your table.

Avoid using a wristwatch. There is no way of checking the time unobtrusively. Looking at your watch requires an arm-swinging motion that telegraphs to the class that there you go, checking the time again. It interrupts their concentration on the subject matter.

If you are always aware of where you are against your time plan, you know whether you need to speed up or can afford to slow down. If you're behind time, you'll need to foreshorten the time you have planned to spend on some subject coming up. If you have already planned some speed-up options, you need to put them into effect. Otherwise you have to improvise.

Team exercises can be shortened by eliminating questions or by assigning different questions to different teams instead of all questions to all teams. With fewer questions to consider, the teams will need less time to reach a consensus. Another option is to use group discussion instead of team exercises. Also, you can speed up your treatment of less important subjects by referring the class to appropriate sections of the workbook and briefly summarizing them. Whatever you do, it is better to foreshorten *your* portion of the seminar—not the participants' portion.

If you are running ahead of schedule, you are better off than if you are running behind. You can introduce optional work exercises or group discussions already planned for such an eventuality. You can throw out some provocative questions to generate group discussion and keep it going: "As you reflect on the subject we've just been discussing, where in your experience are managers most likely to go wrong?"

A final thought on controlling time is to start as well as end on time. Let the latecomers feel a slight embarrassment that the seminar has already begun. They'll quickly get the point. One seminar leader, who has a particularly rich collection of funny stories, starts the afternoon session with one of them. If you're not back from lunch on time, you'll miss it. In rare cases, you may have to raise the question of timeliness with the group. Without making a threat of it, you can point out that starting late means ending late because there is so much material to cover. A subtle tactic is to "synchronize watches" at the start of each day. Also, give them a precise time to return. "Please be back by 10:35" is better than saying "let's take a 10-minute break."

Another aspect of time control is to make sure that discussions don't take too long or don't get too far off track. You want to allow a certain amount of leeway, but if your control is too loose, you will annoy and frustrate some of the group.

Exactly how long to let a discussion continue is a matter of judgment. You have to sense the extent and degree of group involvement. If you can see that every member of the group is keenly interested and the discussion is relevant, let it continue. Sooner or later you'll pick up some non-verbal clues that interest is waning, or perhaps the comments will become obviously repetitious.

Sometimes continuation of the discussion is being maintained by a single highly involved individual. In such cases it is usually time to move on. If you have the gift of cutting in with a humorous one-liner, by all means do it. Sometimes you can seize upon a comment made in the discussion as a natural bridge to the next subject. If all else fails, calling a break is an easy way to terminate an endless discussion.

Controlling the subject matter of discussions also means making sure that all the key points are made. Leader's guides typically include "anticipated responses" to help you know when you have to ask some appropriate questions to draw out the points that have not been mentioned. "What arguments can you make on the other side of the case?" is one good question to use. If necessary, fill in the missing ideas yourself.

How to Deal With Behavior Problems

Fortunately it doesn't seem to come up very often, but sometimes you have to deal with individual behavior problems. These appear in a variety of forms: the intellectual bully who takes personal charge of every group discussion; the joker who is always out to get a laugh from the group; the wallflower who won't participate. One of the most disconcerting is the silent sphinx whose unchanging facial expression can be interpreted as disagreement, detachment, or sheer stupidity. You're never sure which. Once in a rare while you *do* run across hostility.

In a surprisingly high proportion of the cases, the group itself will deal with the behavior problem. I can remember a particularly troublesome individual, early in my presenting career. He was openly disrespectful to me and to other participants, and he would inject inappropriate comments into group discussions. His behavior was apparently particularly annoying to an older, hugely proportioned plant manager from Buffalo who happened to be sitting next to the offender at luncheon on the second day of the seminar. The plant manager, reacting to the problem participant's most recent remark, said, "You know what? You're something of a son of a bitch!" To my great surprise the comment drew only a laugh, but from that point on, the problem disappeared.

In another instance, I had to deal with a persistently hostile, articulate fellow. It was a workshop in which the participants were being trained to develop objectives and measurable standards of performance. He insisted repeatedly on raising the question of why anyone should need these things. He also stated quite positively that he could write his own objectives and standards in half an hour without any need for a workshop.

After trying to reason with him on these questions and calling upon others to help, I finally said that if he felt he didn't need the training, he was free to leave the seminar. After a moment's reflection, he got up and left—much to the collective relief of the whole group, not to mention the seminar leader!

Behavior problems usually don't come up in such a forceful fashion and are not too difficult to handle. The discussion dominator can be deliberately passed over and questions fed to others in the group.

Sometimes a quiet word with an overly talkative participant at the end of the day will help. Dozers and daydreamers can be roused by a direct question or by moving into the U-shaped table and stationing yourself directly in front of the offender. Direct questions will also get the shy members into the action. Those carrying on private discussions can be asked to share their ideas with the whole group.

At various times during the course of the seminar, you are called upon to take some action to keep the group under control. Fortunately, peer pressure is a powerful control on behavior problems. Use the other participants as necessary, but remember you have to keep control of the subject matter and the flow of proceedings against the established time schedule.

Skilled seminar leaders have the capability of maintaining full control over the group while seeming to allow every opportunity for free participation. They know exactly where they are in terms of the schedule, making departures to take advantage of the special interests of the group. They never appear to be rushing even if in fact they are. This firm but relaxed control engenders the respect of the group and enhances the effectiveness of the learning process.

How to Assign Application Exercises

An important role of the seminar leader is to organize the participants into subgroups or teams and assign application exercises to them. An easy way to do this is to assign seat locations in such a way that you can form teams from people sitting together around the seminar table. Once they get used to the idea of breaking up into teams, the group will welcome it. It gives them a greater chance to exchange ideas with their colleagues.

A rule of thumb here is to provide for constant change. You can rearrange name cards every evening to make up new teams for the next day. If you wish, you can actually make up charts to ensure that each participant gets the greatest exposure to the other participants. You can explain this as a desire for them to "share their special intelligence with others." It also helps to free them from team members they have found difficult the day before.

Another way to provide for change is to use teams of different sizes. Teams of two or three people can conveniently be formed without leaving the seminar table. Teams of four or five will work better at breakaway tables or in breakaway rooms. The larger teams will also need more time to reach conclusions. It's best to avoid teams larger than five people since it will be too easy for some team members to take on passive roles.

Before these teams can function effectively, you have to have clearly in mind just what they are supposed to do and how much time they should allow themselves to do it; and you have to communicate this clearly to them. I have found it helpful to put the assignment on the easel after I give it orally. It helps to prevent misunderstandings. I also make a point of visiting with each team to make sure they understand what they are supposed to do. It also gives you a chance to get to know them in small group settings. Alert them a few minutes before the time is up to give them a chance to wind up their discussions.

Another reason for visiting with each team is to sense when a team is off the track. You can then help them get back on track and save them possible embarrassment when they report out to the group as a whole. There are some challenging cases that I use in which I deliberately "salt" some ideas with different teams. In this way, I can be surer that enough substance will be forthcoming for me to make a summary that will be most useful from a learning point of view.

Let the teams choose their own leaders to provide feedback from the team to the whole group. As a rule, they will rotate this assignment among their members, so most people will end up getting a chance to report on their team's deliberations.

To summarize, whether it is getting subgroups to work effectively, steering group discussions, planning and controlling the progress of the seminar, or ensuring the necessary support services from the seminar facility, seminar leaders function as the on-site managers of the seminar delivery.

Change team composition
team sizes   5 or fewer
choose own leaders - maybe
give starting points
 └ how to start
   instructions
   warning before finish

11

How to Present Successful Programs: Tips from the Pros

The exciting challenge faced by seminar leaders at the start of each program is to communicate ideas and information in such a way as to create full understanding and enthusiastic acceptance. They have considerable help in doing so. The seminar design has already structured the subject matter in a sequence and schedule that should facilitate understanding. The seminar leader's guide provides a fairly precise course to follow. Educational materials and visual aids have been developed to add impact. Care has been taken in establishing the seminar setting.

But seminar leaders have to put it all together. They also have to improvise from time to time and depart from the basic design. Let me share with you some guidelines that come out of 19 years of personal experience, reinforced by inputs from many other seasoned discussion leaders. Let's look at them; then we'll discuss each in turn.

1. Know your seminar
2. Know your participants
3. Get and keep them motivated

4. Secure their understanding

5. Ensure retention

6. Get feedback

7. Secure application

8. Follow up

Know Your Seminar

The first and perhaps the most important guideline is to know your seminar completely. Know its objective so that you are always able to determine what is relevant and what takes priority. Know the subject matter so well that you don't have to worry about it when you are conducting the program. You will then be confident that you can handle any question that comes up, and you can put your full attention on the participants and their reactions as the program moves ahead.

I've often compared this process to playing golf. There are four stages of development. First, there is *unconscious incompetence*. You don't know enough about the game at the outset to realize how inept you are.

Then as you begin to take up the game, you realize how difficult it is. You enter the second stage: *conscious incompetence*. You realize that you don't know how to play the game very well. But let's say you keep at it. You're determined to do better. You practice and practice until you become fairly good at the game. But every time you hit the ball you have to concentrate hard on how you swing the club. You've crossed the threshold into *conscious competence*.

Let's say you're now hooked on the game and work your handicap down and down until you become what they call a "scratch golfer"; you don't need a handicap any more. You have become *unconsciously competent.* You don't think about every element of your swing any more. It's grooved. You're now concerned with tactics and keeping the right mental attitude. It's all automatic.

You go through the same four stages in mastering the seminar. At the end, you know it so well you don't have to worry about what's coming up next. You can give 100% attention to your seminar group: listening to what they say, sensing their attitudes, watching for non-verbal clues.

Knowing your subject matter gives you a great deal of confidence. You know you can answer any question the group throws at you. You are almost eager to have someone challenge points that you make. It becomes a stimulating intellectual challenge instead of a fear that you won't make the right response. Your command of the subject matter will become apparent to the group and greatly heighten your credibility.

A good example is Louis Allen, founder and head of our firm, as described to me by the training director of a large and prominent company. "You know," he said, "Lou Allen is not a very dynamic or forceful discussion leader. In fact, his voice drops down so softly that you can hardly hear him. But everyone leans forward with rapt attention because they recognize his vast knowledge of the subject."

Know Your Participants

Knowing your participants ranks in importance with knowing your seminar. Here are the reasons why.

1. You can talk at the right level. If you talk over their heads, the participants won't understand what you are trying to get across and may not care to admit it. If you talk down to them, they'll resent it and lose interest in the seminar. To some degree, the first guideline helps you here. Know the subject matter so well you can more easily concentrate on how well it's coming across to the group. You can see it in their eyes and postures.

2. You are better able to call on the right people to add meaning to a group discussion. If you know the background which each of the participants brings to the session, you can make the most of the valuable experience you have at hand. The group can learn a great deal from each other. You are like the conductor of a symphony orchestra, calling on the right people at the right time to add impact to the performance.

3. At the same time, it gives you the opportunity to provide recognition to the participants, which is important in maintaining their positive motivation. "Martha, with your extensive experience in the use of on-line computers, you can surely add to our discussion of this point." Martha will undoubtedly rise to the occasion and in doing so will experience a sense of positive motivation.

4. On the preventive side, this knowledge can help you avoid potential problems. If you have in the group some impassioned advocates of women's rights, you can be especially careful to avoid masculine pronouns. You might want to use "her/hims" alternately with "him/hers." By the way, McGraw-Hill provides its authors with a 10-page booklet on terms you can use to avoid gender problems. For another example, if you have no golfers in the class, you can avoid

telling your golfing stories. I gambled a little when I used my golfing analogy on the first guideline. Did I lose you on that one?

5. By knowing the interests of the group, you will find it easier to capture their attention by appealing to those interests. If you are conducting a program in the middle of the United States, you might want to make references to basketball. I'm told that it's a much bigger sport there than in the rest of the country. But if you're in Canada with a group of Canadians, it may well be that hockey would be more appropriate.

As mentioned in an earlier chapter, there are a number of ways you can secure this information. You should get as much background information on each individual before the seminar as you can. Then, at the start of the seminar you can have the participants introduce themselves. To add a little fun to this process, you can divide the group into teams of two. Then ask the participants to introduce their teammates, after providing enough time for mutual interviews to secure the necessary background information. During the seminar, there are many informal opportunities to get to know them before and after the formal seminar sessions and during breaks.

Get and Keep Your Participants Motivated

The third guideline is to gain the favorable attention of your group and keep them positively motivated throughout the program. You have to do this or you can't succeed. If they are not listening with interest, they won't understand; and if they haven't developed any inner commitment, they won't apply what they've learned on the job.

You may confidently assume that you have a head start. "They wouldn't be sitting there in the room if they didn't want to learn," you may be saying to yourself. But don't fool yourself. You will be much better off if you make the opposite assumption—and you will probably be closer to the truth. Most of them didn't volunteer for the class. Their bosses told them to come. They may have heard some good reports about the seminar from past participants. At most they will be mildly interested and curious. But they may also be questioning whether they should have been more resourceful in getting excused from the seminar—or at least in getting a postponement.

You have to capture their attention and appeal to their needs—at the outset and repeatedly throughout the seminar. Note that there are two separate thoughts here. One is simply to get them to pay attention. The other is to gain their commitment and, if appropriate, a readiness to change their own behavior on the job.

Capturing Their Interest

If you stop to think of it, you have to capture their interest before you can win their commitment. If they aren't out there listening and interested, you don't have a chance of getting them to understand your subject matter. You have to keep the door to their minds open, so to speak. It usually isn't too difficult if you have matched the right people with the right seminar. But there are a number of useful and practical suggestions.

Get Participation.   The best way to get your group interested is to get them involved personally. Break the group into teams and give them something interesting to talk about with each other. Virtually everyone gets a speaking part in such an exercise. A good deal of this is built into the seminar design, but you may well find further impromptu opportunities.

Suppose you run into an unusually apathetic group, which sometimes happens. The participants just sit there quietly. They may even smile. But they're not about to put themselves out. What do you do? Get them involved in a small team exercise. The worst thing you can do is to talk louder or faster. It is a little easier to deal with a fun-loving group. But you can easily be carried away by the fun and let the group get out of hand. Of course, to a point you *should* relax and enjoy it—but only to a point. You've got to get the group back to the subject matter at hand. Again, small team exercises can be a useful response. Or you can assign a case from the workbook.

Come Across—Personally.   An important aspect of holding the participants' interest is to be an interesting person yourself, in your total impact on the group. It is difficult for seminar leaders to assess their own impact. Yet your total personality can have a considerable effect. Seminar leaders are all different people and shouldn't force themselves into a rigid mold. Nevertheless, our experience suggests three points to remember:

1. *Smile.*   The first is to smile. Be relaxed and friendly. Your open, outgoing attitude will encourage the group to respond in the same way. More than simply a facial expression, you should exude an attitude of sincere enjoyment, treating each participant as a friend, joining in the

fun, but at the same time being sincerely interested in the participants and in the seminar.

2. *Use Humor.*   A ready wit and a light touch help to make the seminar a pleasant experience and provide occasional moments of mental relaxation. Sometimes you can tie humorous stories to specific points to be made in the seminar. If done well and not overdone, the technique can release tension and prevent boredom.

I knew a seminar leader years ago who was so expert at getting laughs that his seminars were a continuous series of humorous asides and funny stories. The participants loved it. They would emerge from the seminar room each day with tears of laughter still twinkling in their eyes. But as a learning experience, it was a failure. Joke retention was high, but subject matter became secondary.

Sometimes jokes can be offensive to people. Ethnic, racial, and sexist stories are, of course, to be avoided; they are simply in poor taste. But different individuals may have quite different views as to what is in "good taste" or "bad taste." What strikes one group as uproariously funny may impress another group as "coarse." A good rule is: when in doubt, don't tell it.

Nevertheless, humor has an important place. Plan your stories in advance and key them right into your notes. Use the reactions of different groups to your stories as a means of sorting them out. Keep the ones that always get a good laugh and illustrate a point and you will have little risk of offending anyone. Get rid of the others. This means you have to be on the alert to collect stories that could be used in your seminars to provide a change of pace and make a relevant impact on the group.

3. *Be Alive.*   The true test of the professional is an ability to be keenly alive, even enthusiastic, though conducting the same program over and over again. Stop to think about it. If you act bored or placid, others will surely lose interest.

Be careful of your own non-verbal cues. Do you keep a lively eye-contact with individuals in the group? Do you stand up most of the time? Do you move around? Are you effusive in recognizing the useful contributions of individuals to the discussion? Do you consciously vary the tone and loudness of your voice? Or, on the other hand, are you seated most of the time? Leaning on your elbows? When you do walk, do you slouch with hands in pockets? It all adds up to your own personality impact.

Make Everything Relevant.   Seminar participants have to see the relevance of the program to their own goals to awaken their interest and provide for continuing motivation. If they see its relevance, they will become favorably motivated. They will get the impetus they need for going through the seminar process. If they can see a real pay-off for themselves, their motivation will be enhanced.

One special challenge here is that sometimes participants are already generally familiar with the subject matter of the course. Take, for example, my own experience in management training seminars. Many managers already know something about setting objectives, delegating, and other subjects covered in these seminars. They probably think they know a lot more than they actually do. The challenge, then, is to get them to realize that the seminar teaches a systematic, logical way of doing many things they are probably already doing, a way that has been thoroughly tested by many generations of successful managers "on the firing line." This is the pay-off: a short cut to improved effectiveness in getting results through others—a result that can be translated into a better chance for advancement and faster compensation progress.

For other types of training seminars, the pay-off may be even easier to find. "If you really learn and apply this step-by-step selling method, you'll be able to increase your sales effectiveness, revenue, *and* your annual bonus."

Selling the course to participants at the outset is critical; but it is also important to point out the relevance of each new idea as it comes along in the seminar. Everything you do must appear to be relevant to the participants.

Keep a Good Pace. If you keep the pace moving properly, with frequent changes of approach, it will help to keep the interest level high. It's not always easy. If you try to keep everyone productively learning, you may lose the fast learners who are likely to be the informal leaders in the group. If you cater too much to them, you may leave the slow learners behind. Your best bet probably is to steer a middle course, giving the fast learners opportunities to show off. If necessary, give the slower ones some after-hours coaching.

The rationale for changing the pace and method from time to time is to avoid boredom. Adults need mental rest periods to maintain a high involvement level. They need opportunities to move around physically to help avoid mental fatigue. What you want to hear from the participants are comments like these: "Boy, the morning sure passed quickly." "I wasn't looking forward to this seminar. My boss made me come. But now I'm really glad I'm here."

You cannot set and keep the right pace unless you are constantly alert to feedback from the group. You have to observe and react to many kinds of signals you'll get. A puzzled look is a clue to repeat, restate, or probe. A sudden gesture often announces the arrival of a good idea to a participant, suggesting the opportunity for a direct, open question. Watch out for frowns and head shakings; they are clues that you have disagreement. Get it out in the open or it's likely to fester. The same is true with side comments. If they're worth sharing with a neighbor, they need to be shared with the group.

Gaining Their Commitment

Getting the commitment of your participants becomes possible only after you have captured their interest. If you are working with a good seminar, the material itself will go a long way toward gaining the emotional commitment necessary for the participants to truly want to learn and to become eager to try their knowledge out on the job. But there are certain things you can do that will be an important help.

Provide Self-Satisfaction.   Give your participants the satisfaction that comes from learning. Every time you pose a challenging question or make a work assignment you are, in fact, providing your participants with an opportunity to test their own understanding. If they pass the test to their—and your—satisfaction it has a positive motivational impact. The response is more positive to the extent they feel they have been truly challenged. If it was too easy, they won't get any satisfaction. In fact, you may get a negative impact.

Give Recognition.   Closely related to creating self-satisfaction is to provide recognition to individual participants, when it is earned. The recognition that you give in the classroom can have a significant effect. Don't underrate your influence here. If you find the opportunity to tell some participant, in front of the whole class, that he or she did a fine job, it is really appreciated. It evokes a very positive emotional response.

But remember to be specific when you give out these "strokes." Simply making a general statement about a piece of "good work" does not have the same impact as when you make some very specific reference to something that was good, and explain to the class why it was so good. It is especially important to recognize good performance immediately after it occurs. It is still fresh in the participants' minds at that time and your power to provide reward will have the greatest impact. Specifying precisely why the recognition is being given also gives you an opportunity to do a little coaching.

Remove or Lessen Anxieties.   Remember, too, to deal effectively with people's natural anxieties. There are a number of possible anxieties that participants may have that can interfere with their learning. Some may be afraid they will look bad in the class. Others may be worried that their poor performance will be reported back to their superiors. The way to deal with these anxieties is to let the participants know that you respect their expertise in their own fields. Show them this respect by your attitude as well as your words. Tell them the seminar is designed to help them use their experience more effectively. Make sure they understand there is no negative feedback to their superiors.

Anxieties can prevent participants from really getting involved in the seminar. Remember, you are after their emotional commitment as well as their intellectual understanding. You have to capture their attention, hold their continuing interest, and build step by step a sense of personal commitment if you are going to get them to put the teachings of the seminar to work on the job.

Secure Full Understanding

When you have the group properly motivated, you have cleared the way to get the subject matter of the seminar across to them. Here are some ways you can communicate ideas and information, together with some practical guidelines with each. Although each of these methods can be isolated for purposes of analysis, they will be carefully mixed together in a well-designed seminar.

Telling vs. Asking

Broadly speaking, there are two alternative approaches to securing the understanding of ideas and information by the participants. You can tell them, using a variety of methods. Or, through asking questions and providing cases, you can get them to come forward themselves with the ideas and information.

Using the Participants. The more powerful, but more time-consuming alternative, is to draw out the ideas and information from the participants themselves. A welcome change of pace, especially for more experienced groups, is getting the participants to think up ideas for themselves which fix the information more surely in their minds. "Teams one and three, will you draw upon your accumulated experience to develop the seven most prevalent sins in performance appraisals? And teams two and four, what in your view are the greatest potential benefits to be derived from doing an effective job of performance appraisal?"

"Can you give me some specific examples of how we can provide meaningful rewards to subordinates, other than monetary rewards, to enhance their motivation?" This question recently sparked a lively and productive discussion among a group of top-level state government administrators who went into the discussion thinking there was little that they could do to provide rewards to employees in light of Civil Service regulations. Drawing specific examples from the group, as in this illustration, is an effective way to get participants to assist in the communication process. Their examples are quite likely to be more impressive to the other participants than your own. The examples will appear to come more from the "real world."

Demonstrations can also be arranged within the participant group. Some years ago I had an experienced director of personnel in a public seminar. Partly to stimulate his interest, but primarily for the benefit of the group, I asked him to role play a performance counseling session in which I took the part of the subordinate and he the part of the manager. He did a superb job — and incidentally enjoyed the visibility — with the result that the participants got a much more dramatic idea of the process than I could otherwise have conveyed to them by words alone.

The participants themselves should be used at many different times during the seminar to generate the ideas and information that becomes the subject matter for discussion and analysis. You can draw them out by asking questions, or by giving them exercises or cases to analyze in subgroups or teams.

Leader Exposition. The less powerful, but less time-consuming alternative, is to present the ideas and information yourself. Direct leader exposition is particularly useful with less experienced groups. Typically, such a presentation involves some mixture of direct statement, visuals, demonstration, and examples.

Direct Statements. The direct statement is the most commonly used of all the different methods of leader exposition. The direct statement takes the least amount of time and is directly under the control of the seminar leader. You can carefully plan in advance exactly what words to use to make the clearest possible communication.

But having the leader introduce and explain the subject matter has its disadvantages, too. Sometimes complex ideas or abstract concepts are not easy to state clearly. If the leader talks too much, the others lose interest. A seminar, by its very name, requires a sharing of ideas and experience, which cannot be done if the seminar leader is too busy lecturing. Talking too fast has a special disadvantage. If the ideas are coming across too rapidly for some of the participants to grasp, the communication will fail in its purpose. In addition, fast talk is often accompanied by a lack of clarity. The leader hasn't had enough time to select the most appropriate words or think through the most logical thought sequence. On the other hand, speaking too slowly will produce boredom and mind wandering.

Despite these disadvantages and potential problems, the direct statement, often accompanied by a restatement or rephrasing, is by far the most commonly used teaching method. Used alone or in conjunction with other methods, the direct statement is an essential tool for providing ideas and information, for correcting mistakes, for answering questions, and for summarizing a seminar sequence before advancing to the next. For these reasons, some practical suggestions for making these statements as easily understandable as possible are worth considering.

1. *Use Simple Words.* Language can be a formidable barrier to understanding, and not just foreign languages; more frequently, it is technical jargon which causes the problem. Some disciplines are worse than others, but it is easy to build into your vocabulary, quite unconsciously, phrases, words, or acronyms that mean a great deal to you, but may not communicate at all to others. Fortunately, this problem is more likely to appear in written rather than oral communications. But you need to be on constant guard. Make "dry-runs" or practice presentations and have your audience watch especially for opportunities to use simpler, more specific words.

2. *Communicate in Small Bites.* Beware of "overload." If you pack too many ideas or too much information in too short a space of time, you can't expect to get understanding. Instead, throw out one idea at a time. Provide an example. Contrast it with another idea. Only when you sense the understanding of the group—or test it through questions—should you move on.

3. *Build on Prior Information.* Proceed from what has already been understood and accepted to new material, relating it logically to the prior information. Often there is a natural order into which ideas will fall, like a step-by-step sequence of action steps.

4. *Go From the General to the Specific.* Provide some overview or perspective at the outset. Then get down to the details. It will be easier for people to grasp. Deductive Reasoning

5. *Break up Complex Ideas.* A number of smaller, simpler ideas can be the best way to get people to understand some complex concept. You want to present something that is not so complex as to be confusing, nor so simple as to be obvious or boring.

6. *State and Restate.* If a few participants were lost on another thought when you first made a point, you need to give them another chance to catch on. Repetition also adds emphasis and contributes to re-

tention of an idea. A summary of some sort is indispensable before moving from one subject to the next and is itself a form of repetition.

Visualizations.   Visualizations have the great advantage of conveying the whole idea at one time. Verbal communications have to present a sequence of words to establish an idea. Not so with visuals. Furthermore, many people actually need to see what you are saying as well as to hear it. They need to hold on to the idea and reflect upon it, which visuals permit.

   a.   Using Prepared Visuals

In well-developed seminars, you are provided ahead of time with a variety of visual aids complete with directions on how to use them. If this is the case, you still need to know how to use them most effectively. Here are a few suggestions.

1. Let the visual speak for itself. Elaborate on it, but—as a general rule—don't read it word for word. There may be rare exceptions for special emphasis, but your participants can read—and read it faster to themselves than you can read it aloud. Don't insult their intelligence.

2. Talk to your audience, not to the screen. If you maintain eye contact with the participants they are encouraged to pay attention. You will also get the benefit of any non-verbal feedback or response to the visual. If you are projecting 35mm slides onto a screen behind your speaker's table, you can place a hand mirror on your table in such a position that you can see what is on the screen. Even though the image you see in the mirror is reversed, you can get necessary reassurance that the visual you are talking about is the one that is actually before the group.

3. Remember to keep the screen in view of everyone. Don't let your own body, an easel flip chart, or anything else get in the way.

4. If necessary to do so, get a participant to dim the lights for you or turn a remote projector on or off. Ideally, the seminar room and layout should make this caution unnecessary. But if it has to be done, you are better off getting someone else to do it for you rather than interrupting the flow of proceedings by doing it yourself.

   b.   Using Flip Charts

Your flip chart, a large pad of paper, usually 30 by 40 inches, on an easel, should be of great help to you, whether or not you have a complete set of prepared visuals. As an alternative, some presenters prefer to use acetate sheets (or a roll of acetate sheet) with an overhead projector on which they write with a special marker, projecting their writings on the large screen behind them. This alternative is especially good for larger groups and may make writing legibly somewhat easier. But it has one disadvantage over the flip chart: you can't tear off pages and hang them on the walls of the room.

There are a number of specific instances in which it is quite useful to write something down on the flip chart or blank acetate sheet.

1. Recording team exercise response. One is to record the responses of a subgroup to some work exercise or case. Their response is kept before the whole group long enough for others to reflect upon, absorb, and comment on it. You can use a different-colored marker to indicate comments that are from another team to create a little friendly competition.

2. Providing special emphasis. Another use of the flip chart is to add importance to a statement made by a participant or by yourself. Writing it down gives the point special emphasis.

3. Preserving for later reference. A third use is to save ideas generated, say, in a group discussion for later reference. For example, it may be helpful to collect the group's thinking on the advantages or benefits of delegation, which can later be used in summarizing the subject.

4. Showing relationships. Sometimes it is useful to provide a visualization of certain relationships not provided for in the prepared visuals. It may be something you have planned for this particular group, or an idea that comes out of a question presented or out of a group discussion.

5. Making work assignments. As a wise precaution, it is useful to write down as well as give orally individual or team exercises, especially evening assignments. Even if stated in participant workbooks, the assignment will be more surely understood and remembered if it is up there on the flip chart in writing for all to see.

Although extremely useful, flip charts can be used improperly. For one thing, don't write down too much. It takes time. Everything stops while you are writing. Furthermore, you'll be tempted to write quickly, which usually makes writing less legible. Use key words. Paraphrase your thoughts.

Another caution is to avoid putting everything in your own words. Try to use words provided by the participants, if you are capturing a team response or points derived from a group discussion. It's a good way to provide recognition to individual participants. If you put it in your own words, you are claiming some of the credit for yourself.

Finally, write large enough for everyone to see and clearly enough for everyone to read. After all, your objective is to communicate. If people can't see it or can't read it, you have failed in your purpose.

Make sure as well that you put a title above your writing, e.g., "Barriers to Planning." The title helps focus everyone's thinking. If anybody's mind has wandered, it can more easily get back into the stream of discussion.

Appropriate use of handwritten visuals will add greatly to the prepared visuals in gaining impact and total understanding. Visualizations, both impromptu and prepared, can communicate some ideas and relationships much more quickly and easily than words. They can provide an instant impact, where verbal explanations require a sequence of thought. Visual aids have to be considered an indispensable component of successful seminars.

Demonstration

Another method of communication, demonstration, is of special usefulness in teaching technical skills such as sales training or machine operations. Actually showing someone how to do something can be much more effective than telling them how. Just think how much easier it is to demonstrate how to use a can opener than it is to explain it in words. Demonstration is usually accompanied by direct statements for purposes of introduction, and audio-visual aids may be used as vehicles for the demonstration. The demonstration may dramatize incorrect behavior to be critiqued by the group, or the desired behavior to be emulated. Undesired behavior should not be demonstrated unless the desired behavior is also shown. To do otherwise would run the risk that only the dramatized, unwanted behavior is remembered.

Sales training programs are especially appropriate for videotape dramatizations. A sales call by its nature has a lot of human interest and suspense. Will the sales representative be successful in getting the prospect to reveal needs that his or her product will meet? What obstacles will the prospect throw up and how will the sales representative handle them? How well did the sales person identify and react to the attitudes exhibited by the prospect? The dramatization can offer more excitement than the average TV soap opera.

You may find demonstration opportunities in addition to the sequences incorporated into the seminar design. For example, you might assume the role of the manager providing on-the-job coaching to a subordinate. Such a demonstration can offer a high-impact change of pace to the seminar. Impromptu role playing can sometimes clear up a point of confusion or answer a question much more effectively than verbal explanation.

Examples

A fourth way that leaders communicate ideas and information is through the use of examples. The method is especially helpful in seminars teaching concepts and principles to be applied on the job. Many people have trouble thinking in conceptual terms. Unless they can see how a concept can be applied in a specific, familiar situation, they may be at a loss to understand it. Seminar leaders can make abstract ideas come alive through the adroit use of examples.

Despite their great usefulness, though, examples can pose some dangers and have their limitations. Sometimes the precise relationship between the idea and the example is not understood by everyone. With certain groups, the example you have built into your repertory appears too naive or too unrealistic to them. If it's an example you've borrowed from someone else, you may be embarrassed by aggressive cross-examination. If the example is contained in a funny story, the joke may overwhelm the intended message in the minds of the participants.

Clearly, the usefulness of examples far outweighs their disadvantages. But try to make them relevant, easily understood, and not too lengthy. Draw from your own experience, orienting your examples to the particular group at hand to the extent possible.

Examples, mixed with other methods, are useful both in leader exposition and in drawing information out of the participant group. Getting participants to provide examples is a good way to get participation. Participants will get a motivational boost by the opportunity to tell a few "war stories" about their own successes and accomplishments. By all means, make liberal use of examples.

Ensure Retention

People tend to forget too easily; they have to be helped to remember what you want them to remember. No matter how effectively you have used all the available methods for securing understanding, you have to ensure retention. It is a truly sobering thought to realize how quickly people forget. I'm told that unless you do something to prevent it, your participants will forget 25% of what they have learned within 24 hours, and 85% in 1 week. It's an appalling thought.

What this means in conducting seminars is that you have to state and restate; you have to find opportunities to review, and opportunities to associate your subject matter with familiar ideas so as to fasten it on participants' memories.

Use Repetition

"Tell them what you are going to tell them (the introduction); then tell them (the main body of the communication); then tell them what you told them (the concluding summary)." This advice is age-old. You have heard it so many times before that stating it now is in itself a form of repetition to ensure the advice is remembered.

A proven technique used in a lot of seminars is "The Three Most Important Points." Participants are asked, as part of their evening assignment, to think through the subject matter covered during the day and select what they consider to be the three most important points. They are asked to be able to explain on the next morning why they thought each point was important. This forces them to review the material individually as an evening assignment. Then, the next morning, individual participants are asked to tell the group what their most important points were and why they believed they were so important. A discussion develops naturally that provides a second review of the material and helps the participants to remember it.

Another, less-structured form of repetition is simply to state an idea twice. State it with one set of words. Then rephrase it for an immediate repetition. Those whose minds were wandering on the first go-around will pick it up the second time around. Those who heard it the first time will benefit from the reinforcement.

"How would you describe this principle in your own words, Mildred?" is another form of repetition frequently and effectively used. The question also serves to test understanding (and may be a way to get Mildred to participate). If Mildred really can state the principle correctly, it will give her some satisfaction and give you the opportunity to provide a little recognition. Now, if you look back over this paragraph, you can see that some repetition was used here in references back to portions of the chapter on motivating participants.

Associate with Familiar Ideas

The other usual way to ensure retention, association, is the concept behind some well-known memory feats. Perhaps you have witnessed some performer recall correctly and in the exact sequence a long list of objects that had previously been stated. How? The performer has memorized a long list of verbs. As each object is mentioned, it is visually associated with each verb in sequence. The performer visualizes himself or herself, for example, shaking the lamp, kissing a desk, patting a clock, and so forth. The sequence of actions associated with each object provides clues leading to the feedback of all the objects in correct order.

You don't want to play this game in a seminar; but you can still use association. An association that I frequently use is to compare a manager who doesn't take time to plan with an old water-soaked log floating in a harbor. The log is at the complete mercy of wind, tide, wave, and current with no control over its own destiny. So, too, a manager is at the complete mercy of events and conditions unless the manager attempts to influence his or her own destiny by planning.

Get Feedback

A communication isn't complete without feedback. A face-to-face meeting or a telephone conversation that permits two-way conversation is much more effective than a memorandum or a letter. You get immediate feedback. You know immediately whether the receiver of your message has understood it in the same way that you intended.

Here is one exercise that is frequently used to get participants to experience the importance of feedback. One team member is asked to describe a somewhat complex diagram of equal-sided triangles to his or her teammates while they attempt to draw it from the description they are receiving. The first time the exercise is run, the team member describing the diagram stands with back to teammates who are not allowed to ask any questions. Then, the exercise is done a second time with a different diagram of equal difficulty. This time the group is allowed to ask questions and get answers. Needless to say, the participants do a much better job reproducing the diagram on the second try. With the help of feedback, the communication is far more successful.

There is another important reason to get feedback from the participant group: to test their understanding. Wholly apart from the give-and-take of ideas built into the seminar design or induced by the leader for motivational reasons, you have to take stock from time to time of the learning process. Both the seminar leader and the group benefit from this testing process. The leader learns how well the group is grasping the subject matter being presented, information necessary to deciding whether to keep going on the same subject or to move ahead. The participants are also given the opportunity to assess their own progress, which is quite important to achievement-oriented people. They either learn where they need to secure better understanding or improved skills, or they are given a kind of reward—the satisfaction of progress in their learning.

How to Do It

The simplest and most direct way to test understanding is through the use of questions: open questions to the group as a whole or, more usefully, questions directed at specific individuals. You can ask a direct question to test understanding of an idea, or you can pose a hypothetical situation and ask some participant a question which requires making use of the idea. If you get a successful, appropriate response, you know that the idea is understood. If not, you know that you've got to do something about it.

It's a good idea to develop your test questions in advance and put them right into your crib notes. In this way you can be sure that your questions are clear, directly relevant to the material you have just been presenting, and have a sensible answer. They should be important in terms of the subject matter and challenging enough to command the interest of the group. Try to avoid questions that are too difficult. You may have to end up answering them yourself. In that case the participant doesn't get the satisfaction of coming up with the right answer, and you run the risk of appearing to show off your superior knowledge, which may irritate the group.

It's all right for the group to know that your question is designed to test their understanding. But it should be asked in such a way that it doesn't threaten anyone. You should avoid the appearance of being personal or prying. Your question should force the participant to think, not just to remember something that was said earlier. The question should have a ready answer if the participant really understands the idea involved. If so, the correct answer will generate a feeling of gratification. Both the question and the answer should contribute to the learning of the group as a whole.

Generally speaking, there are two kinds of questions that you ask. One simply tests how well a participant understands some idea. The other is intended to find out if the participant know how to use or apply the idea. Here is an example of the first type of question: "How would you define 'delegation' in your own words, Carolyn?" If the answer is "Delegation is what makes people think," you will have to keep up the line of questioning. For example, you might say, "Well, give me an example." What you are trying to do is test Carolyn's understanding, not her memory. If she can use her own words or translate the idea back into her own job, she understands it. However, if she cannot do this, she does not understand it.

Another way to test understanding is to ask "why" questions. For example, "Harold, why do we have to have standards of performance before effective performance appraisals can take place?" In this instance, you are asking Harold for the relationship between the two ideas. If he can explain it, he's got a good working understanding of the idea and its application. If not, you have to keep after him.

Here's another example: "Why would we want to put an objective in writing, Bill? Isn't that just paper work?" In this case you're trying to get at the reasoning behind the need for writing down objectives. If Bill can't explain the reason why, you might have to rephrase the question. If he still doesn't know the underlying reason, you can be sure he doesn't really grasp the idea.

Understanding can also be tested by asking a participant to differentiate between ideas. "What's the difference between performance appraisal under the leading function and performance evaluation under the controlling function?" In this case the participant has to understand both the definition of the idea and its relationship to other ideas. Again, if the participants cannot do this, they probably have not fully grasped the idea and certainly won't be able to use it effectively on the job.

The second kind of question tests understanding of *how* an idea can be used: "What practical benefits do you get out of becoming a better delegator, Nancy?" If she understands what you are trying to teach her about delegation, she'll give you some very specific reasons—such as freeing up her time to do more management work or getting more work done.

A more direct question of the same type is simply to ask a participant how to use some idea. For example, "How would you go about trying to get your subordinate to identify his or her own performance deficiencies, Paul?" If Paul can give you some specific thoughts on this that are acceptable, you can be sure he understands it.

Another way to test understanding of use or application is to describe a situation and how it was handled and then to ask, "What would be a better way of doing this?" In this type of question, you ask the participant to analyze what was done in relation to what might have been done. The answer should also tell you how well the idea is understood.

Sometimes you can use a more complex question for this purpose: "What is the reason that you want to secure understanding and acceptance in any delegation situation, Margaret, and how would you actually go about securing it if you were giving a project to one of your subordinates?"

These, then, are some specific illustrations of how you can go about getting feedback from the group. A lot of feedback is coming your way anyway in the course of carrying on the seminar, which in itself may be valuable in gauging the understanding of the group. But, in addition, from time to time you have to use test questions to make sure you are getting the understanding that is central to the purpose of the seminar.

When to Do It

You test understanding at frequent intervals but in different ways. You do so whenever you want to find out whether or not your participants have learned what you have taught. You will probably find yourself testing understanding several times during a morning and similarly in the afternoon. It may be quick, but at least you do take a reading.

Sometimes you can sense from the reaction of the group that they are having trouble understanding. If so, ask a few questions to find out. If they do understand, you move ahead. If not, you go back over the point again. You test whenever you think the learners haven't understood or you aren't sure whether they have or not.

Be sure to test understanding after presenting an idea that is particularly significant, or one that is essential to understanding the next step. The more important the idea, the more important it is that you know how well the participants understand it. If you assume that a critical idea has been grasped, and you build on that idea, you will be in trouble if it turns out that the idea hasn't been understood. You will have to go back over it later and clear up the confusion. It is better to find out that something is wrong at the time it happens, rather than later.

A good time to test understanding is when you complete one subject and are about to go ahead to the next. In this way, your testing acts as a summary. It helps you to close off one subject and make a natural bridge to the next.

Whom to Ask

Usually it is not too significant to whom you direct your question. Sometimes you'll have another purpose in mind that will determine whom you select. Perhaps you want to get a passive participant to get into the action. Perhaps you want to give someone a chance to perform successfully before the group for motivational purposes. You may be asking the question simply to get someone else to summarize material that you have been covering. If so, then you may want to ask somebody who will give you the best answer. But if your main purpose is to assess the group's understanding of some subject, you might want to ask someone you think is a slower learner. If that participant understands, the others probably do, too. But you do have to be careful not to keep picking on the same person. Give everybody a chance.

Sometimes you will see someone looking puzzled during the discussion. If so, direct your question to that person. If for some reason you want to avoid embarrassing that person, then call on someone else and see if this resolves the problem.

Directing your questions to named persons from time to time, whether for testing or other purposes, has a special benefit. It keeps everyone alert. Nobody knows who will be next. If you depend on volunteers to do the answering, the less assertive may never get a chance to participate.

How to Listen

When you get a response to your question, you have to concentrate on the answer you are getting. It is easy to let your mind wander to the next subject that you have to introduce. But nothing is as discouraging to participants as to feel that you are not paying attention. It is a way of telling them their answer is unimportant. It is disrespectful and likely to create hostility.

You may think that listening is easy, but it is not. Many natural barriers prevent you from hearing correctly what someone says and understanding correctly what someone means. Sometimes you think you know what it is that Florence is going to say before she says it. So what you actually hear is what you think she was going to say, not what she really does say. Sometimes your own biases or attitudes get in the way. You tend to hear the things that you agree with and that are pleasant and not to hear the things with which you disagree. Similarly, you tend to pay a good deal less attention to someone whom you do not respect or like. You may not even be aware of all your own biases. The point is, however, to try to overcome all these barriers and truly understand the intent of the individual who is trying to communicate with you.

One of the most important rules is simply to pay attention. Look at the person who is talking and try to concentrate on what he or she is saying. Watch for facial expressions and other non-verbal clues to true meaning. Above all, don't daydream. Don't be thinking of that telephone call you have to make during the next break.

If you should lose your concentration and not hear what someone said, don't be afraid to ask for a repeat. If you are not sure, a useful device is to restate what you think the individual said and see if you get a positive or negative response in return.

Most people don't realize this, but listening is as much a part of effective communicating as speaking. To be a good communicator, you have to get feedback from your group. Unless you get it, you cannot be sure that you are truly creating understanding.

How to React to the Answer

Now you have to do something with the answer you listened to and understand. You have posed a good question and you have paid careful attention to the answer. What do you do next? It depends. If it is a reasonably acceptable answer and you sense that the group is ready to do so, you move on to the next subject. Other times you may have to make some kind of specific response.

Suppose that the answer you get is absolutely wrong. What do you do? The best approach is to rephrase the question and ask it again to make sure it has been understood. Repeating the question also gives a little more time for the participant to think. If you still get the wrong answer, pass the question on to somebody else.

What if the answer is unusually good? Here the best technique is to give your participant an opportunity to enjoy a little public recognition and satisfaction. Try to avoid rephrasing the answer or repeating it. It will have a greater effect on the other participants if you simply let it sink in as it was phrased. This is difficult to do. Your temptation will be to jump in and put it in precisely your own words.

Now, let us say you got a more-or-less correct answer but it was not particularly well-stated. Sometimes at this point the other participants will jump in and clear up the confusion. If not, probably the most useful thing to do is to restate the answer in your own words, sharpening it up as necessary. Be sure to give full credit for the answer. Make sure the participant involved doesn't think you are trying to take the credit yourself. But you have to be honest. The group will see through you if you give false praise.

As you deal with the answers you get to your test questions, you want to liberally award "strokes" if you can conscientiously do so. Misunderstandings and misconceptions have to be corrected. But, above all, be careful to treat your participants with respect and consideration. They are all good people, they are all your friends, and they are trying to learn from you. The way you treat them will have a major influence on their willingness to give you the feedback you need to ensure full understanding.

Secure Application

The final guideline in conducting the seminar is to provide opportunities for the participants to apply their new knowledge to cases, work exercises, and role playing so they can build new skills and behavior patterns. Most of the value of actual application will take place on the job. But nevertheless, there is a great deal that can be accomplished in the seminar itself, where you can provide feedback and coaching assistance as the process of application takes place.

Work Exercises

Work exercises represent one way to simulate application in the seminar room. These exercises can be either assigned to individuals or to teams.

Participants are required to apply the ideas presented in the seminar to a relatively simple situation. The exercises are ordinarily contained in the participant's workbooks, but may also be contained in handouts.

If there is a choice, use team exercises rather than individual work exercises. The latter bring a prolonged silence to the seminar room, which can cause a loss of pace and interest. Individual work exercises do have one potential advantage: they can be used to require each participant to make some specific relation between the seminar ideas and his or her own job situation. On the other hand, team exercises will take longer, but they do provide for interaction between and among different individuals, which is generally preferred by the participants.

The purpose of work exercises is to get participants to apply the ideas they have learned in a more or less ideal environment. There are no interruptions, no erroneous information, no particular pressures. The exercises are probably more useful in gaining an understanding of ideas than they are for recognizing opportunities in which the ideas could be used. Be sure to let the subgroups resolve the problems in the workbook exercises themselves. Try to stay out of it — at least for a while.

Have each of the subgroups elect a leader who will then report back to the full group. You critique their performance when they report back. You tell them what they did well and what they did wrong. Try to give as much credit as possible. Relate the lessons learned to on-the-job situations as well as you can. Remember, your job is to see that they learn everything they can from the work exercise that can be useful to them back on the job.

Role Playing

Another form of practice application is role playing, which can be highly structured or quite impromptu. Role plays are usually structured directly into the program design. Seminar leaders simply have to follow that design, which will differ for different programs. Sometimes individual participants are asked to perform before the whole class for a group critique. At other times, they make their skill demonstrations in small subgroups in which they evaluate their own and each other's performance. The use of videotape playback equipment is becoming more and more widely used for these demonstrations because of the unique opportunity offered for self-evaluation. The playback feature makes evaluations no longer dependent on remembering details of the performance. The role play can be recreated through "reruns."

Sometimes seminar leaders can very effectively improvise role plays. "John, let's say I am a prospective purchaser and you are a salesman trying to sell me some office equipment. You have sized me up as being a fairly dominant person. Show me how you would go about closing the sale." If John handles the situation properly, you know he has understood. You have also reinforced some learning with the other participants who observed the role playing.

Skill Demonstrations

In some types of seminars, participants can practice the skills they are supposed to be developing under the supervision of the seminar leader and get direct coaching assistance. The practice serves to test the current stage of their training progress as well as to provide actual application experience. Skill demonstrations are particularly useful in training seminars designed to develop specific technical skills, such as the operation of equipment, or the use of a new computer language.

The Critique

Once you have given participants the chance to apply what they have learned in some work exercise or through role playing, you have to provide some coaching assistance for them to get the most out of it. This need is especially strong if skill building is an important behavioral objective in the seminar or workshop. It is a particularly difficult part of the seminar leader's job because no one really enjoys constructive criticism. That is why it is wise to emphasize the reward for doing better rather than the specific deficiencies to be corrected.

Accentuate the Positive. The purpose of critiquing is positive. If you point out participants' weaknesses, it is so that they can improve. Your purpose is not to make people look stupid or to make yourself look smart. Nobody really enjoys being criticized. Therefore, you should make clear on the first day of your class that performance is going to be criticized and tell them why in positive terms.

Watch out for the relative weight of your negatives to your positives. You don't want to criticize so much that your negative comments outweigh the positive ones. Try to leave the participants with the feeling that they are in fact improving. Of course, your positive comments should be sincere.

Be Selective. In providing feedback, you want to focus on participants' most important opportunities for improvement to make these visible and help them recognize these points. Then you want to help them overcome these identified weaknesses. You cannot expect to create perfection. If you insist on mentioning every single thing that they did wrong, you can weaken their self-confidence and commitment. However, if a fundamental is not used properly, you must bring it to the attention of the participant.

In deciding what to comment upon and what to pass over, your rule of decision should be based upon the importance of the specific weakness to their performance on the job. By following this rule, the participants will learn that the points you are making are important to them. They learn that they should listen carefully to what you have to say and try to take advantage of it.

Get Help From the Participants. One way to make the critiquing job easier is to get help from the participants themselves. The least threatening way to critique is to ask the participants to evaluate their own performance. You can ask them directly what they would do differently if they were to do the assignment another time. If you've created a good seminar environment, you'll discover that people are not loathe to critique themselves. In the alternative, you can ask other participants what the performing participant did well and what improvements could be suggested. This indirect route is not always appropriate. Sometimes the point to be made is fairly obvious and needn't be belabored. You simply describe what was done wrong and how it could be corrected. In any event, it is your obligation as the seminar leader to endorse or overrule the self-criticisms or the comments of the group. In many cases you will find they will be tougher than you are.

In critiquing performance, try to keep a light touch. Remember that you are criticizing some individual's best effort, which makes most people feel uneasy. Using a little humor can help to put a person at ease and soften the impact of the criticism. Always remember: never use humor that will cause embarrassment to anyone. And don't overdo it, either. Otherwise you will be regarded as not taking the course very seriously and people will react accordingly.

Wholly apart from which approach to criticism you use, make sure the participants understand the reason why the right way is better and the wrong way was wrong. Participants have to be able to understand the underlying rationale if they are going to be able to use your ideas in many different situations.

People Are Different. Another point to remember in your critiques is that people are different. Some will quickly grasp the ideas you present and take an active part in group discussions. Others will be less able and less willing to do this. Some may be very sensitive to performing before a group of their peers. These differences will show up in their reaction to receiving criticism. Some people may take this in full stride. Others may feel unusually sensitive and threatened. With such a person, you are probably well advised to take it easy on them in class. It would be better to give some after-hours coaching to such an individual.

Give Them a Vision.   If you are going to get your participants to continue to use the ideas you have been giving them, you will have to make them feel that somehow they will profit by doing so. It is up to you to help them see the benefits they will receive personally. If they understand all the things that you have taught them, if they can see how to use them on the job effectively, and if they truly feel some sense of personal benefit from using them, then you've got them. They will continue to use what you have taught them long after your seminar has been completed. This will be one of your great satisfactions as a seminar leader.

You have to provide them with a vision. They have to see some pay-off or benefit in increased job satisfaction in some form. If your participants see that this is likely to happen, in whatever specific form they may visualize it, they will really want to improve their performance. They will be keenly interested in their own progress and improvement. What you have to do, then, is to help them see this in themselves. Sometimes you can provide specific illustrations of improved performance that you can feed back to the participants. Sometimes, at the end of the course, you can get participants themselves—perhaps in an unstructured group discussion—to evaluate and share their own improvement perceptions with other members of the group. It is even better if you can get the participants to identify improvements in each other. But regardless of how it is done, it is of great importance that the participants emerge from your program with the conviction that the ideas are sound and really work and that they can benefit personally from putting them to work. The greatest satisfaction a seminar leader can get is carrying his or her participants through to this point of conviction and enthusiasm.

As the participants file out of your seminar room, you experience a feeling of gratification in a job well done. You knew the seminar thoroughly— its objectives and subject matter. You got to know this participant group and were able to make adjustments and relate to them well. You captured and kept their favorable attention. All the various methods of communication were employed with professional skill to secure their understanding. With repetition and association with familiar ideas, you reinforced and ensured retention of the key ideas. You know from the feedback you received that the subject matter was truly understood. And finally, you gave them opportunities to apply their learning and get constructive feedback from your and the other participants. From all this, you can be sure that this group will demonstrate a significant improvement in productivity on the job. You have indeed presented a successful seminar.

8. Follow Up

12

How to Present Successful Programs: Tales of Woe

Whenever seminar leader professionals get together informally, the conversation often turns to "horror stories," disasters that even the most successful of them can find in their backgrounds somewhere. I'm not sure why this is so. Perhaps the storytellers want to project an image of such self-assurance that they can laugh at themselves. Maybe it's to avoid appearing too pompous and detached.

In any event, we can learn a great deal from looking at what can go wrong. Naturally we don't want to become too obsessed with this point of view. It is essentially negative. But we all learn from making mistakes, and we can benefit from the misfortunes of others as well as from our own.

All the anecdotes collected in this chapter are known to be true either from my own experience or by report from a reliable source.

Program Leader Problems

There are a variety of sad tales focused on program leaders.

The Missing Program Leader

Picture a seminar room with a class of participants gathered around a U-shaped table, but no seminar leader. They are gathered together at the Marriott motel in Tarrytown, New York. They are shaking their heads, looking at their watches, and getting increasingly frustrated.

One venturesome individual goes to the wall telephone and starts making telephone calls. Eventually he succeeds in reaching the regional manager of the company sponsoring the seminar. We'll call him Bill Williams.

How let's shift the scene to the waiting room of a medical clinic on East End Avenue in New York City. Bill Williams was midway through his annual physical examination. It was Monday morning at about 10:30 A.M. when he was called to the telephone. Much to his horror, Bill learned that the whole group of attendees at the seminar had been waiting around for an hour and a half for the program leader, which was to have been Hank Meyers, a semiretired ex-partner of Bill's firm. Hank Meyers was happy to make himself available to conduct seminars from time to time to augment his retirement income. He knew the material well and had great platform presence.

You can appreciate the panic that grabbed him as Bill assessed the situation. Here he was sitting in a hospital gown in New York City, between medical procedures. He was trying to prevent his anatomy from being visible to the two other patients, similarly attired. It wasn't easy. His gown, which was literally all he was wearing, didn't even reach his knees and was open in back.

He was at least a 1½-hour drive from the seminar site in Tarrytown. Up there was a room full of unhappy people whose companies had invested substantial money to enroll them in the program and provide for hotel and transportation. At least two of the participants represented very attractive prospects for future consulting services.

Bill leaped into action. He thanked his telephone informant for taking charge so effectively and asked him to adjourn the class until 1:00 P.M., at which time Bill said he would be there to take over. He explained that his partner, Hank Meyers, was scheduled to give the program and surmised that something must have happened to prevent him from getting there. Bill was sincerely concerned because Hank was very reliable and a good friend. He must have had some terrible accident on the way to the seminar.

When Bill arrived in Tarrytown, he found that the seminar participants were not as upset as he was. They were really quite understanding, as it turned out. Bill explained that something must have happened to Hank and assured them that he would be able to cover the material they missed. He also invited them all to join him for cocktails in the lounge after class at his expense.

At about 5 o'clock, Hank Meyers calmly entered the room and looked around with astonishment. He had believed the seminar didn't start until Tuesday morning and had arrived to check out the meeting room in advance. What made this particularly embarrassing to both Hank and Bill was that Hank had spent a whole day with Bill in Bill's New York office 10 days earlier to be briefed on some changes to the program. They covered everything in great detail. But each assumed the other knew what day the seminar started!

Looking back, it's hard to believe this incident really happened. But it did. The good news is that Hank took over on the second day and the seminar was a great success. In fact, one of the participants became a client within the year. Years later another one joined Bill's firm, opening an office in Paris.

The story does demonstrate that people can easily make assumptions about what the other knows. A written confirming memorandum would have avoided the problem. When we put things in writing, we are generally more careful to provide a complete communication.

Personal Crises

Here are two true stories about seminar leaders who faced personal crises while their seminars were being actively presented. Most seminar leaders don't have to face such a conflict. Or if they do, there are substitute program leaders available to take over. If no substitute is easily available, there is a strong tradition, much like in the theater, that "the show must go on."

The first of these situations involved an associate of a middle-sized training firm who was presenting a management seminar in Singapore. On the second day of the program, he received a cable from his wife stating that an elderly aunt had died and asking him to return at once to San Francisco for the funeral. He promptly dismissed the class and took the next plane home.

He was roundly criticized by his firm, no so much for leaving the seminar but for not even trying to find a replacement. Although not mentioned, it was believed that an elderly aunt was hardly a close enough relative for such an extreme action.

Something quite similar happened years later during a seminar being conducted at Buck Hill Falls in the Pocono Mountains in Pennsylvania. The program leader had the class working in small teams on an application exercise toward the end of the first day, when he was called to the telephone. It was his wife, semihysterical, calling from New York City. She ordered him to come home at once. Her sister's husband had dropped dead of a heart attack without any prior warning at the age of 39.

What to do? It was a considerable personal shock. The program leader and his wife had just recently spent a weekend skiing with his wife's sister and brother-in-law. At the same time, the program leader happened to know that there was simply no one available to take over for him. It was a fairly high-level group of participants in a major new client. The penalty for calling it all off just seemed unacceptable.

It was an agony of a decision, but he telephoned his wife at the end of the day and told her it was impossible for him to come. She had subsided a little by then but was still furious at his decision. She hung up on him and said she'd never speak to him again.

The discussion leader, in true theatrical tradition, did not mention his personal problem to the class. He carried on as though nothing had happened. He had gotten to know them well enough to know they would have been interested and sympathetic, but he didn't want anything to interfere with the fullest success of the program. (By the way, his wife later did forgive him.)

It's difficult to know what you or I would have done in cases of this kind. Certainly there is an obligation to find a replacement before calling off a program. The nature of the personal problem is of prime importance too. Death of a spouse or child would have to be viewed quite differently from that of an elderly aunt. Logistics are also a consideration. It would be easier to cancel and postpone a program in which no participant travel or facility expense was involved. But the tradition of carrying on is strong. "The show must go on!"

Problems with Program Materials

You might think that the worst thing that can happen is to arrive at a seminar site and find that there are no workbooks to distribute to the participants. To be sure, it's a difficult situation, but you can usually arrange for a duplicate shipment. And if you know your material well enough, all you need is an easel pad and a glib tongue to survive for at least half a day.

There's also another recourse, well known to seasoned practitioners. Divide the group into teams and give them some assignment that will capture their interest and produce feedback for a useful group discussion. You can usually buy perhaps an hour at a time this way. And they'll love it!

No, far worse is to have the wrong workbooks. I hope it never happens to you. I've got two stories on this. The first one involves a major space-age company which commissioned a partner in an outside firm to produce—at considerable expense—a customized version of one of the firm's standard programs. The special workbook was replete with examples and cases especially relevant to the client. It also featured the client's logo and official colors on the cover of the workbook.

The outside consultant, let's call him Jerry Johnson, checked with the hotel in Atlanta, Georgia, in advance to make sure the workbooks had arrived. He was particularly concerned because the participant group was composed mostly of higher-ranking executives in the client company. He was informed that the shipment of workbooks had in fact arrived and would be brought to the seminar room early next morning. With this reassurance, Jerry had a good night's sleep.

His tranquility was lost in an explosion of despair the following morning at 7:15 A.M. When he opened the cartons containing the educational materials, he saw the familiar covers of the firm's standard program! A quick look through the inside pages confirmed that his company had sent the wrong workbooks. He had so looked forward to seeing the finished version of the customized workbooks on which he had lavished some $25,000 of the client's money.

What added to his frustration was the time difference between Atlanta and his firm headquarters in Palo Alto, California. He had to wait until 11:30 A.M. before he could telephone the office and vent his fury.

The other story has a slightly different twist. It wasn't until he distributed the workbooks to the participants' places that Larry Francis realized that it was the recently updated version of the program with different cases and enough text changes to require new page references. It was not the same version contained in *his* workbook, which was carefully marked with all his crib notes. Fortunately, the changes were not so great that he couldn't use the overhead transparencies he brought with him.

As the magnitude of the problem hit him, Larry's fast-moving mind thought of a possible solution. If at least 1 of the 20 participants scheduled to attend the seminar failed to show up, he could appropriate one of the new workbooks and use it together with his marked-up old workbook to conduct the session.

As people gathered to attend the program, Larry as his usual charming self, greeting them as they arrived. Behind his affable exterior, however, he was busily counting the participants as the class gradually assembled. He counted only 17 with 5 minutes to go. But the number had increased to 19 when the clock registered 8:30 A.M., the scheduled starting time. Just as he was feeling a grateful release from his tension, the twentieth participant arrived in a rush! There would be no new workbook available for him to appropriate.

The morning was a nightmare, although it was not apparent to the class, with one exception. Larry had to enlist the help of the nearest participant to double check page references. Then at every break and during the lunch hour he reviewed this attendee's workbook to take fast notes on the new cases and make necessary changes to his crib notes. He survived, but it was a scramble.

From that day forward, Larry always ordered at least one extra workbook. He never experienced precisely the same problem. But on occasion he had to steal pages from the extra workbook to replace defective or missing pages in some participant's copy. It turned out to be a useful precaution.

Facility Problems

Let me review a series of actual situations in which the facility served as a significant deterrent to learning.

1. This facility was a charming, historic country inn nestled in the foothills of southern New Hampshire. I suspect it offered a bargain price to the sponsoring company. It had only recently been modified to attract seminars and meetings. The conference room had been an outside porch which was now walled in by plastic hangings attached to the underside of the roof and extending to the concrete floor. A bare wood table was surrounded by folding wooden chairs of minimum width and comfort.

All this was bad enough. But the seminar was scheduled in early February, during what turned out to be a spell of freezing weather. When the first few people came into the seminar room, they could literally see their own breaths as their exhalations condensed in the frigid air. It was quickly agreed to adjourn to the living room, where one attendee kept a Franklin stove supplied with wood and the rest of the group sat around in a strange assortment of New England chairs, workbooks in lap.

2. Several hours drive outside of Mexico City lies an old plantation with aged stone walls and gracious trees. It had been taken over as a conference center, a fascinating, beautiful place. In an interior part of the main structure was a large room, fitted out for conferences. The workshop being conducted there was one which required the participants to develop measurable standards of performance on acetate sheets. Several of them would then be selected to put their work on overhead projectors to show to the rest of the class for critique. It would be a valuable learning experience for all.

What made this seminar memorable was that there was an electrical blackout for several hours. Because the conference room had no windows, it was cast immediately into complete blackness. You couldn't see your hand in front of your face. There was no way to know how long it would last. The seminar leader tried valiantly to carry on but finally had to adjourn the group to the outdoors. As you can imagine, the coefficient of learning (if there is such a thing) took a nose dive.

3. Shifting scenes again, put yourself in a small, aging hotel near the St. Francis Hotel in the center of San Francisco where a public seminar on management concepts and methods is being held. Representatives from various organizations came from as far away as Florida and Canada to attend the session. The program leader came from New York and had not seen the facility until he arrived to conduct the seminar. It had been secured by his firm's local office, which had assured him of its adequacy.

The hotel had been built in the late 1920s and had not been redecorated for at least 10 years. The carpeting in the public halls and elevators was badly worn, as was the upholstery on the chairs in the small lobby. The whole effect was somewhat dark and Victorian. If you stretched it a bit, you could say the place had a lot of old charm. Several of the participants took one look and found a nearby hotel instead.

The seminar room, on the second floor, was quite acceptable, however, or at least until the hammering started! It happened after lunch on the first day. The noise was so deafening, the discussion leader had to call a 15-minute break while he hastened to the front office to make loud, angry complaints. But, incredibly, the hotel could do nothing about it. The owner of the building was doing some important reconstruction work over which the hotel had absolutely no control.

The hotel management tried to be helpful. They offered the "Royal Suite" on the twelfth floor or space in another hotel. Neither alternative was acceptable, but the program leader opted for the twelfth floor, moving the whole session up there. The suite was intended for comfortable residential use. It was too small and narrow for a seminar. But it had to do.

The curious thing about this experience was that the participant group had developed some comradery by this time and was very good natured about the change. The seminar turned out to be very successful. Many months later, the seminar leader learned that the group almost played a dirty trick on him. They were going to have someone burst into the seminar room with a noisy vacuum cleaner. But at the last minute they thought the better of it. The poor fellow had suffered enough!

The moral of this story? Check out the facility yourself before you put on a seminar.

4. Let's move now to New York City to a large conference room on the second floor of a hotel facing Fifth Avenue where a 1-day session

for a prestigious professional firm is being held. Everything had gone smoothly until 11:00 A.M.

It's Columbus Day folks! And the Columbus Day parade is right outside the window. The blaring, booming sound of marching bands ebbs and flows as new marching elements pass by to take the place of old ones.

The message here is obvious but sometimes overlooked. Be alert for outside interventions, in this case attributable to the day selected for the meeting.

Equipment Failure

I can still see him trying to put a good face on it, but it was a complete disaster. It wasn't exactly a "seminar," but it could have been. The speaker had been asked to put on a program for the New York City chapter of the American Society for Training and Development. The subject was the march of technology and its impact on human resource development. Specifically, it was a demonstration of computer-driven image projections from data stored on compact disc.

The speaker had assembled an impressive array of computer equipment and related hardware on the front of the stage. Just behind this equipment was a giant screen. On each seat in the meeting room was a complex handout, the first page of which was a "menu" that listed many subjects of interest to the audience.

He explained that the presentation was intended to be more of an experience than the usual presentation. He stated that in a moment he would display the menu on the large screen in front and ask for the group to select any subject of interest. He would then switch to that subject on the screen and show us an outline which he would use to describe all the things that were happening relating to that subject. After questions and answers, he said, we could then choose another subject for similar treatment.

If there had been a musical accompaniment, there would have been an attention-getting fanfare as he turned his and our attention to the screen. He flipped the master switch and stopped frozen before us for a full minute. The large screen lit up, all right, but it was so dim that none of us could read it! He fiddled a bit with the controls and connections, but it didn't help. See what I mean about a disaster?

By way of contrast, we had another speaker appear before our chapter at another time. His subject was communication. He arrived with two assistants an hour before he was scheduled to speak. They carefully placed and tested the two 35mm projectors that he was going to use, the lighting at the speaker's stand, and the microphone equipment. Weeks before, one of his assistants had telephoned five members of our chapter to get some background on our existing knowledge of communicating techniques and subjects of special interest to us.

It won't surprise you that his presentation was outstanding, nor that he was the head of a consulting firm specializing in communications. How does the Boy Scout motto go? "Be prepared."

Troublesome Participants

Every professional in the field will be heard to say on various occasions that it is the participants who determine the success of a seminar. They can also contribute to its failure. Let me review a few cases.

1. The Western Electric Company used to have (and may still have) a huge training facility near Princeton, New Jersey. They put on most of their programs themselves but supplemented their own effort from time to time with outsiders.

One such outside presenter, let's call him Morris Fields, was conducting an advanced workshop on management planning and control when two of the participants complained to the management of the training center during a break that "their needs were not being met." The two were particularly articulate, leadership types. As a result, when the class reassembled, a representative of the training establishment was present. He interrupted the proceedings to report on this complaint and asked for a general discussion from the whole class.

Points of view were exchanged for about half an hour. At that time, one of the participants asked for a show of hands as to how many in the class had read the advance description of the course given in the catalog distributed by the training people. Less than a third of the class held up their hands! Needless to say, the two complainants had never read the advance billing. The class voted to proceed with the course, but Morris Fields was psychologically crushed.

He should have been. If he had asked for each participant to state his or her expectations of the course at the outset, the problem could have been avoided. It sometimes helps to collect these on an easel pad and use that page at the end of the program as part of the summary.

2. This case involves a similar corporate training center and a participant who was a particular problem. At the outset, each attendee was asked to get up, introduce himself or herself to the group, and state what he or she hoped to get out of the seminar. When it came to our troublemaker, who was fourth from the last to get up, he said "I don't know why I'm here. I didn't want to come, and I don't expect to get anything useful out of it."

For the space of perhaps 15 seconds there was absolute silence in the room. When the program leader finally recovered his poise, he muttered something about hoping the participant would, in fact, find something useful in the program. He then continued with the seminar.

Curiously enough, it turned out later that our troublemaker made a complete switch in attitude as he worked with the others in the group. He became a leader of the group and made a presentation to the seminar leader on behalf of all the participants at the end of the program. I guess he must have thought he was being funny, but nobody took it that way.

3. The setting for another tale of woe was the seminar leader's own office, 2 days after she had completed what she thought to be a very successful public seminar. The telephone rang. When our leader picked up the instrument she heard the voice of a training director whom she knew well complaining about the seminar. It seemed that a director of research from his company was very upset because he wasn't given enough of an opportunity to participate during the seminar. When the seminar leader reconstructed the situation, she realized that she had allowed a young, articulate MBA-type from a prestigious Wall Street firm to dominate the group discussions, to the disadvantage of the research director, among others.

4. At a 5-day course for new managers sponsored by a leading manufacturer of hair products and held at a conference center, everyone was told to dress informally, which meant slacks and open shirts for both the men and the women.

This time, I was the seminar leader, although for only one half of the day. I got one half of the total student group in the morning and the other half in the afternoon. This was the morning group. It was a little on the large size, about 30 people, but manageable.

As is my custom, I very shortly divided them up into teams for an appropriate exercise. After the teams had had enough time to develop their conclusions, and as I was writing their responses on the easel pad, I was aware that a young woman on my right had put her feet up on the table and leaned way back in her chair. She seemed to be challenging me with her facial expression, as though to say "what are you going to do about this, you old fogey?"

I didn't do a thing about it, although I was more than a little upset. I concluded that there was a generation gap here of about 40 years. Perhaps I *was* a bit old-fashioned to think that students shouldn't put their feet on the table. The others didn't seem to mind, so why should I? In any event, she looked as though she could hold her own in a showdown!

I suppose I could have made a humorous remark about her pretty feet or dirty socks. If I could have thought of a good one-liner, I might have gotten a chuckle out of the group and induced her to assume a more decorous posture. But I am not that quick with the quip. I usually think of the perfect response afterwards. This situation resolved itself when I redivided the group into teams and they had to pull their chairs back from the table.

The list of woes could go on. But perhaps enough has been said to warn you that these things will happen. Some, like equipment malfunction, are preventable. Most just happen and you have to deal with them as well as you can. If you have developed a good rapport with your class, they'll be understanding. If you have a good sense of humor, you can use minor adversities as a chance for a quick witticism.

13

How to Evaluate
Your Seminars

You and I have come a long way together since you first picked up this book. Putting on successful training seminars requires a lot of planning, a lot of up-front work, as well as the use of professional skills in the actual delivery of the program.

But if you remember that far back, you'll recall that we appear to be entering a decade in which greater and greater emphasis will be given to improving the productivity of human resources. At the same time, companies are facing a toughening, worldwide competition for survival. You may well expect to have increasing resources for your training function, but you also have to expect that a close look will be taken at what those resources are generating in terms of concrete results. There will be few if any companies investing in training because they know it's the "right thing" to do. They will want to have a strict accounting for their investment, much as they have long been accustomed to for capital investments. How will you deal with that?

In most cases, the objective of a training seminar is to improve performance on the job. It would seem therefore that this should be the thrust of any seminar evaluation effort. Some laudable efforts have been made in this direction, but for many practical reasons, most training directors depend almost exclusively on the evaluations of the participants in the seminar.

Participant Evaluations

The most generally used postseminar evaluation takes place right in the seminar room. The participants are asked to fill out a form to give their opinions on the quality of the presentation and subject matter and the relevance of their new learning to their job responsibilities. There are differences of opinion on the reliability of these judgments. The main criticism voiced is that the participants may be unduly influenced by the pleasure of the experience rather than its value in terms of improved performance. This criticism is especially directed at evaluations made in the glow of the seminar leader's last impassioned summary. One training director flatly states he doesn't care what the participants say, so long as he can show a measurably improved performance on the job.

Why to Do It

Despite these criticisms, participant evaluations can be helpful, if interpreted with good judgment in light of all the surrounding circumstances. Even if the performance of the presenter produces an upward bias, you still get a picture of the strongest and weakest portions of the program. The evaluations can be helpful to the presenter in improving future seminars. In some instances, the comments of participants can result in a redesign of the seminar.

Furthermore, patterns may emerge from one group to the next, if the seminar is a continuing one. For example, if the visual aids are consistently rated lower than other aspects of the seminar, you can reasonably conclude there is the need for improvement in the visuals. If your favorite cost-effective facility is always rated on the low side, you might want to get another place for your seminar. If a change in location is not practical, you might find it worthwhile for the presenter to mention the favorable economics of the site at an early point in the seminar.

The participants' "smile sheets" may also offer a motivational advantage. In this democratic country, "the voice of the people" has an important value. If some participant has a very strong reaction, either positive or negative, some tension can be created if there is no outlet through which to express it. And remember, all these participants are going back into your organization, influencing the total "climate." Some day they may be influential members of the higher management hierarchy.

How to Do It

In using participant evaluations, there are some guidelines that can be developed from accumulated experience. You may not agree with all of them, but perhaps they will start you thinking about the subject.

Develop a Standard Form.   The first suggestion is to develop a standard form that is partly structured and partly unstructured. The structure makes it easy to make statistical summaries. The unstructured portion encourages creative contributions. We favor a rather simple form
that focuses separately on the presentation, the subject matter, and the
overall impact of the seminar, while providing a few "open end" questions (see Figure 11). You will note that our form features a five-point
scale to provide a range of scoring options but without too much definition on the precise meaning of each. Our own experience would indicate that successful seminars will get at least 80% of the responses in
the 4 and 5 categories. *Use evens cale force off neutral*
Use descriptors on scale

Get Immediate Evaluations.   Get the evaluations filled out before the
participants leave the seminar room, even at the risk of a positive bias.
Why? A simple answer: to get 100% response. If you try to get the responses at a later date, you may get only 60% to 70% and cannot be sure
how truly representative they are. Members of the "silent majority" may
not be fully represented. It takes time and effort to fill out the form—
time and effort more likely to be expended by those with something
particular they want to say, often negative.

Ownership
Encourage Signed Forms.   Try to get the participants to sign their
evaluations. But do it gently. You don't want to force them, if they prefer to remain anonymous. The reason for getting their signatures is to
help in reviewing the evaluations. If, for example, you know that some
individual participant was forced to go to the seminar against his or her
will, you might expect a less favorable evaluation. Furthermore, you
may value the judgment of some individuals more than others.
less honest

Use With Care.   Participant evaluations are valuable, but after all, you
are the professional in the training business. It is your professional
judgment that should have the greatest weight.
   Let me offer an illustration from recent experience. A management
seminar specially designed for higher management levels had been getting excellent ratings from three prior groups when it suddenly was
rated just satisfactory with a few strongly negative votes. Was it the presenter who had gone stale? Was it due to unusually poor timing (the
participants were constantly on the telephone with their subordinates to
finalize strategic plans that were due on the day after the seminar)? Was
it the makeup of the group (there were two "angry young men" represented)? It was extraordinarily difficult to sort out these possibilities.
Some changes were made in the seminar to step up the pace and to pro-

LOUIS ALLEN ASSOCIATES, INC.
CONFIDENTIAL PARTICIPANT EVALUATION

Program _____ Presenter _____ Dates _____

City _____ Public _____ In-Company _____

Presentation (Circle your answer)

1. How would you describe the presenter's knowledge of the subject matter?	Limited 1	2	3	4	Extensive 5
2. In general, how did the presenter treat differing viewpoints?	With Antagonism 1	2	3	4	Acknowledged them 5
3. How did you find the presenter's style of delivery?	Uninteresting 1	2	3	4	Dynamic 5
4. Were the concepts, principles and techniques explained in an understandable manner?	Seldom 1	2	3	4	Consistently 5
5. Did the presenter invite and encourage individual participation?	Seldom 1	2	3	4	Consistently 5
6. Did the presenter maintain control of the discussion and work groups?	Seldom 1	2	3	4	Consistently 5
7. Did the presenter use visual aids for reinforcement of discussion points?	Seldom 1	2	3	4	Consistently 5

8. Did the presenter hold your interest?

	Seldom				Consistently
	1	2	3	4	5

Program Content

9. Was the program content organized so that you could under-stand it?

	Difficult to Understand				Easy to Understand
	1	2	3	4	5

10. Did you find the workbook clearly outlined the content of the program?

	Not very clear				Very clear
	1	2	3	4	5

11. How often could you relate the situation in the case studies to your own job?

	Seldom				Consistently
	1	2	3	4	5

12. Did you find participation in the application exercises benefi-cial?

	Seldom				Consistently
	1	2	3	4	5

13. How useful did you find the visual aids used? (slides, Vu-graphs, etc.)

	Of no use				Very Useful
	1	2	3	4	5

Program Overall

14. Do you think that you will be able to apply what you learned in this program to your job situation?

	Seldom				Consistently
	1	2	3	4	5

15. Did you feel challenged by the content and the exercises?

	Seldom				Consistently
	1	2	3	4	5

16. To what degree did you feel that the content and exercises were relevant to your job?

	Not relevant				Very relevant
	1	2	3	4	5

Figure 11. Louis A. Allen Associates, Inc.: Confidential Participant Evaluation.

LOUIS ALLEN ASSOCIATES, INC.
CONFIDENTIAL PARTICIPANT EVALUATION

Program _____ Presenter _____ Dates _____
City _____ Public _____ In-Company _____

17. How would you rate the facility in which the program was held?

Poor				Exceptional
1	2	3	4	5

18. Please comment on any question (Presentation, Program Content or Program Overall) to which you gave a rating of 1 or 5.

Question
Number: Comments:

_____

_____

_____

_____

_____

_____

19. Do you have any additional comments regarding program or presentation strengths and weaknesses?

_____

_____

_____

_____

_____

_____

Participant Profile. Your answers to the following questions are for our research purposes only. You may sign or not, as you wish.

A. Type of business or enterprise _____   C. Years in management _____

B. Your position title _____

D. Educational level _____   Signature _____

Form No. 640.1 (1/81)

Figure 11. (*Continued*) Louis A. Allen Associates, Inc.: Confidential Participant Evaluation.

vide more team exercises on "real world" problems. With these changes, and a more sensitive eye on timing, the training director was pleased to see the "excellent" ratings resumed. If he had taken the evaluations at face value, he might have abandoned a seminar that had been having a positive impact with other groups.

Securing Postseminar Implementation

The "bottom line" is improved performance on the job. Many training directors realize there is a need to go further than participant evaluations of the seminar. There is a need to put in motion some specific efforts to induce participants to put their new knowledge to work on the job. In some instances it is relatively easy. If they were being specifically trained on new equipment or new procedures, they are *required* by the organization to use their new skills on the job; no further effort is necessary. They simply have to put the training to use.

But if the participants are not compelled to use the new knowledge, it is much more difficult. They may sincerely want to, if the seminar has had a positive impact; but a backlog of paperwork has accumulated while they were at the seminar. Their superiors may be making certain demands that have to be given high priority. As time goes on the probability of self-implementation declines. For all these practical considerations, not to mention that old habits die hard, you have to consider the available means for "building a fire" under the participants.

Postseminar Assignments

One way to motivate your ex-participants is to set up an assignment for each participant to carry out after the seminar is completed. For example, let's say the seminar included training in holding effective performance counseling sessions. Then an appropriate assignment would be for each individual to use the newly learned method in the next performance counseling session that the participant is required to conduct, completing and forwarding a self-evaluation form provided for this purpose.

There are a variety of assignments that could be made. Participants could complete and forward self-evaluation forms as they next delegate a project to a subordinate, or next make a formal oral communication, or next analyze a problem for decision, or next make an important sales presentation.

Postseminar assignments should ordinarily be developed by the participants themselves or at least have their understanding and acceptance for best results. Thus, if some participant has an organizational problem to face, then his or her project might be to apply the seminar-taught technique for organization improvement. Another participant might elect to use an action-planning process covered in the seminar to realize some specific cost improvement.

Reviewing the possibilities reveals one important implication: the training director has to provide for some way to follow up to collect the self-evaluations. An administrative requirement is imposed which has to be staffed by qualified people with the time available to do the follow-up.

Superiors' Completion Certificates

Postseminar assignments can be made more effective if a certificate from the participant's superior is substituted for or used in conjunction with the self-evaluation form, and if the certificate of completion of the course is awarded only after receiving the superior's certificate. We have used this technique with some success, the requirements for receiving the certificate being included at the end of each participant's workbook (see Figure 12).

The involvement of participants' superiors is particularly desirable. The superior is a much surer source of motivation than the training department. However, it does require cooperation from the participants' superiors, which may or may not be forthcoming. We abandoned the practice in our public seminars years ago for one simple reason: we had to depend on the participants to get their own superiors involved, which didn't happen often enough to warrant continuation of the practice.

Superiors' Orientation Sessions

Group sessions involving the superiors of participants are beginning to be used in influencing postseminar behavior. One instance, reported by the New York Stock Exchange, involved a series of informal group sessions with the superiors of a group of supervisors who had gone through a time-management course. The participants' superiors there were given an understanding of the subject matter of the program and participated in informal group discussions on how they could help improve their subordinates' performance in managing their time.

Other Motivational Methods

Two other methods for postseminar participation have come to light: one is publicity and the other is use of refresher courses. One manage-

Managers who have participated in the Profession of Management Seminar may qualify for the Professional Manager Certificate of Completion, which attests to demonstrated achievement in professional management.

This certificate is awarded upon satisfactorily meeting the following requirements:

1. Completion of the prescribed Louis A. Allen Profession of Management Seminar.
2. Completion of the Management Work Assignment A, *signed by your superior.*
3. Completion of the Certificate Review Form B, *signed by your superior.*
4. Receipt of one copy of the completed Forms A and B, with attachments* to Ralph MacDonald, Louis A. Allen Associates, Inc., Palo Alto, California.

A distinctive vellum certificate will be awarded each successful applicant, certifying to his study, analysis, and practice of professional management.

Ralph MacDonald
Management Services

*Attachments will be treated with utmost confidence and returned to sender if so requested.

© Louis A. Allen Associates and reproduced with permission

Figure 12. The Louis A. Allen management program: Requirements for the Professional Manager Certificate of Completion.

ment development firm used newsletters for this purpose. Performance improvement projects would be developed by each of the participants during the seminar. At the end of the seminar, the participants agreed to complete 45-day and 90-day progress reports on their projects which the firm would then use as the basis for developing a newsletter to be distributed back to all participants. The method proved to be administratively onerous and was abandoned, primarily because it required a great deal of telephone follow-up. Nevertheless, it might be more successful if administered internally by a training department.

Another publicity method is use of the organization's internal publication. For a period of many months, the Bank of America devoted a regular column in each issue of its internal newsletter to some management principle or concept. Each story was accompanied by enough specifics to make it newsworthy and give some individual recognition.

"Refresher" courses represent another approach to motivating participants to apply their seminar knowledge to their jobs. It adds a sense of importance and brings forward to their consciousness many of the ideas and information that may have been forgotten through disuse.

Measuring Performance Improvement

If the final pay-off of your training program is improved performance on the job, how do you measure it? You need to be able to measure the impact of your seminars if you are going to evaluate your own performance as a trainer. Isn't this the rationale that we started with 10 chapters ago? Namely, training is part of a broad-scale effort to improve the productivity of human resources.

Yet with a few outstanding exceptions, measuring performance improvement is not being done at all, or is not being done well.* The reasons are very practical. For one thing, the methods for measurement are generally considered either too crude or too costly or both. For another, you have to be able to call upon the cooperation and efforts of the participants' supervisors, which is difficult to do in many organizations. In any event, considerable administrative support is required by the training function, which may have all it can do developing and conducting its higher-priority programs.

The methods available, as one might expect, range from the highly sophisticated to the very crude. We have not attempted any exhaustive survey, but can report upon a fairly broad base of experience.

Internal Consultants   link b/t performance + training

One extreme of sophistication is illustrated by the Fiduciary Group of Bankers Trust Company, as reported to us. In this organization, a highly sophisticated, computerized system has been developed that ties training directly into job requirements backed by standards of performance and productivity measures. A small cadre of qualified internal consultants analyzes performance deficiencies to identify training

*See Lookatch, Richard P.: "HRD's Failure to Sell Itself," *Training & Development*, American Society of Training and Development, July 1991, p. 47.

needs, and measures the impact on productivity of the training given. The provable gains in productivity are said to offset the cost of this staff by a large margin every year.

Control Groups

Another sophisticated approach† involves measuring productivity gains by groups going through the training against those not going through the training. Intellectually, this rather scientific approach would seem to offer the highest accuracy. But it has some practical disadvantages that perhaps explain why it does not have widespread use. The method is difficult to use—with scientific precision. You have to make sure, through matched pairs, that the control and non-control groups are as identical as possible. Then too, because of the difficulty, it is time-consuming—hence costly. Some training directors worry about the reaction of those who are given no training in order to serve as control groups. And finally, the method would seem to be inapplicable to seminars that are not directly skill-building in purpose.

Measuring Specific Project Results

Sometimes you can measure specific cost savings or productivity improvements generated through action plans developed in the seminar and tracked after the seminar. One major city in the United States using this approach reported annual benefits of $9.7 million from twenty-three such projects and a one-time benefit of $1.3 million. Arguably, some of these savings might have been realized without the benefit of training in the action planning process used. But even if you discount the totals by 50%, it is still rather impressive. More importantly, follow-up of specific projects is much easier to do for most training directors than either the control group or the internal consultant approaches.

Survey of Superiors

The American International Group makes effective use of a method that rests on a very sensible premise: that the immediate superiors of those going through training seminars are in the best position to assess the results of the training (see Figure 13). Questionnaires of this kind of

†Parker, Treadway C.: "Statistical Methods for Measuring Training Results." In Craig, Robert L. (ed.): *Training and Development Handbook*, McGraw-Hill Book Company, New York, 1976.

Borough of Manhattan Community College
American International Group*

1. Have you noticed any change(s) in your employee's work performance
   since completion of the following course(s)

                              Mathematics
                              Language
                              Grammar
                              Office Skills

           YES _____   NO _____

   If so, describe these changes by checking off the appropriate statement(s)
   a. Improvement of skills _____
   b. Able to handle more responsibilities _____
   c. Shows initiative and creativity _____
   d. Is more aware of job expectation _____
   e. Is more effective in general _____

2. In your opinion, do you feel that this course was worthwhile?

           YES _____   NO _____
   COMMENTS:

   _____

   _____

   _____

   _____

   _____

   _____

* Used here with permission.

Figure 13. Evaluation form.

structured interviews of the participants' superiors offer a good compromise between the most sophisticated and the crudest approaches to
measuring the impact of training seminars on the job.

A prominent insurance brokerage concern, Johnson & Higgins, uses
the participants' superiors in another way. It asks the supervisors of

participants to identify their development needs *before* the seminar and then to assess their improved performance relative to these needs *after* the seminar.

Past-Participant Self-Evaluation

Probably less effective, but still useful, is an approach that calls upon the participants themselves to make postseminar evaluations of their own performance. It is personally less threatening than methods providing for the close involvement of their superiors. It is also easier to administer. On top of that, there may be a side-benefit: self-evaluation is a powerful source of motivation for self-improvement.

Informal Feedback

Despite all the other methods available, unstructured, informal feedback is by far the most prevalent method for evaluating results achieved through training seminars. Companies using this informal approach say it is one thing to consider the ideal "textbook" approach, and quite another to deal with the fast pace, constant change, staff shortages, and major unplanned interventions that represent the everyday world of the training director. Perhaps so. But this argument could have an element of excuse or self-deception as well.

Peer Review

Another way to evaluate the effectiveness of a seminar is to institute a process of peer review at key steps in the development of a seminar and later in occasional audits of seminars in the process of delivery. The approach is similar to methods that have been developed by manufacturing companies to build quality control into their production processes and rely less on inspection at the time of the shipment.

We suggested in Chapter 6 that you bring fellow professionals into the picture to review your seminar design before going into the production of your educational materials. It seems to me that this is an ideal point to get this kind of a check on quality.

But you could do it at other times as well. How about participating in a review of the needs analysis that started the whole process? How about a brainstorming session at the start of the seminar design process? A review of the final educational materials?

In these days when there is so much emphasis on teams, the use of peer reviews at these critical points could do more than give you greater assurance of quality. It could also have developmental and motivational benefits.

It is a comfortable idea for a training director to consider the seminar completed when the seminar participants have left the seminar room. One might say: "After all, we do have the participant evaluations. As professionals in the field we can rely on ourselves to determine our training needs. We know a good seminar when we see one, to meet these needs. And with the evaluation of the participants themselves (fortified by an occasional personal visit) we have a way of reassuring ourselves on the quality of the seminar. All of these things added together have to give us a major impact on improving performance on the job. If they didn't, we would learn about it soon enough."

14

How to Evaluate Overall Training Performance

It is not enough these days to evaluate individual seminars. You have to assess in some acceptable way the overall impact of the total training effort over a period of time. You have to try to determine if this is acceptable in light of what others in the industry are achieving. And you have to be able to show continuing improvement, in keeping with the powerful movement toward strategic quality management that has been so widely embraced. How do you do this?

I would suggest that you apply an approach that has been tested and found useful in many areas of business, including staff services such as training. Here it is:

1. Identify the critical dimensions of success in your total training effort.
2. Develop measurable standards for each of these dimensions.
3. Establish the means for getting reliable information on actual performance to compare to each of these standards.
4. Discipline yourself and your people to use the system to make regular evaluations and take corrective action as necessary.

It doesn't sound too difficult, does it? Let's give it a try.

Short term
long term

How to Determine the Critical Success Factors

The first step then is to identify the most critical dimensions of success in managing a corporate training function. You'll have to do this for yourself to fit the precise environment in which you are operating. But let me offer some possibilities for your consideration.

In efforts of this kind, you first ask yourself some broad questions and then keep probing until you hit pay dirt. Here's another area, by the way, that lends itself to a team approach. The broad questions relate to *quantity*, how much; *quality*, how good; and *cost*, what resource constraints?

KEY INDICATORS

Scope

In thinking about quantity, you are really concerned with the *scope* of the programs and services you are offering and the *productivity* or total output of your department. In days gone by, you could select a safe array of courses to meet generally recognized needs: management training, sales training, problem solving, team building, computer literacy, and the like. Today, you have to increasingly put yourself to the test of relevance and priority. You have to be familiar with the strategic thinking of your company and what that means in terms of the training function.

For example, your company might foresee (as most companies do these days) a work force that will be increasingly multi-cultural. Such a situation requires special treatment in your supervisory training programs so that your supervisors will understand how to deal with this diversity.

A case in point is Handy & Harman, a prominent company in the rare metals business. In making a survey of employee attitudes in Attleboro, Massachusetts, the company wanted to provide questionnaires in the native language of each employee in an effort to get more reliable responses. The company ended up with questionnaires in six languages: English, Hindi, Cambodian, Laotian, Urdu, and Spanish! At other locations they had to have versions in Arabic, Chinese, Italian, Portuguese, and Vietnamese—all in a little town in Massachusetts!

What it all means is that the programs you offer have to meet identified needs—not just the needs of individual employees, but the needs of the company as well.

Productivity

You have to be concerned with another specific that comes from thinking about "quantity"—the productivity of your function. The main thrust here is the productivity of your human resources, but you have to think beyond this. What about the utilization of your training facility? Your investment in high-technology equipment and software to deliver your training? These are involved too, if you are responsible for investments of this nature.

In fact, you may feel particularly sensitive about it. Since your function is being relied upon to improve the productivity of human resources throughout the company, you may rightly believe you have to serve as a model. Surely you want to feel comfortable that the productivity of your department is improving each year.

We're not just talking about "filling seminar seats," although that is involved. You have to fill seminar seats for top-quality programs that are probably directed to high-priority needs, which brings us to the second line of inquiry: quality.

Participant Satisfaction

In thinking about how good your programs and services have to be, you also branch out into several channels. The first, mentioned in the first part of the chapter, is probably participant satisfaction. To some degree this would be a perception of quality, but it's still important. You want these customers to feel their experiences are worthwhile. You want them to spread the word so that others will keep on coming.

Performance Improvement

In most cases you are trying to improve job performance, so that probably has to be a critical dimension of success you'll want to be able to measure. But how do you know whether the improvement you may be getting is good enough? Do you need to compare yourself with other companies? Do you need to think about continuous improvements, year to year, which is being stressed in so many other areas of business these days?

Technical Excellence

Another aspect of quality concerns the professional quality of your educational materials and the technical capabilities of your people. Are you doing something to keep on the forefront of developments in these matters, or are you assuming your people will maintain their technical skills on their own? Is this a critical success factor in your operations?

Cost

The third general line of inquiry has to do with the resources you are using to get the results you want. My sense is that this factor will be getting a lot more attention in the future. The American Society for Training and Development is advocating that an amount equal to 4% of payroll should be directed toward training and development.* That's a lot more than most companies are spending now. And the proposal comes at a time when companies are downsizing and economizing in a variety of ways to preserve profit margins in a toughening, globally competitive market. It seems inevitable that if they continue to spend more on human resource development, they are going to be extremely concerned with the cost and more particularly with justifying the cost.

How to Set Measurable Standards

1. choose indicator
2. determining standard for indicator

2nd step

Once you have identified the critical success factors, you have to think through the measurable level of performance on each that you need to achieve. You have to concentrate on one at a time, and you have to establish a standard that is better than average performance. There should be some "stretch" in it, but not too much; otherwise it can be discouraging to your people.

"Measurable" does not necessarily mean quantitative, although that is highly desirable. For example, if "innovation" or "continuous improvement" becomes a critical success factor for you, you can measure it by the evaluation of the management committee with respect to your annual plan: "Annual departmental plans demonstrate a commitment to innovation and continuous improvement as determined in the review of the plan by the management committee."

We need to make a distinction between "measures" and "measurable standards." Thus, "cost per trainee" is a measure; and "average cost per trainee does not exceed $300" is a standard. It is something against which you can compare actual performance to see if you have met the standard. Note, that in this example it is essential to define what costs are included in the calculation. It can make a huge difference whether or not you are including salary costs of trainees in the calculation.

What level you choose to define as acceptable performance is perhaps even more challenging than identifying your critical success factors. One way to do it is to look at past performance and add a little "reach"

*Carnevale, Anthony P., and Gainer, Leila J., "The Learning Enterprise," a 2-year research project of the American Society for Training and Development and the U.S. Dept. of Labor, U.S. Government Printing Office, 1990, p. 48.

to it. In the example, if for the past 2 years you see the cost per trainee moving down from $350 to $325, you might believe that $300 is a good target. But then again, if you have invested in some new facilities and equipment which have to be amortized over, say, 3 years, you have to take it into account.

Sometimes you can find some benchmark companies with whom you can trade information. If so, it gives you more to go on than your own past history, which may be good or bad.

Other times you may have to make a reasonable guess, recognizing that it might take a year or two of actual experience before you can be confident of your standard. If you do so, make sure your people and your manager recognize this so they won't place undue importance on any failures to meet such a standard.

You'll see in Figure 14 a collection of standards that are purely hypothetical, but it may help you to see the way they are constructed, even if the level of performance specified would be inapplicable to your situation.

Scope.   All programs offered in the company training catalog each year are backed up by needs analyses conducted in accordance with established departmental procedures.

Productivity.   The number of participant seminar days delivered per trainer each quarter is at least X and not more than Y.

Participant Satisfaction.   80% of all seminar attendees evaluate the seminars they attended 4 or better on a 5-point scale where 3 is satisfactory and 5 is outstanding.

Performance Improvement.   At least three seminar classes, chosen at random, are selected each year for in-depth, follow-up evaluation in accordance with established procedures. The evaluations establish that significantly improved job performance, as determined by the participants' immediate supervisors, has been demonstrated by at least 75% of the participants in each class.

Technical Excellence.   Annual surveys performed by multi-company teams against jointly established criteria covering training facilities, equipment, trainer/trainee ratios, program development, learning methodologies, program delivery, and use of high technology places the company in the upper 50th percentile of all companies included.

Cost.   Average total cost per trainee hour each quarter is X, plus or minus 5%.

Figure 14. Examples of measurable performance standards.

The examples are given purely as "thought starters." You will probably be able to do better.

How to Measure Actual Performance

As you are developing your standards, you have to keep one eye on the practicality of getting information on actual performance that you'll need in order to compare it to the established standards. For example, if you have selected cost per trainee hour as a standard, you're going to have to record and assemble information on the number of seminar hours logged in such a way that you can easily total them each quarter. You're also going to have to keep track of all the costs you had decided to build into that measure, again so that you can total them up easily at the end of the quarter.

If this kind of scorekeeping is going to be too onerous, or too expensive in work hours or workdays, you have to weigh the value of having the more precise standard against that extra cost.

Let's take one more example. The one on technical "excellence" presumes that you can get some fellow professionals from other companies to cooperate with you in jointly developing criteria and making annual surveys. Perhaps you could retain an outside consultant to make the surveys and report back. Presumably, it would operate in much the same way as salary surveys. But instead of getting salary data for benchmark jobs you would be sharing information that would usefully add up to technical excellence. It may or may not be feasible to do this. If it isn't, you have to find another way. If you are in a division of a larger company, perhaps some qualified person or group at corporate headquarters could make the survey for you.

As these two examples show, you have to develop your standard first, and then find some way to generate the data that you need on actual performance afterwards. You then may have to do some "cutting and fitting" until you get a practical balance between the ideal and the doable.

How to Evaluate Performance

Let's say you now have an acceptable set of standards and practical ways to record and report information on actual performance. You've got your system; but now you have to use it.

But are you going to do all the evaluating for the department? Or do you have an established structure of accountabilities that requires a further breakdown of standards and information flow to individual sections within your department? It's well established that the more you can get people to evaluate their own performance, the better off you are.

Now, let's say you have thought that one through and you are left with some items that you have to evaluate personally. How are you going to discipline yourself to do so in a systematic way? Maybe you are well organized by nature and don't have to worry about it. But for a little insurance, I would suggest building evaluation events into your personal work planner. It works for me. Maybe it will work for you too.

How to Take Corrective Action—Constructively

When it comes to what corrective action to take and how to take it, we are opening up a door to the whole subject of interpersonal relationships. You have to know your people and how to deal with them constructively. If you have used them as a team in building the whole performance evaluation system, they'll be predisposed to accept it and work with it. The essential point here is to ask, "What is the right thing to do?" rather than, "Who is the person to blame?" Every performance deficiency can be viewed as an opportunity to improve the system or help some individual's performance.

Keeping Management Informed

Perhaps I should have warned you at the outset that you need the support and participation of your own manager in setting up this system of standards and reports. You should view the system as established primarily for you and your people. But it's also going to give your management a much better way to understand what you are trying to accomplish and a better way to work with you in helping you to accomplish it. It should facilitate teamwork at all levels.

It occurs to me as I reflect on what we have been sharing together that if I were a training director in some company, I would want to be sure to take the initiative in this whole process of evaluating results: the results from individual seminars as well as the overall results of the whole function. With the heavy pressures that can be foreseen to improve human productivity and at the same time to keep a tight control over costs, I can expect if I don't do it, it may be forced on me. And then someone else will get the credit!

15

Eight Steps to Vital Training Seminars

You and I have come a long way together since you first picked up this book. We've considered all the preliminaries that have to be done properly to ensure success in putting on training seminars. We've spent some time on the firing line, thinking through together the actual delivery of the seminar. Then we examined the difficult question of evaluating the effectiveness of a seminar and a total training program. Now it's time to see if we can put it all into perspective.

Perhaps a useful way to do this is to ask this question: If you were to start up a series of training seminars for an organization that had previously had no formal training function, how would you go about it? It's a way that we can think back together over all the material presented in the preceding chapters.

The answer to the question can conveniently be structured around eight steps. Let's consider each in turn.

1. Assess the Organizational Climate

Internal + external

The first step would be to do some serious thinking about the environment in which you find yourself. What is the overall mission of the organization? What strategic directions has it embraced in order to carry out that mission? What are the major events and developments that make up its history? What market or markets is it serving? What products or services does it offer to meet the needs of these markets? What are its strengths and weaknesses? What are the directions and probable pace of future growth?

The answer to some of these questions may be found in annual reports or other written materials. Much of it will have to come through discussions with knowledgeable people in the organization, which is probably just as well. It will provide a meaningful way to get to know these people.

Within this broad frame of reference, you would then review the kind and quality of training given in the past. Even if there was no formal seminar program, people had to be trained. Was it all done on the job? Is there any record of success or failure in the past that could affect the overall receptivity to training?

You would go about this fact-finding mostly through interviews, legitimately passing yourself off as "needing to get acquainted." But you would probably have to supplement the interviews with any published articles about your organization or perhaps informational brochures developed for new employees. The net result would be to give you a feeling for the organizational climate, which you know has a major impact on the success of training activities.

2. Build and Maintain a Base of Support

This round of interviews will help you with step 2: building a base of support. As you meet and talk to these managers, you would be alert for those you might be able to build into an informal network or, better still, a formalized advisory board or training committee. You know how helpful such a group can be in determining training needs, developing and getting approval of training plans, providing two-way channels of communication with user groups, and generally providing a useful source of counsel and advice. You cannot successfully function in a vacuum. You need to develop a source of advice and a base of support.

3. Base Programs on Identified Needs

Your third step is to make a determination of training needs. Your needs analysis will become the basis for deciding what training programs to set in motion. You'll want to involve top management in your needs analysis, if you sense that it is feasible to do so. In any event, you'll want to work with your board of advisers or training committee. You'll probably decide to take a leading part yourself in the needs analysis, through questionnaire and follow-up interviews, because it gives you a further chance to get acquainted and build support. When you put it all together, you want to make an attractive, well-organized presentation, using tables, charts, and graphs as appropriate to illustrate your findings and recommendations. After all, the first end product of your work will be to help create the image you want: a true professional who is thoroughly practical.

4. Manage Your Resources to Support Corporate Objectives and Strategy *alignment of goals*

If you are going to win the continuing support of top management, you'll have to position your overall effort in line with overall corporate objectives and strategies. The background you have gained in step 1 gives you the means to do this. You have to think broadly and creatively in terms of present and future corporate needs.

You don't simply inaugurate a sales training program; you relate it to the established corporate need to increase market share in specified areas. Similarly, management training isn't offered per se; it is tied to a need to supply a specified future stream of qualified managers required to support planned growth. Courses in managing change are related to the turbulent decade ahead as foreseen in company forecasts.

5. Choose and Develop High-Impact Trainers

As you build your training function, it is critical that you look forward to the time when you can become a manager of the training function and spend less of your own time in actual training. I have seen newly appointed training directors become so bogged down in doing the actual training that they didn't find time to think creatively about making a success of their functions. It's easy to fall into this trap. Presenting successful seminars is personally very rewarding.

In order to avoid this danger, you have to plan at an early time to build a top-quality training staff. Think about what we said on selection criteria, providing a sound organization structure, and motivating your trainers.

6. Use Outside Resources—
Selectively

Once you have established your needs and have gotten them understood and accepted by the training committee and top management, you would see if there are good-quality vendor programs available to meet some of your high-priority needs. You know that if there are, you can make a much earlier impact than if you have to develop these programs yourself.

Here's what you would do. You would first telephone your friends in other companies to round out your own knowledge of what is available. You would solicit brochures and references from the reputable firms that could meet your needs, making sure to telephone their clients for a check on the quality of their programs and the overall service they provide. After reducing the possibilities to a relatively few, perhaps two or three, you would arrange a personal meeting for each side to learn more about the other. You would also request written proposals so that you could get a more specific look at cost and compare it with the cost and time delays of internal development. At the face-to-face meetings, with the outside consultant, you would try to gauge how effective they are in terms of personal impact and flexibility. Personality is particularly important if they are to provide the seminar leaders. You would involve the training committee in the final evaluation and decision: whether to use outside vendors at all and—if the answer is yes—which one.

7. Succeed Through
Successes

The seventh step you'll take is to start a seminar program; but make sure the first one is a winner. Whether you use outside resources or develop the program yourself, there are a number of points to remember to maximize your chances of success.

Seminar Design

In adapting or developing the seminar design, you'll make sure that the seminar objective and target group are clearly defined, that the subject matter is directly relevant to both, that the design incorporates a high level of participant involvement, and that it meets all professional training standards.

Pilot Program

You'll select a representative participant group and a suitable facility for conducting a pilot or test program. By running a pilot program first, you minimize the risk and open the door to program improvement. You want to be sure to select a seminar leader who is skilled in using all four methods of communication: direct statement, visualizations, examples, and demonstrations. You also want one who will be sensitive to the participant group, who will be able to capture their interest, and keep them motivated throughout the session.

Program Strengthening

No matter how outstanding the seminar leader is, you know that there are ways that even an "excellent" program can be made better. You'll want to incorporate the inputs of the presenter and the evaluations of the participants into this improved version.

Program Implementation

At this point, you would launch the full program. The enthusiastic evaluations of the participants in the pilot program should help you merchandise it. And continuing groups of satisfied participants should establish the program fully.

Evaluation

You would use participant evaluations plus a survey of participants' superiors to develop conclusions on the overall impact of the program. You'll try especially to get some measurement of improved productivity, even if this has to be a sampling. In the whole process, you would keep your training committee involved.

Only after your first effort, would you develop a multi-year training plan. Now that you have a highly visible success, you are in a much better position to get acceptance of your plan. Even though you may be asking for funds for the first year, you want to start conditioning management on the need for the programs you have pushed off to future years.

8. Blow Your Own Horn—Discreetly

Many highly qualified staff specialists, including human resource development professionals, overlook the real need to sell themselves and their functions. It's helpful, I believe, to think of yourself as being in business to meet the needs of your clientele. In doing so, you have to realize that their *perceptions* are what counts. *You* may know what a powerful force you represent for enhancing the productivity of human resources in your organization. But if *they* don't know, you are not doing a fully professional job.

Naturally, you have to do this with a great sensitivity to people. But this is something that comes naturally to those in the training function. Nobody responds positively to "bragging." But there are many quiet ways you can make sure that information about your successes gets into the right hands.

Well, there they are: eight steps. If you are able to take these steps effectively, you should be well on your way to making the training function in your organization a vital, successful force in continually improving the productivity of human resources. You should yourself be feeling a great sense of personal satisfaction in your job—satisfaction from the demonstrable bottom-line impact of your important work. Keep up the good work!

Index

About the Author

Lawrence S. Munson is vice president for Louis Allen
Associates, a major management development firm. He has
spent more than 30 years providing consulting services to
business organizations, and estimates that he has personally
conducted well over 600 training seminars for both small
companies and large conglomerates. In addition, Mr.
Munson has been active in the American Society for
Training and Development and is currently Board Chair of
the New York metropolitan chapter.